THE MAN

WHO LIVED A

HUNDRED LIVES

THE MAN

WHO LIVED A

HUNDRED LIVES

a memoir

MARK PERES

ShelbyPress

This is a work of creative nonfiction. This memoir reflects the author's present recollections of experiences over time. The events and conversations in this book come from the author's memories and notations and are not written to represent a word-for-word transcript. The author has retold events in a way that evokes the feeling and meaning of what occurred and what was said. Some names have been changed or omitted to protect the privacy of individuals. Although every precaution has been taken to verify certain factual assertions, the author assumes no responsibility for any errors or omissions.

For my parents

"The distinction between past,
present, and future is only
a stubbornly persistent illusion."

ALBERT EINSTEIN

CHAPTER ONE

"WHAT DO YOU remember about Itacoatiara?"

"I have these memories that are so vivid. Itacoatiara was a very small town. Itacoatiara means 'painted stone.' The first settlers found mysterious engraved painted rocks on the shores of the Amazon River. The town had nothing. I grew up not knowing about the radio or telephone or automobiles. We had none of those things. I saw so many things that I don't think I would have seen had I not been born there. Snakes eating other snakes. Jaguars eating chickens. I saw wild pigs. I saw so many alligators. Itacoatiara is on the left bank of the Amazon River, and along the banks, on the river, it is infested with alligators. My father didn't like for us to take a bath in the river because sometimes on the street you could see a man without an arm or a leg. You took a chance in the water and an alligator would strike out and eat you. I saw all those things, the torrential rain, the insects, the ocelots and vultures, but that was my world, you understand."

Ambrosio Benchimol Peres sat across from me. No one I knew called him by his first name, or even Mr. Peres; they simply called him *Peres*, as my mom did, or *Andy*, as Americans did, or called him *Papai*, *Daddy* in Portuguese, as my brother and sisters and I did. Then there was the way he signed his name, *APeres*, a contraction, but beneath the names we knew him by and the abbreviated way he presented himself, was a fierce pride for the many lives he led and unspoken regrets for doing what he had to do to provide a life for us and redeem a secret he took to his grave.

But I get ahead of myself. I know this now. Then I was a young man with a tape recorder.

How do you honor a parent whose life confounds you? How do you capture the stories of a person when your moral sense objects to so much of what they have done? How do you come to understand someone so different from you but whose imprint influences everything that you are? I was there to interview my dad and capture his life, as if I could truly capture it, before his memories and his stories and the sense for what anything is for was lost, in the hope his life story would help with a pressing decision of my own.

And I worried at any moment he would disown me again.

My mother had set the dining room table for lunch. The plates were chipped, and the knives and forks didn't match. The embroidered white lace that covered the table had begun to fade. My mom had placed folded paper napkins beneath the tableware, and a plate of picadillo at the center of the table, my father's favorite and mine, warm ground beef made into a soft fragrant stew with tomatoes and chopped green olives beside white rice and black beans. My dad took his seat at the head of the table. I sat to his left in an old wooden chair with a carved stiff back. I mixed my picadillo and beans and rice together. My dad kept them apart. My mom served me soda before serving my dad a cold beer. Beer was new for my dad, at least in front of me. He smoked his entire adult life, because that's what men did, until he stopped after an incident with his heart. I rarely saw him drink alcohol, unlike my mom who liked a glass of wine when she felt good about herself, or when she wanted to leave it all behind. I took it as a good sign that my dad had a beer with me. Maybe having a drink was his own way of preparing himself to talk about his life.

"How's the judge?" he asked.

"Good. I wish I could stay there forever." I didn't add more. Not about my clerkship coming to an end, or the novel I wanted to write, or the position at the firm I had accepted. I had long mastered a perfunctory response with my family that didn't give too much away. I wasn't different from my brother or sisters in that regard. We led private lives to avoid inviting complications from any family direction.

"And your friends?"

"They're good too." I didn't name names.

We ate quickly. I had time on my mind. Time and story. We didn't say much as we heard the evening news on the radio in the background. Something about the election being the most important in our lifetimes. They always are. My mom cleared the plates.

I took out two cassette tapes from my backpack. We had practiced a few questions and were ready to record. "Where do you want to talk?" I thought we might stay at the table.

My dad put his napkin down and gestured instead to the balcony, which I knew meant he wanted to talk away from my mom. I forced open the sliding glass door, which was stuck in its track. Outside, there was just enough room for two chairs and a small plastic table where I put the tape recorder. We were surrounded by white gardenias in pots my mom purchased at K-Mart. The waxy deep green leaves leaned in as if listening to us. Taping a conversation outside on the balcony, eleven stories up in the wind of their apartment building in Sunny Isles, didn't strike me as a good idea, but the afternoon skies had cleared and there was not much sound from below.

I'd taken Biscayne Boulevard north to 163rd Street to get to my parents' place, each lane busy with traffic. No surprise there. Miami is known for many things, and traffic one minute away from danger is one of them. Tall condominiums accented in pink and blue lined the way toward the beach. Then a right turn on Collins Avenue, and a right again on Kings Point Drive, before I found a parking spot across from their building one block from the ocean. Of all the places my parents lived in, this was better than most, bright with color because my mother had chosen it.

As a slight breeze rose on the balcony, I pushed the red record button. My dad looked at me waiting for his cue.

"So, Daddy, tell me your name."

"What?"

"Tell me your name."

"My name is Ambrosio Peres. But you knew that."

"I did. And I do. I'm testing the tape recorder. Can you speak a little louder?"

"My name is Ambrosio Peres."

There is something about how a person says their own name. The intonation. The emphasis of vowels and consonants. His name was my name. How he said *Peres*, the accent over the first syllable, the 's' sound that distinguished it from *Perez*, the mispronunciation I heard my whole life, modeled how I said it, rolling my 'r's for special effect. *Mark Frias Peres.* Son of Ambrosio and Lourdes Peres. The youngest of five. Me.

What to ask next? I arrived with a short list of questions I had written on my legal pad. I conversed well with people who interested me, discovering and uncovering and going deep quickly. I could banter and charm. It was my magic power. But not with my family. In law school I had practiced taking depositions, pinning down facts and tying up loose ends, and it was as good an approach as any now. I would depose my dad.

"Do you want something to drink?" I had been taught to put a deponent at ease.

"No." My father sat stiff in his chair, looking at the tape recorder.

"What we want to do is go back as far as we can. We'll start with your grandparents, who they were, what they did, where they came from, and how they came to Brazil."

"That's not an easy question. There is no record of these things, but the oral tradition is—"

"Let's start on your father's side."

"My father? He was from Tangier—"

"What period of time are we talking about?"

"The middle of the last century—"

"The 1800s?"

"Yes—" My father raised his hand.

I knew what that meant. I had not allowed him to finish one sentence. That was hardly the way to start a deposition and hardly the way to begin a conversation with my dad. The one thing my father knew how to do was tell a story. If this was going to work, I would have to put my legal pad aside. I pushed the stop button on the recorder and flipped over the ninety-minute cassette.

"I don't think it recorded," I said.

"The tape was turning."

"I know. But I think we could start again."

"Are you going to use what we just did?"

"Maybe."

"So, it recorded?"

"Yes. But let's start again."

"How my family came to Brazil?"

"Yes, how it all began."

It was Saturday, March 21, 1992.

If I was going to live in Miami again, I was going to live somewhere full of promise and a neighborhood of my own. I moved into a small apartment in South Beach on Collins Avenue between 7th and 8th Street, one block from the News Café, the new gathering spot for locals, tourists, and goings-on well into the night on Ocean Drive. South Beach, once relegated to retirees sitting forlorn in metal chairs on the front porches of faded Art Deco hotels, had come alive with cafes and restaurants and trendy New York-Euro fare. I lived in the middle of the daiquiris and neon, the sand and breeze, the artists and hustlers and dealmakers. I walked the red-stained sidewalks of Collins Avenue, and the grime-filled streets of Washington Avenue, from the 5th Street Gym to Lincoln Road. The shops and hotels and faces passing by were new and old to me. South Florida had an ever-present illicit air, the languages and accents and greed and gaudiness of the people, and the buying and selling of tokens of desire.

My apartment was a haven and a lure, a single bedroom with a galley kitchen, the décor presenting a liberally educated young man, the man of letters that I wanted to become, with the latest books and a marble cafe table and sea green couch and posters from MoMA. I wrote letters to classmates from college and received cards and letters in return that I kept in chronological order bound in rubber bands. I listened to NPR and Dylan and Zeppelin and had *The New York Times* delivered. On weekends I watched movies in the Grove and ate at restaurants in the Gables. It took me twelve minutes to drive from Miami Beach over the sun-drenched Venetian Causeway to the postcard views of downtown Miami.

I was a newly minted attorney. My life was on the clock. My one-year federal appellate clerkship with Judge Peter T. Fay on the U.S. Court of Appeals for the Eleventh Circuit was coming to an end, about as plum a career-launching position a young law student could get. I had a good run during law school. I didn't love most of it, not contracts, not torts, not taxation, not commercial paper, but I had a talent for writing and a knack for constitutional law. In my third year at Florida State University, I applied for a clerkship to the U.S. Court of Appeals in Miami. The application was a complete long shot. The odds were not good that I would get selected because federal appellate clerkships were generally reserved for students at the top of their class. When I told the dean I had been selected, he gave me a long look and told me to say yes "with alacrity."

Eight months into my clerkship, I faced a big decision about what to do next, and what might be next left me completely uncertain. I had been searching for something that felt essential, whatever the next stage of my life would be that would fill an unsettled part of me, and I had weeks to decide on whether to show up for a job I had accepted.

My mom and dad had moved into their two-bedroom apartment ten miles north of me just as they had moved into countless other places during their thirty-seven-year marriage.

Their building, overdue for renovation, overlooked the Intra-coastal Waterway with a sliver of a view of the ocean if you turned your head sharply to the right on their balcony. They paid rent with their combined Social Security checks and the intermittent money my dad earned. Their apartment was furnished with photographs and throw pillows and things that accumulated from living in Brazil and America and from raising five children and moments of joy and endurance and despair and wondering where the time and hopes and dreams went.

My parents were in a period of detente. My dad drove to work in a car that leaked oil to his office in a strip mall that had an old fax machine where he made phone calls and sent catalog listings to customers while doodling arrows and parallelograms in the margins. When too much was on his mind, he would stop by Dunkin Donuts for coffee and sit at the same seat at the end of the counter or go to a nearby Cuban restaurant where he spoke Spanish and befriended the owner and flirted with waitresses thirty years younger than him. My mom cooked and cleaned at home, shopped for fruit and cheese and roast chicken at Publix, watched Nikki and Victor on *The Young & The Restless*, wrote letters that she sent in airmail envelopes to her sister back in Brazil, and served my dad dinner at night when he came home and sat at the head of the table. Every time I visited their apartment, they fed me the food that I craved, and they were clearly proud of me even if my personal life was completely unknown to them.

On 123rd Street off Biscayne Boulevard, my dad made his living as the sole proprietor of KrystalKraft, the latest iteration of the many companies and lines of business that had become his life. He imported mineral specimens, semiprecious stones, and handcrafted gifts from Brazil. The latest imports were small crystal birds with feathers in them. He sold them to one-off retail stores. He could sell anything, he said, and he did, until he didn't or couldn't or lost funding or a relationship went sour, or the hustle of the street caught up with him. Times change and what people want change and his life changed and so his business changed. What remained the same was his relentless work ethic because rent needed paying and mouths needed feeding and what else could he do? He was near the end of his life, and he had no savings. He might be learned and well-spoken and cultured, he might speak several languages and have the mind of a philosopher and the spirit of a teacher, but his fate was selling baubles to whomever would buy.

That's how I saw him. An old man who betrayed his talents, whose temper could erupt at any moment, whom I was wary of, and yet loved, as loyal sons love their flawed families.

I wasn't home much during college and law school, visiting once or twice a year for the holidays. It was during my second year of law school that my parents had a terrible fight. I helped my mom move out. My dad sent me a blistering typed letter on tissue-thin paper writing that "I had decided poorly," that "I was co-responsible and a co-participant in the destruction of my parents' home," that "I would come to be very sorry and ashamed of myself." As to my relationship with him, I could "keep it or throw it in the wastebasket. I was no longer his son." Months of silence and recrimination between us followed.

There was more to it, but for now we had put it behind us, but not too far behind us that it couldn't happen again, this time ending our relationship permanently.

During the years when I was away, when we were still speaking, holidays at home were like they always had been. My dad carved the Thanksgiving turkey with an electric knife and my mom decorated the same plastic Christmas tree out of a box. My sisters who lived nearby brought their children, and we gathered around Brazilian and American food and took pictures of the nephews and nieces. My dad never smiled in pictures, but it didn't mean he didn't enjoy being photographed. Not that he would ever say a word about being left out as people posed around him. No matter how much or little my parents had for themselves, they gave gifts to each of us and the grandchildren. Even if they were strange and peculiar gifts that immigrant parents give. We always had presents under the tree, hearing no talk on Christmas day of the financial strain my parents bore to pay for them.

When I graduated from law school, my mom and dad, and my oldest sister Rachael and her boyfriend Jimmy, drove five hundred miles from Miami to Tallahassee to see me receive my diploma. My dad wore a blue blazer that didn't quite fit, and cream-colored pants and black shoes. I introduced him to my dean and professors. My dad and mom toured the grounds of the newly opened Rotunda, walking slowly so not to trip. I showed them the townhouse I lived in and drove them around campus. They were tired at the end of the day. There was no question they would come to my graduation.

No matter what might be happening between them or us or anyone else in the family, no matter what I kept private and only shared reluctantly, no matter the months of estrangement between my father and I that could come back at any moment with one strong word, I knew they would be there when I crossed the stage.

My parents were genuinely glad that I was back in Miami. They had a son that had become a lawyer. Even if they didn't fully appreciate what a law clerk to a federal appellate court judge did or the steppingstone that it was, they understood enough to know that it was the life of the mind and a noble pursuit. I had a position of honor that gave them pride. All their work, all their sacrifices, all their choices, and the chaos and drama and instability of their marriage, had somehow worked out. If not for them, then for me.

My dad wrote me a birthday card after I moved to South Beach. He said it was a great joy for him to celebrate the day, and he wanted me to know that whatever I strove for would come to pass. He said the good Lord would reinforce my strength and determination, and that I should stay close to books, which would be my best friends, quenching my thirst for knowledge and feeding my soul. That's the way he wrote, Old Testament damnation one day, Old Testament blessing the next, his hurt and hopes for me right on the surface. I knew, yet again, that between my father and my mother, I was divinely charged, even if I couldn't make sense of the lives they led.

One night when I was at my parents' apartment for dinner, I asked my dad if I could interview him about his life and our family history. I made the remark casually not really knowing what I had in mind. He'd just told a joke that I heard many times that still made me laugh. The light in his green eyes behind his glasses softened. It was as if he had been waiting for me to ask, never expecting that I would. His many lives would be remembered. I told myself if I could understand his choices, then maybe it would help with the decision I would soon have to make.

"How would you do it?" he asked.

"Well, I could just come over with a tape recorder and ask you questions."

"What would we talk about?"

"I would ask about Brazil and your parents and grand-parents and how you grew up, the jobs you had, how you met Mommy and moving to America and what my brother and sisters and I were like when we were young and why we kept moving from place to place to place and how we got to where we are now."

"Well, these things can be hard to remember."

We were still at the table discussing the idea when my mom looked at my dad with a worried face. I could see her considering how much my father might reveal and what to make of my intentions. They spoke briefly. Afterward my mom went to the kitchen and came back with green grapes and sliced cantaloupe in a bowl.

We were on.

CHAPTER TWO

MY DAD WORE black pants and the same black shoes he always wore and a striped short-sleeved button-down shirt. His hair was slicked back and gray. For many years, he had a pencil-thin mustache but was now clean shaven. He wore oversized metal-rim glasses over a prominent nose. He looked like an older Robert Mitchum if Robert Mitchum had been Jewish and wore glasses and was from South America.

We sat three feet apart.

I felt part of him but not part of him. I was twenty-nine years old. My dad was seventy-five. I was forty-six years younger than him and felt the advantage of every year of it. I was tall and lean and strong and growing into the body that my dad once had. I had my mother's smaller nose, but my father's ears, cheekbones, lips, and chin. The color of my eyes was a hazel blend of my mother's dark brown and my father's pale green eyes.

I liked my dad most of the time. I admired his work ethic and intelligence and his curiosity about the world. I liked his ease connecting with people. I liked those things in him because I liked those things in me. I didn't like the wounded pride he

could show, his authoritarian ways, and his instability and inse-
curity. I was embarrassed about those things in him and saw
none of those things in me. He had strived and taken risks but
always seemed to make the wrong decision. Success eluded him.
My habits were different. I was certain that everything I wanted
for myself would happen. I just wasn't sure what that would be.

As the youngest of five children, I had escaped much of
the brunt of the most chaotic years of our family life or at
least I had less of a memory of it, unlike my older sisters and
brother who'd moved on with their lives with various wounds
and compensations. I was giving my father an opportunity to
tell his story, to explain what always seemed inexplicable, to
give reasons for all the disruptions we experienced as a family.
He knew he would never have this opportunity again.

"This time I won't interrupt," I said.

"Ask your questions."

"Let's start with the Amazon."

What occurs in our lives is set in motion long before we're
born. For my father, causal events began with nineteenth
century Jews migrating from Morocco to the deep interior
of the Amazon jungle. It's a long-ago story at the core of our
family history. The immigrants who carved European civilization into the Amazon, for better or for worse, what they wanted
and how they made their way, was infused in everything my
father did, and shaped how we were raised.

I was fully aware of the backstory:

After winning the Battle of Granada in January 1492, which completed the centuries-long Reconquista, the Christian reconquest of the Iberian Peninsula from Muslin rule, King Ferdinand II of Aragon and Queen Isabella of Castille issued the Alhambra Decree in March, expelling Jews from Spain. The decree followed decades of growing suspicion and persecution of *conversos*—Jews who had converted to Catholicism under pressure but were suspected of secretly practicing their faith. In 1478, Pope Sixtus IV had authorized the Spanish Inquisition through a papal bull, granting Ferdinand and Isabella the power to root out heresy and enforce religious orthodoxy. Under the guidance of Tomas de Torquemada, the first Grand Inquisitor, the Inquisition used brutal methods, including torture and public trials known as *autos-da-fé*, where Jews and alleged heretics were scourged and killed before large crowds. The Alhambra Decree, or the Edict of Expulsion, gave Spain's entire Jewish population four months to either convert to Christianity or to abandon land and property that had been part of their heritage since King Solomon. Jews were forced to sell everything they could not carry to avoid the horrors and tortures of the Inquisition. The punishment for any Jew who did not convert or leave by the deadline was summary execution.

Tens of thousands of Jews fled, leaving all their possessions behind, many to Morocco, on the far-western edge of North Africa, just south of Spain, seeking accommodation under Muslim rule. Upon arrival, Spanish Jews encountered severe famine gripping the Mediterranean. Many Moroccan cities refused to allow Jews in, leading to mass starvation among the Jewish refugees. Many Jews, without means or protection, were enslaved. The swell of arriving Jews caused overcrowding in Jewish quarters in urban and rural cities as desperation and the summer heat took hold.

In October, Christopher Columbus, sponsored by King Ferdinand and Queen Isabella, arrived on an island across the Atlantic, called Guanahani by the Taíno native people, now called San Salvador, claiming the land for the Spanish Catholic monarchs. For Gentiles, the Year of the Lord 1492 became excitingly and disruptively new – a time of Christian ascendency and expansion of empire. As roars went up about discoveries of exotic lands and trade routes to the Indies that would make adventurers and European kingdoms wildly rich, the edict to eliminate Jews and Jewish culture from Spain went into further terrifying effect. By December, nearly 100,000 Jews had been expelled from Spain, while those who stayed were forced to renounce their faith or be killed. For the Jews, the Year 5252 of their Hebrew calendar was one more year in a notorious and brutal age.

Most Jews who settled in Morocco were small traders and peddlers who sold trinkets and exotic goods in Arab marketplaces to survive. Others were tailors, cobblers, and jewelers. Many were physicians, teachers, and scholars. They developed a hybrid language, a sometime secret code, that protected them from people outside their community, a variant of Spanish with Arabic and Hebrew jargon called Haketia. Jews in Morocco were itinerant, moving from town to town, from market to market, traveling restlessly between Tangier, Tetuan, Rabat, and Casablanca, alert to plagues and persecution, pursuing opportunities, keeping whatever valuables they could hold in their bags and pockets. Back and forth they went from one place to another to survive. Movement was central to how they remained alive. In the decades and centuries that followed many Moroccan Jews emigrated from the Iberian Peninsula to Gibraltar, which had become a British overseas territory in 1713. In the early nineteenth century, life in Morocco for the Sephardim, as Jews from the Iberian Peninsula are called, had become hard. The economic climate in Morocco became depressed, an influx of Spaniards made jobs scarce, and drought and disease worsened poverty. Young Jewish men cast their hopes farther and farther away. The New World beckoned. In 1808, the Portuguese empire issued an edict permitting the private practice of religions other than Catholicism in the colony of Brazil. In 1822, Brazil became an independent nation, encouraging immigration to its shores and foreign investment. The signal went up. Moroccan Jews, and many from Gibraltar, took up the quest, migrating across the vastness of the Atlantic Ocean to the other worldliness of the jungles of Brazil.

Traveling first by sail and then by steamboat, Jews wearing orthodox garb and brimless hats arrived in Belém, a port city on the eastern coast of Brazil and gateway to the interior of the Amazon basin. These Jews were as alien to the Brazilians as the land was to them. Jews that followed went westward into the jungle, seeking natural resources and territory to settle, working mostly as merchants and traders, selling food, medications, ammunition, and wares to indigenous Brazilians and native tribes. They bought fruits, nuts, minerals, leather, hides, and skins from Indians to export back across the Atlantic.

In the 1880s, Jewish migration to Brazil boomed. A new product promised untold wealth to those who could farm and manufacture it: rubber. The Industrial Revolution in Europe and North America led to rising demand, and at that time, latex from rubber trees was exclusively found in the Amazon. Speculators and entrepreneurs purchased swaths of land in the jungle and established rubber tree plantations, employing large workforces of indigenous people to tap the trees for latex. The rubber trade became lucrative for many business owners and for the nation of Brazil, which taxed those transactions. Belém, and other cities and settlements in the Amazon, such as the towns of Manaus and Itacoatiara, hundreds of miles inland, prospered. In short order, second- and third-generation Jewish merchants opened banks, municipal markets, customs and opera houses, theaters, schools, libraries, cemeteries, and synagogues. The Amazon jungle transformed. Languages, religions, and cultures collided. Roads, housing, technology, amenities, consumption, and human creation came into primordial habitats.

All this was background to the first questions I asked my dad.

"What was your house like? Can you describe it?"

"I remember it so well. We lived in a very large house with two living rooms, one very large dining room, and about five sleeping rooms, and a kitchen. It was in the middle of a lot, and it had a very, very long backyard full of wild trees and animals. The climate was very hot and humid. We had many windows that were always open. The house was on the main street. That street, the main street, was named after my father."

"Did you have your own room?"

"Yes, together with an Indian boy named Rosendo. A captain of a local vessel on the river found him in the jungle and gave the boy to my father."

"What do you mean? As a gift?"

"Yes, sometimes Indians were given as gifts. The boy was naked and violent and tied up when my father brought him home. My father tied him to a tree in the backyard to keep him from running away. The boy fought and fought against the ropes. After several weeks, he calmed down and my father moved him into my room. He became my friend. He spoke an Indian language and then learned Portuguese. My father taught him how to read because he believed everyone should become educated. Rosendo and I became brothers. Together all the time. We slept in hammocks in my room. We made our toys together."

I imagined my dad carving toucans and dart frogs.

"What happened to Rosendo?"

"He became a public-school teacher. And he married and had eighteen children."

"You're kidding. Did you stay in touch?"

"No. No."

I waited for more, for a story about how my dad became a mentor to one of Rosendo's children who grew up to become governor of a state, or a movie star, but my dad seemed lost in memory. Was he going somewhere in his mind he had not gone to in years? I watched him as he closed his eyes.

In the 1880s, Joseph Peres, a tailor, and his wife, Cota Mhaudy Peres, left Morocco and crossed the Atlantic to Breves, Brazil. Breves was a small but strategically located and vital trading center southwest of the major port of Belém. With a population of a few thousand at the time, Breves was experiencing remarkable growth because of the rubber boom. Joseph and Cota had two sons, Isaac and David, and two daughters, Esther and Mary. The family placed their hopes on the two sons, each brilliant and driven in their own way.

Young Isaac completed primary school in Breves. When Cota, his mother, died in 1893, Isaac and David, and their father Joseph, returned to Tangier. Isaac and David continued their education at the Alliance Israelite Universelle, a Zionist organization that had opened in 1860 with the mission of safeguarding human rights for Jews around the world. The AIU promoted Jewish self-defense and self-sufficiency through education and professional development. Students were encouraged to venture to South America to fortify the diaspora and to bring values and customs that would allow Jewish life to prosper. Isaac and David studied language, science, history, geography, religious studies, and business. In 1898, when Isaac was twenty-two years old, and David was fifteen, they returned to the Amazon.

Isaac moved to the town of Cameta, a rough and tumble river town south of Belém. Finding prospects dim, Isaac reached out to his sisters, Esther and Mary, who had moved to Itacoatiara, a small settlement deep in the interior of the Amazon. Esther had married a local businessman named Moyses Ezagui. In 1900, after Moyses died, Isaac followed his sisters to Itacoatiara and took over the remnants of his brother-in-law's business, a latex extraction and rubber processing business called Casa Moyses. Isaac kept the business in his brother-in-law's name and provided for his sister Esther and her family. Mary would later marry Moyses' brother, Marcos. The Peres and Ezagui families became intertwined.

Isaac met and married Rachel Benchimol. The Benchimols were from Gibraltar, with British bearing and manners. Rachel's father, Leon, was a merchant sailor on ships that carried Jews to South America. Isaac and Rachel made Itacoatiara their home. Although not strict Orthodox observers, they followed the precepts of Jewish law and custom. In the years ahead, Isaac and Rachel had eight children: Leon, José, Cota, Esther, Mary, Clarita, Ambrosio, and Simita. Everyone was named after someone. My father, Ambrosio, was the youngest son, born in his mother's bedroom in the jungle, in 1916.

"What do you remember about your dad's business?"

"I remember being very young and hearing about places importing rubber from my father. Places like Brooklyn,

Liverpool, London, Marseilles. We were in the middle of the jungle, and my father was doing business with cities around the world. My father would write letters on his big desk that would be taken on boats that would cross the ocean."

Shipping commerce that crossed the seas. I loved it. "How did the war impact your dad?"

"The first war? It made him a wealthy man. Rubber was a commodity in demand during the war."

A wealthy man. A measure of ambition, of competence, of habits and choices. It's so much of what I wanted to explore with my dad. The man he could have become. "Did he own a lot of property?"

"Yes, he did, at times. My father hated to have land for no reason. He was very practical. He liked to have cash, jewelry, and some objects of art that he could turn into money. He didn't like to have properties or buildings. I don't know if it was the idea of anti-Semitism. The Jews learn through their own history. When you have money or valuable things you can carry, that you can hide or sell or bury, you can leave quickly."

"Did your father enjoy having money? Was he comfortable with it?" I was pressing the point comparing his father's mindset with his own.

"Everybody knew he had money. But nobody knew how much he had. Not even his family. My mother didn't know. But it was a small city, everybody saw, everybody knew, nobody was blind. What I admired about him most, even though we lived in the jungle, was that he was a very avid reader. That was more important to him than money. He placed education above everything else. He was very proud that all his children were educated."

And that was my dad's retort: there were more important things than money. The education that a parent gives a child, for one.

I went with it, for the moment. "Was your father an intellectual man?"

"Well, intellectual in the sense that he was very much interested in reading, especially history. He bought books, he used to go to Manaus, to Belém, to larger cities, and buy books, and books, and books. He went to Europe two times, to Portugal and France, and he shipped so many books back in crates, and he spent his time reading."

"And you enjoy reading."

"Yes, you know that."

We both did. That was the legacy I was most proud of: that his bedroom had books on Roman history, the Jewish diaspora, on Christian theology. My most cherished possessions were the dozens of books assigned to me in college on history, literature, and religion that I packed and unpacked everywhere I went. Yes, I cherished my books; they were essential to me. "Did your house have a library?"

"Oh yes, yes." My dad beamed. "I was exposed to books at a young age, when I was very, very small. I was four or five years old when I started learning Hebrew to say the prayers. I remember there was an old man named Annanias. Yes, Annanias. Very religious man. He was old. Maybe eighty-five years old. Long beard. He spent his whole life studying the

Torah. He was our teacher. I was in a class with three or four other small boys. One of my classmates' fathers was the Moher. He performed circumcisions. This was our tradition. I was circumcised by him. That's what they told me. It was a very natural life. We had no pharmacy. We had no doctors. Everything was home medicine. Using plants and herbs. Asthma was very common. We all learned."

"Did you study in synagogues?"

"There was only one synagogue, which was my Aunt Esther's house." My father paused again, then continued. "You see, there were Jews scattered all over the state, in the jungle, but on the high holy days, they came to Itacoatiara to celebrate the holidays, and we didn't have a synagogue, so we used my Aunt Esther's house."

I wasn't sure what houses in the Amazon looked like. Wood? Brick? Concrete? I made a note. "Was your family a religious family?"

"Yes, but practical. We lived in a different environment, and the only way to survive was to accept it, not to assimilate, but to accept our circumstances. For instance, most of the population was Catholic, so my father wanted to be very friendly with this majority. We had a Catholic church that was in bad shape, covered with wood, plaster, and straw, falling down. My father used his money to rebuild it in brick, and he gave it to the priest."

There you go, wood, plaster, straw. And brick.

My dad added, "The priest was a Portuguese man who used to come to our home every night to play cards with my father. Catholicism in that area, in that time, was very fanatical, very ignorant, and still is, but this priest used to say that as long as Señor Peres was alive, he loved the Jews."

I laughed. "I bet he did if your father was building a brick church for him. What did your father look like?" I had an idea already as I had a framed photograph of my grandfather in my apartment.

"My father? He was tall. Very agile. And very healthy. A strong man. A nice-looking man. He had a big mustache. Old style. He wore a white linen suit and a straw hat. We had an Indian maid from one of the tribes who pressed his suits every day. People liked my father very much. He was a very happy man. He liked to laugh. He liked to talk. He didn't have enemies." My dad said it with matter-of-fact pride.

"And your mother?"

"My mother was a very quiet person. Very calm. My father used to call her 'My English lady' because her family was from Gibraltar, and she was very phlegmatic. Do you know that word, phlegmatic? She accepted things as they were. She didn't complain because it didn't help to complain. She had a tremendous sense of balance. My father depended on her a lot. My father could be very excited, very nervous sometimes, and make the wrong decisions. Maybe I was like him. The family at that time was a different thing. There was a kind of a hierarchy. He was the head of the family, he had to be obeyed one way or the other. If you had something to tell my father, you went to my mother first. She would give you advice. She would tell you what to say."

There it was: my dad's ideal. How he believed a family should be. A husband and father in charge. A wife and mother always calm, loyal, and loving, balancing his moods, acting as the go-between with the children.

"What did you look like when you were little?" I didn't have any pictures of my dad as a boy.

"Me? I was skinny. Blond hair. Green eyes."

"A blond-haired, green-eyed, Jewish boy in the jungle?" *I loved it.*

"Yes. And active. Active. Always moving. Running. Climbing trees. I didn't like staying too long in one place."

"I guess that started young." My first real shot across the bow.

My father didn't react. At least not in a way I could tell.

I flipped over a page of my legal pad. "You were the youngest son in your family. Did you spend time with your older sisters and brothers?" Not something I did in my life.

"Yes, with my sisters. I lived with my sisters, but not my brothers. My older brothers were gone. They had already left the house. Leon and José were very good students and went to university in Belém. And my cousins all went to school. It was very competitive between the cousins to succeed. They became professionals. Two or three engineers. Two or three lawyers. Two or three doctors. They all did very well in life. My sisters were educated too."

Again, my dad underscoring the values of his family that had become my values too.

"And your uncle David, your dad's brother, also did well."

"Yes, yes. He was a great man. He went to school in Belém and then went to Rio. He studied law and economics. Journalism. He became a teacher, a professor, he became one of the most respected scholars in Brazil, a university teacher of Portuguese, Hebrew, Latin, and Greek. A man of letters. Very respected."

If that hadn't come to describe my father, then he could take consolation that it described his uncle. I took consolation in it too.

My dad added, "My father and David were very close. Stayed close as brothers."

That was his shot at me. My older brother Edison and I lived separate lives, and my father didn't like it. *Cat and mouse.* I knew where to go next with my questions.

"What was school like for you?" I knew the story he would tell.

"The schools were very simple but very tough. The toughest thing you can imagine. I used to go to school with my sisters, Simita, Clarita, and Mary. The teacher was so tough. We would learn in her backyard with chalk. Aurora. Professor Aurora. I still remember her name. Every day she used to make a revision of what she taught the day before. She would ask you questions and if you didn't answer she would hit you - POW! - with a stick."

My dad clapped loudly when he said "POW," startling me.

"She hit you?" I knew the answer.

"Yes. I don't know how many times. Now, if you made a mistake writing or spelling, you had to write that word a thousand times. One thousand times. Hours and hours."

"How old were you?"

"Young. A boy. I remember one day I made mistakes in school, and I went back home and an hour later I saw her coming, I saw her by the gate. Professor Aurora. Like a witch. I ran into the house and hid myself under my father's bed, which was the only bed in the house because we all slept in hammocks. And at that time the bathrooms were way outside the house, so they used those bedpans under the bed, so when I hid myself under the bed, I saw one of those things there smelling so bad. I stayed there as long as the teacher stayed in the house talking to my mother. When I heard her say goodbye, I ran outside to the backyard where I vomited."

"Nice," I scrunched my face to keep from laughing.

"And she used to do something else. She cut donkey ears. Big ones and put them on you when you made a mistake, and made you walk in front of the school, back and forth, back and forth, back and forth, for two hours. Everybody would walk by and see me with those big ears, but I would not stop walking."

I pushed the stop button.

I got him to say it. I was certain the story explained everything in his life that followed. My father was different from his high-achieving father and brothers. He was rebellious and proud. He would screw up and endure. He would wear his donkey ears, even if it killed him.

CHAPTER THREE

MY MOM SLID open the balcony door. She had a plate of little blocks of orange cheese with toothpicks in them. I loved her toothpicks with the red plastic frills on the end. She put them in slices of salami, green olives, strawberries, melon. Whatever was bite-size that she could serve. She brought another soda and beer for me and my dad. "What are you saying?" she asked in Portuguese.

"It's not about you," my dad said. "Not yet."

She let out a *tsk* and turned back around. It was one of many sounds and faces she made that expressed annoyance or anger or embarrassment or joy. She was easy to read.

We waited for my mom to leave. Even if I wanted her to listen in, I deferred the decision to my dad, and he wanted his time alone with me. I'd ask for her side of the story, but as my dad said, not yet.

I kept an eye on the cassette tape and how far the tape had turned. We were both up for the game. What encouraged me the most was how unguarded my dad was being with me. There was a genuineness and trust to his answers that I expected but also took me off guard. I turned to questions about his father, a measure and standard of success in his life, and one in mine.

"Your father became mayor of Itacoatiara."

"Yes, in 1926. My father became interested in the administration of the city. You see, what I'm going to tell you reflects his soul. The first thing he did when he became mayor was to build two schools and a library. Many people were illiterate and without education. My father said a library is symbolic. It is a small building with very few books, but let's call it a library, and then from now on we must educate the people to know the meaning of a library and start going there. In three or four years, this small building had over a thousand books and people going there to read. He used to give incentives to families to send their children to the library. So, this shows his soul."

A soul we shared. "He did other things too," I said.

"Yes, he wanted to build the city he wanted to live in—"

"Wait, I love that." I wrote it down. "Tell me more."

"He built buildings, parks, infrastructure, he brought electricity to Itacoatiara, a big project. You see, Itacoatiara was in bad shape when he took over. Bad governance. Corruption. The price of latex had collapsed. My father was honest and ambitious. He opened the municipal accounts and balanced the books. He was fair with everybody. He met federal officials and ambassadors. He brought business, commerce, and the arts to the city. The main street is named after him. Rua Isaac Peres. The street runs across the city. Our home was there. You can go there and see it."

One day. I wasn't sure when.

My dad added wistfully, "I used to visit him in his office."

I imagined my dad as a young boy visiting his father. I had a photograph of my grandfather in a dark wood-paneled office with elaborate carved wooden chairs with portraits and maps on the wall. I had read articles touting Isaac Peres as one of the most visionary mayors in the north of Brazil. He built the central public walkway inspired by the Champs-Elysees, the retainer wall for the city's port, access stairs from the river throughout the city to keep goods and people moving, a renovated Public Market, restored heritage sites, major roads to coastal cities, and tree-lined boulevards and bridges. He reformed municipal codes, funded the first synagogue and Jewish cemetery in the city, completed construction of a Catholic church, established a municipal statistics service to provide data for decision-making, and kept the city clean, well-lit, and free of epidemics during his watch. I imagined my father's feelings as a boy: his wonder and pride that *his father*, the mayor, was the father of the entire town. Ambition was in that office. Achievement was in that office. All that was good and possible was in that office, for my father to inherit and become.

But that's not what happened. "Everything changed then," I said.

"Yes. Everything changed. You see, this is life. 1930. I was thirteen years old. I remember that it was 1930 because that year we had a big revolution in the country when Vargas took power and started that dictatorship."

"Your brother, Leon . . . "

"Well, this is a sad event." My father took a deep breath. He folded his arms and looked into the sky. "My brother came home from university in Belém. The oldest son. He came to pay us a visit. He was twenty-five. Accomplished. Intellectual. Kind. Everything an older son and brother should be. My parents were so happy to see him. They welcomed him with a feast. They invited people to the house. Everyone talked late into the night. They sent me to go to sleep, but I watched from around the corner of a room."

I imagined him peeking in as his older brother and parents talked in the living room. "Leon met Einstein, didn't he?"

"Yes, this is the story. Leon was an engineer in school. Albert Einstein had come to Brazil in 1925 and spoke at the Brazilian Academy of Sciences in Rio. Brazilian scientists had helped prove his theory of relativity during the total eclipse of the sun in 1919. Einstein said, 'The problem conceived in my head was solved by the luminous sky of Brazil.' So, he gave this talk, and my brother was there. He met and spoke with Einstein. This is what I was told. This is what my brother talked about with my parents."

"And you listened in."

"Yes, everyone expected Einstein to speak about relativity in Rio, but he spoke about quantum light and photons instead, and trying to understand how photons behaved both as a wave and a particle."

"Did you understand that at the time?" I was impressed my dad had the terms down.

"No, no, no. I did not understand any of that. I was a little boy. I just heard them talking. Since then, I've read about the important talk Einstein gave in Brazil. I know all of that now."

"Got it. Then Leon got sick."

"Yes, then one day, while Leon was visiting, he got sick. Maybe the water. He got a terrible fever. He had fatigue, headaches, nausea, and pain in his stomach. Suffering terribly. He contracted typhoid. Typhoid is a bacteria that invades the blood and intestines. My parents took him to Manaus to see several doctors. They tried everything. My father tried everything. But he could not change the situation. Leon died there in Manaus. He's buried there. He's still there but not there."

Still there but not there. I let his words linger. "How did it affect the family?"

"My father was not the same person. My mother was not the same person. I saw them crying all the time. They used to praise him because he was such a good student, and he was a good brother, and he was a good son, and he died anyway. It was a different atmosphere. My mother finally accepted it. 'It's God's will,' she said. But my father never accepted it. 'Why, why, why,' he asked. It made him very, very unhappy through the years. None of his authority and skills and achievements prevented his son from dying. He began to question everything."

"How did it affect you?" This is what I wanted to get at, events that explained my father and the many lives he led.

"It shocked me. Our whole life was disrupted, and I started having a different sense of life. Life started having a different meaning for me. There was life and death around me every day in the jungle, animals killing each other, the violence of nature, people I heard of who died, but no death in my family. I didn't know someone in my family could die. I didn't know that. Then I realized that life was nothing."

I looked carefully at my dad. "What do you mean?"

"Why be good? What is the point?" My dad clasped his hands. "If my brother could die, then I could die too. Then, my father said, 'Enough, no more Itacoatiara.' He couldn't take it. He didn't want to be there reminded of his son's death. He decided to no longer be mayor. After everything he did for everyone, God still took his son. It became very tense at home. Arguing. Sadness. He moved the family to Manaus. No warning. I didn't like it. I left all my friends behind. I wasn't happy. But my father made the decision, and we didn't have too much to say about it. We moved fast and I had to take it."

"I know that feeling." I said it too quickly, making it about me and my brother and sisters, and the many times we moved and had to take it, but my dad was in his own thoughts.

"What happened next?" I asked.

"Manaus was a more modern city. I saw automobiles, that thing running on the street without a horse. It was funny to me. I saw a telephone for the first time. I didn't understand it.

I went looking for the wires all over. My father opened a new business, this time under his name. Casa Isaac Peres. Everyone in the state knew him anyway. I went to gymnasium. High school. I started doing things on my own, becoming more independent. I started doing things I shouldn't have done. I was not a good student in Manaus. I didn't apply myself. I was with students of bad caliber. Not criminals, but we fooled around. I got mixed up in fights. I came to Manaus with that attitude that is peculiar to the people of the jungle: don't step on our toes."

"You got into fights." I said it expecting that he would, like the new kid always does, like I did in sixth grade finding my way in a new school.

"Yes. You have to understand. I came from the jungle, I was Jewish, I looked different. My hair, my eyes, my skin, I spoke different, different accent, and things of this kind. I got into problems, the teachers hit me, and it was bad because when I got home my father hit me too for disobeying the teachers. I started rebelling against my father. I shouldn't have done that because I didn't see that he wasn't causing the problem. I was causing the problem. I didn't understand his pain. And he was always calling my attention to my brother Leon who died, and to my other brother José, and my cousins, that they were good students, and I was not. So, I said, that's the way it is, that's the way it is. I said why does everyone have to be intelligent in this family, somebody's got to be stupid."

My dad got up from his chair. He had not eaten a single thing from the plate my mom had prepared. He went inside.

I began eating the melon and strawberries, spearing each with a toothpick.

My conversation with my father that afternoon didn't end there. Minutes later he came back onto the balcony. I wasn't sure what emotions were coming up for my dad, but he clearly felt wounded. I felt for him when he talked about being hit by his dad and feeling stupid compared to the rest of his family. It was such a departure from what I knew about his intellect and how I experienced him. He spoke so many languages, he knew history and literature, he wrote beautifully. But when he brought up those memories, I didn't comment. I didn't offer any consolation. Part of me thought he could be so infuriating in the decisions he would later make in his life, and his disclosures felt like a win in my column.

He looked out over the condominiums as the wind picked up on the balcony. He had gathered himself.

"You see, I didn't like Manaus at first, but the move was good because I came face-to-face with civilization. It opened new worlds for me and maybe that was what my father had in mind all along. Manaus was a brand-new city at that time, a beautiful city, built up by English engineers with a floating harbor, the only one like it in the world. Beautiful street cars. Good water treatment. Electric light. Nice pavement. Famous opera house. Beautiful courthouse based on French design. It was a beautiful city. A clean city. And a very important city as far as business was concerned. It was the main place for rubber in the world."

It was as if he wanted me to say that sometimes fathers know best, that they know their children better than children know themselves, but I didn't say it. I just listened. Impassively.

My father added, "In 1933, we moved again. This time to Belém, eight hundred miles away from Manaus. I was sixteen."

And his life was about to take a dramatic turn. I stopped the tape. "Thank you, Papai." That's all I said. I kissed him and my mom on the way out the door. My own concerns began pressing on my mind.

Five days after my conversation with my dad, I was out on the water one mile south of Cape Florida on the edge of Biscayne Bay. The afternoon sun sparkled on the waves. Judge Fay invited everyone in chambers to a staff party in Stiltsville, a group of old wooden shacks that sit ten feet above sand banks at low tide. Judge Fay stood at the helm of a thirty-five-foot Cabin Cruiser. No one looked more the part of a captain, more at ease on the water, than him. At the age of sixty-two, he had a perennially athletic bearing. On the boat was Maryanne, his faithful administrative assistant who brought humor and affection to the office; a U.S. Marshall to keep us safe; my fellow law clerks, Ed, a graduate of the University of Miami School of Law; Ed, a graduate of St. Thomas University College of

Law; and Christine, who, like me, graduated from The Florida State University College of Law, three years prior. I had asked permission to bring a friend, so Suzanne was onboard too. She had just started her residency after graduating the previous year from the University of Miami School of Medicine.

It was Suzanne's birthday. During my clerkship year, Suzanne accompanied me to events as a plus-one. She was thoughtful and considerate and kind. We would talk for hours. She was the former girlfriend of my friend Bob from college who I roomed with during law school. They had a complicated relationship, and I was a friend to each of them. There were moments when I wanted my friendship with her to be more than it was, but we never dated. The most that ever happened was when she asked if she could practice taking a patient history and listened to my heart with a stethoscope and I felt a spark move through me. She came along to enjoy her birthday on the bay.

Stiltsville had an illicit past that made it fun to visit with a federal judge. Set on the edge of sea green flats where the waters of Biscayne Bay met the Atlantic Ocean, the area became famous as an outpost for rumrunners and smugglers during the 1920s. With the end of Prohibition, "Crawfish" Eddie Walker built the first shack on the flats in 1933. He sold bait and beer, played jazz and swing, and celebrities and Miamians motored out to drink and gamble and cavort on the deck surrounded by ungoverned turquoise waters. Soon other colorful characters built wooden shacks on the flats. Before long, invitation-only social clubs opened their doors, including the Calvert Club and the Quarterdeck Club. The Quarterdeck, with its "couple's cubicles," became one of the most popular spots in Miami, profiled cheekily in *Life* magazine in 1941, as an "extraordinary American community dedicated solely to sunlight, salt water and the well-being of the human spirit." In the 1950s, between gambling raids and hurricanes, Stilts-ville attracted lawyers, bankers, and politicians who sought a place away from shore to drink and make deals. In 1962, a man named Harry Churchville, also known as "Pierre," grounded a 150-foot yacht in the shallows and called it the Bikini Club. He offered $1 memberships and free booze to sunbathing women while poaching lobster out of season. In the decades that followed, police raids, fires, and changing times reduced the number of shacks from a heyday of twenty-seven to fourteen ramshackle houses by the time Judge Fay took us out to the flats. We docked by a bright yellow and white double-decked A-frame wooden house on the water that had rocking chairs and hammocks, a generator and a grill, and a proudly waving American flag.

Between the beer and soda, hot dogs and hamburgers, it was a good time to talk with Suzanne. What I wanted to do next and who I wanted to be after my clerkship had been weighing on me for months. Unlike my classmates who had started job searches during the fall of their third year, I had a few more weeks to figure it out during my clerkship, but time was running out. One clear option was to work at a law firm. It's what most law school graduates hoped to do: jump into private practice and begin their careers. Law firms offered cases, mentorship, salary, benefits, paying-down-of-law-school-loans, and just-out-of-law-school prestige. I began a search shortly after starting my clerkship. I created a handwritten spreadsheet on a letter-sized yellow legal pad, and listed law firms in Miami, Tampa, Chicago, New York, and Washington, DC. I knew the clerkship and a recommendation from Judge Fay would boost my chances of landing at a leading firm. I drafted a cover letter and a resume that I sent to twenty different firms, five at a time, two weeks apart. On my spreadsheet, I had columns for dates sent, confirmations, interviews, rejections, offers, comments, and acceptance. One of the last letters I sent was to the Miami office of Jenner & Block, a highly regarded Chicago-based firm. The letter quickly led to a series of interviews, the partners of the local office meeting with Judge Fay, and an offer of employment. With a bird in hand at a notable firm, I accepted. I had a great job in my back pocket ready to begin when my clerkship ended.

But it was not my only option.

"Are you excited about your new job?" Suzanne asked.

"Yes and no." I shaded myself from the sunlight off the water with my hand over my eyes. "I mean I am. I'm thrilled. It's an incredible opportunity, and I know how fortunate I am to have it. I wish I could continue doing what I'm doing now. I'm not sure what to do."

"You want to write."

"I do. I want to stay up and drink bourbon and catch lightning."

Suzanne had heard this before. I wanted to write about dilemmas and choices and passion and tragedy. I had started on a manuscript. I had outlined a plot, researched facts, and written pages and pages. I wanted to live free from discovery requests and motions and briefs and senior associates giving me interrogatories that I found no meaning in. I wanted to drink coffee and eat apple pie late at night at roadside diners. I wanted to capture dialogue as fast as I could on the edges of notebooks and to listen to blues guitar. I wanted my own space in libraries and to ride on trains.

"There is a long list of people who want to join you."

"I know. And that's the thing. It's romantic and naïve. It's also real. I could live that life. I could write novels and short stories and memoirs. I could make that choice."

"You could. What else can you do?"

"I could start a law firm of my own." For months I had been having conversations with two younger classmates from law school about starting a new kind of firm. I'd sent them letters outlining a business plan and the values that would guide us. We could launch a firm that would be artist-driven: an Artist Studio-Law Firm where lawyers would do socially conscious work and paint, compose music, and write essays about the times. The firm would midwife creative citizenry and be a concierge practice for civic change.

"Could you really get that off the ground?"

"Maybe."

"What else?"

"I could go into public practice. Become a public defender or an Assistant U.S. Attorney and prosecute criminals."

"Do you really want to do that?"

"No."

"How's it going with your dad?"

"That's the other thing. He led this crazy life. One place after another. One mixed up adventure after another. We're just starting to capture it all. I don't want to live his life. I want things to add up."

Ed and Ed and Christine joked about *Basic Instinct*, which everyone had gone to the theater to watch. We didn't talk about cases outside the office. Maryanne took a picture of us sitting on a railing, the four of us shoulder to shoulder, the sun in our eyes. I took a photograph of Suzanne in a hammock, smiling happily, and one of Judge Fay in a rocking chair, his cap down and his legs extended, shadows creeping over him. We stayed out on the deck past sunset. The skies turned gold on the horizon.

My life in South Beach and in the office was an active rush of things-to-do and keeping track of notes in my Week-At-A-Glance calendar book. I marked down in pencil what I thought important every day. I noted my hours at work: Fay, 9:00 a.m. to 5:30 p.m., Fay, 8:30 a.m. to 6:00 p.m.; conversations with friends on the phone: talk w/ Adam, talk w/ Kristen, talk w/Bob. I noted movies I watched at CocoWalk:

The Mambo Kings, Silence of the Lambs. I wrote down when I did laundry in my building, my quarters jamming in the slot, and when I took a bin of clothes to my sister Rachael's house across town. I noted who I had lunch with – Richard, Moises, Steve, and Steve – and places where we ate: Pi's near the courthouse, the Passport Café. I wrote down when and where I shopped for groceries, Publix, Pantry Pride, and the Minute Maid Juice Bars and Stouffers French Bread Pizza I bought every time. I wrote down the Friday and Saturday night dates I had, with Linda, Karen, Jennifer, and Amanda, what we did, drinks at the Clevelander, drinks at Tobacco Road, and who stayed over at whose apartment. I noted when I paid a parking ticket, once twice in one day, games I watched on television, Indiana vs. FSU, Heat vs. Knicks, hours blocked to study for the Bar exam and MPRE, when I bought a Brooks Brothers shirt, which rep tie went with which suspenders, and what time oral arguments were scheduled at the Eleventh Circuit. I wrote down when I lifted weights, the day I got new Ray Bans, and when I swam in the ocean.

I was on the make. A young man full of promise. I knew I could do what any employer asked of me. I could write and argue and advocate. I could talk to anybody. I liked wearing suits, and who my suits attracted, and late at night, over a drink, loosening my tie. I felt competent and soulful. I was diligent and responsible. I could do more in less time than most people I knew. I made quick decisions and made and broke rules. Every personality test I took reported I could run companies, be an elected official, manage money, create value. I felt it. I knew it.

But there was another part of me. A part of me that felt alone. Anxious. Underachieving. I wanted to lead but I wasn't sure about what I wanted to make happen. I was grateful for everything that allowed me to live an entirely different life than my parents. I wanted to honor them but break from them.

I called my dad. "Do you want to do it again?"

"Yes, I have more to tell you."

CHAPTER FOUR

MY FATHER AND I arranged to meet one week later on a Sunday afternoon. I sensed my dad's enthusiasm. I was pleased that I made him happy, that I was providing him with an opportunity to reflect on his life, but I didn't say so. On the day we were set to talk again, I called him on the phone, and I told him I was against a deadline for a first draft of an opinion for Judge Fay and today wasn't the best day. For some reason I took pleasure in that too. "I understand," he said. "Do your work first." As soon as he said it, I changed my mind. I didn't want work to come first, I didn't want to be like him when he was a distant presence in my life when I was a child, and I was struggling with writing the opinion anyway. I asked him if he wouldn't mind coming my way. He said he would.

My dad took the Route T bus from Sunny Isles down Collins Avenue all the way south to Washington Avenue on 9th Street. He was a nervous driver, and I preferred that he take the bus. Plus, it was difficult to find a parking spot near the beach. A wrong decision and a tow truck would whisk his car away.

I met him at the bus stop two blocks from my apartment
building. He looked a bit rumpled from the long bus ride.
I gave him a kiss on his cheek, smelling astringent on his skin.
We walked to a favorite restaurant for lunch. Puerto Sagua had
been on the corner of 7th Street and Collins Avenue since 1962.
Laminated wooden tables. Chipped wooden chairs. A faded
3-D mural of Cuba on the wall. I had lunch there at least once
a week and ordered take-out from there in the evenings. The
restaurant was filled with men wearing t-shirts and guaya-
beras, and young women in sundresses over swimsuits. I loved
the basics of the food – the simple vinegary shredded salad
with sliced red onions and cucumbers, the warm buttered
Cuban bread – the efficiency of the staff (Rosalina, Celeste),
and the sound of different languages in the air. I ordered
the No. 9, Bistek Empanizada, Papas Fritas y Ensalada, and
my dad had the No. 22, Pollo Asado, Arroz, Frijoles Negros
y Plantanos Maduros. I had a Materva, a crisp tart soda
made from the yerba-mate plant popularized in Cuba before
the revolution, and my dad had a café Cubano espresso, the
stronger the better.

Over lunch we didn't talk about anything personal. The
previous month George Bush and Boris Yeltsin had proclaimed
a formal end to the Cold War. The Democratic primaries were
underway with Bill Clinton, Jerry Brown, and Paul Tsongas.
Mario Cuomo and Jesse Jackson declined to run for the presi-
dency, avoiding the high likelihood of personal defeat. My dad
loved watching the news and particularly loved listening to
Cuomo and Jackson. He liked the way they talked just like

he liked the way Christian preachers talked. The rhythmic rhetoric. The soaring righteousness. The call and response. My Jewish dad stayed up late to listen to Billy Graham Crusades. On Sunday mornings, he switched between *Meet the Press* and *The Hour of Power*, from election analysis to the baritone voice of Robert Schuller in the Crystal Cathedral. My dad had a particular roadside attraction to Jimmy Swaggart. Cuomo, Jackson, Graham, Schuller, and Swaggart: a Hall of Fame of sin and salvation. I'm not sure what my dad worked out listening to all the Christian human failings and forgiveness and keeping hope alive. He thought Bill Clinton was all the politics and religion of the nation and every hypocritical ounce and boundless infuriating and entertaining talent of America rolled into one oversized shameless person. He said he would vote for Clinton if he could. His Brazilian citizenship and permanent legal status in the U.S. left him a keen observer.

When the bill came, my dad paid with cash. I could see a faded picture of me and my brother and sisters as school children in the fold of his worn wallet. I was probably five years old when the picture was taken.

After lunch we walked from the restaurant to my apartment building on Collins Avenue, which offered below-market rent to residents who could show below-market wages. My salary as a law clerk was low enough to allow me to live a block away from what was becoming the most famous beach in the world.

My dad held onto the railing, climbing the flight of stairs behind me to the second floor. We walked down the hallway to my door. Apartment 13. The same number as Dan

Marino's jersey. Rent cost me $500 a month for 500 square feet. A deal. And I made every inch of the apartment my own.

My dad had not been to my apartment since I first moved in. He took it in quietly. My books from college and textbooks from law school. Photographs of my summer interning in Washington at the Progressive Policy Institute. My CDs of Depeche Mode and Kitaro. My queen-size bed with a white duvet. My closet with perfectly spaced gray and blue Brooks Brothers suits, striped ties, suspenders, and lightly pressed shirts. The apartment was clean and coordinated and organized, inviting for one, and a night over for two.

"You have nice things."

Things that may have reminded him of his bachelor days too. "It's getting there." I pulled up one of the chairs from the café table just inside the door. I turned on the tape. "Are you ready?"

"Yes, I'm ready."

"Is there anything that we covered from our last session that you want to expand upon?"

My father sat at the edge of my sea green striped couch. He opened a thin spiral notebook he had brought with him. He had several notes written. "Yes, I'd like to mention a friend of mine I had in Manaus by the name of Paulo Castello-Branco. We were neighbors and in the same class. We were very, very close friends. Together all day long. We never did anything wrong. He was kind of a poet, and we enjoyed discussing politics at that age. He came from a family of politicians. A very good family with many brothers and sisters and very good friends with my father. I'd like to mention his name because we were very good friends. He died at the age of twenty-one. A very unfortunate thing."

"How did he die?"

"He had cancer of the blood, leukemia. About five or six years ago when I was in Rio, I found out that his father, his mother, all his brothers and sisters died too. All gone."

"I'm sorry that you lost him as a friend." I felt his pain, seeing how he had written his friend's name from decades ago into his notebook.

"And another thing I'd like to add is that the Amazon is a godsend to man. I don't think there is anything in nature like it. It is gigantic, majestic, almost impossible to describe with words. Once a German scientist said the Amazon exploited scientifically can support the world for five hundred years."

"They're destroying it every day."

"Well, they are in a way, but it is so big. Now, there is a Brazilian writer that once said that the Amazon was the last act of Genesis. It was the last thing that God created. God was already tired of distributing gifts all around the world so on the last day he threw everything into the Amazon. Everything is there. Everything is great. There you can see the smallest things in the world and the biggest things in the world. The smallest monkey in the world is there. At the same time, you can see the largest trees in the world. There is one tree called the Kapok tree. Kapok is a tree that produces a kind of cotton that is imported into the United States and Europe as filling for pillows and mattresses. The largest freshwater fish in the world are there."

"Did you appreciate all these things while you were there?"

"To be honest with you, I started to appreciate all these things after I left. I saw all these things myself. It was just my world, I didn't try to compare it with any other region of the world."

"Don't you think that the people who live there, the Brazilians, are the people who least appreciate it?"

"That's right, exactly. The Brazilians know more about Europe and the United States than they do about the Amazon. But this is true in many places. You see, the nature there is such a fantastic thing, the phenomena that you see there, like rivers of different colors. For instance, in Manaus, we have the Black River, Rio Negro, which runs along the Amazon River. And you see on one side the black water, and on the other side you see the yellowish water of the Amazon River. Of course, the water itself is not black or yellow, but the bottom of the river is, so that reflects on the surface. When you look at it, you see black on one side and yellow on the other side. A Brazilian writer called it the wedding of the waters. Now there is another river, the Tapajos River, which is green. You have phenomena like that. So, I think if God has a sanctuary, it is the Amazon."

I steepled my fingers under my chin. "Why is that important to you?"

"Why is it important to me? Well, it is important to me because . . . in the first place, it is unique. In the second place, it is, as it were, God's gift. It makes you feel proud."

"Are you proud?"

"Of the Amazon, yes."

I had drawn a tree on my legal pad while my dad had been talking. And a monkey jumping from a branch. "How do you think growing up in that environment defined you?"

"Well, it would have a tremendous impact on anybody. You are a product of your environment. This is a very funny story . . . I became a kind of a pantheistic man. I forgot for a while of the Jewish god. Of a personal god like we Jews, and the Christians, like to say. And you become a lover of nature, and love in a very mystical sense. You don't know why you love, but you love. When you see all these phenomena and strange things, and tremendous jungle, you come to realize that a Creator exists. You become kind of a mystic. And that has a very big influence on anybody. At least it had on me. The torrential rains, raining for days and days and days. The size of the river. For instance, you couldn't see the other side of the river. It is seven or eight miles wide. And when you see a river, coming down from the Peruvian Andes, crossing Peru, crossing the Amazon, crossing the state of Para, and over-flowing into the Atlantic Ocean, you see, it is so majestic, so fantastic, that you become mystical. You try to understand, you cannot understand. You try to explain, you cannot explain."

I liked when he spoke this way, when he was moved by forces greater than himself, when his mind turned to soulful things.

"Did it lead you to turn away from Judaism?"

"Well, it did not, but it made me a very soft Jew. You see, religion is an indoctrination. You are born without a religion. Your parents make you a Catholic, a Jew. Then as time goes by and you grow up, and you start having consciousness of the world around you, you become conscious of that religion. Maybe as a way of life. For instance, in Itacoatiara, for us Judaism was a way of life. We followed the dietary laws to protect our health. We did not eat pigs, we did not eat alligators, we did not eat monkeys. We only ate what was written in the books. That way we were healthy. Our water was not from the river but from wells, boiled two, three, four, five times because water from the river was a vehicle for infections, especially intestinal infections. Nothing of this kind happened to us, except for my brother Leon, who got typhoid and died. I told you this. Judaism in that sense was very healthy for us. We were a very healthy family. My mother was very strict about these things."

My dad reached for the water I had poured for him. He took a long sip from his glass. We were onto something at the core of who he was. I asked: "You mentioned your brother dying young, your best friend dying young, the physical environment of the Amazon. How do you think those things influenced you?"

"You realize that everything grows, decays, and dies. And you are a part of that nature. I accepted that you are born, that you grow, that you live, that you die. Religion, at least the Jewish religion, despite the great respect for God, the God of Israel, the Jews don't accept death so easily. It is very traumatic for them. Not only for the Jews, but for the Arabs, for all Oriental people. We don't accept death with resignation. But if you live in the jungle, and observe nature, how things develop in nature, you accept the situation. You say, the tree dies, the animal dies, so I'm going to die. The Indians accept these things more easily. They don't rebel against life and death. A Jewish funeral in that area, in the Arab countries, in Israel, in places with large Jewish populations, is a very traumatic thing."

"But how did it affect you?"

My dad put both hands around his glass of water. "I suffered the consequences because I was living in a very sad home. Every day I saw my father crying. Every day I saw my mother praying. It was very depressing."

He put the glass down.

"You suggested when we last spoke that you kind of thought that life meant nothing."

"It means nothing in the sense that it is not forever. You live within that framework."

"I guess what I'm asking is," I paused for emphasis, "you saw your brother and your father and all their success, how they emphasized education and hard work, and it didn't matter. Your brother and best friend died. You realized that everyone dies. That you could die. Did that affect what you chose, the decisions you made, how you lived your life?"

Surely this was it, what guided him, fatalism at the center of his life.

"Well, I don't know," he sat back in his chair. "I cannot answer that question in a positive way. I know that we, man, build up civilization, what we call civilization. Civilization is created by man. Men's deeds and work and dreams and realizations. Then you die, but civilization goes on, history goes on. Why are we here? I don't know. I don't think anyone knows."

"But, Daddy, you are saying this now. What did you say back then? How did it affect you then?"

"It had a very bad effect on me. It killed some of my enthusiasm for realizing things, for attaining things. Do you understand? I lost that urge to say that I am going to be something or somebody. You say, 'What the hell difference does it make?'"

"Is it how you feel now?"

"Now is a different story. Now I am at the end."

I pushed my hands into my face, frustrated. I wanted an admission that early in his life he had given up, that he had become dejected, that he lost ambition, that would explain his decisions that followed. But I knew that wasn't the case. If anything, his life proved the opposite. He never gave up. He persisted and persisted and persisted. Driven by ghosts, driven by ideals, driven by responsibility, driven by shame, driven by pride, driven by love, he would make impulsive decisions and something out of nothing at every turn. He would never stop working.

I didn't want to think of him being at the end of anything. Not for another ten or twenty years.

My dad went to the restroom and returned. There was a wet mark on his pants. I could not imagine being seventy-five years old. I wondered what I would look like at his age. Would I think of myself as a twenty-nine-year-old, a forty-year-old, a sixty-year-old, trapped in a seventy-five-year-old body? I wouldn't have to worry about aging for a while. I glanced at my watch. We were nearing 3 p.m.

I flipped the tape in the recorder. We sat back in our same seats. "After three years in Manaus, your family moved to Belém. You were sixteen years old. Did anything change?"

"Everything changed. I changed. It was 1933. My father finally decided to retire. He said, 'Enough is enough.' Most of my mother's family was in Belém: uncles, aunts, and my mother's mother were in Belém. So, my father decided to move. He sold his business to two nephews. To Esther's children. One was named Ambrosio, the same name as me, and the other was named Jacob. My father sold the business, the building, the supplies, everything. And he bought a house, a good house, a large one, in Belém. And he retired. But his life in Belém was very dull. He was not used to that thing."

"Tell me about Belém."

"A big city. Now it is a city of two million people with big buildings. A metropolis. We call it Belém do Para. It is the capital of the state of Para. Big port. Big airport. Beautiful squares. Beautiful theaters. Beautiful churches."

"What was it like in 1933?"

"Like Lisbon. Narrow streets. Busy. Very European."

"I'd like to go to Lisbon one day."

"One day you will."

"You said everything changed for you in Belém. What changed?"

"When we moved to Belém, I was older. Sixteen. Seventeen. I changed my attitude. I started loving my life, started dreaming, planning, trying to look into the future, becoming active. It was a new place for me. A new start. The sadness and anger of death in my family had lifted. I became a very good student. As a matter of fact, a first-class student. I was at the top of my class during my years in high school. I was studying all the time. I gave my studies all my time, my interest, my enthusiasm. And I felt good about it. I thought I could be somebody."

"This must have made your father happy."

"Yes, he began to see me differently."

"Now you were the successful one."

"I was doing very well. I liked the city. I made good friends. The school was good. The teachers were good. I enjoyed what I was doing. I tried to integrate myself into the life, the social life, political life, of the city. We were living in a very difficult political situation, living under the Vargas dictatorship. Dictatorship of this kind was something unknown to us. We had been a monarchy and then a republic. It was the first time Brazil was under a dictatorship of this kind."

"Right-wing?"

"Yes. There were no more elections in the country, no more Congress, no more representatives, no more senators. Vargas changed the structure of the country. When I grew up Brazil was called the United States of Brazil. Like the United States of America. All the states were independent with their own constitutions. Landowners and businessmen like my father had influence governing each state. Vargas burned up all those state constitutions and changed the name of the country to Republica Federativa do Brazil. The Federal Republic of Brazil. The whole country was now governed by central authority. All the laws came from that source and covered the whole country."

"There was nothing the people could do?"

"Vargas had the power, he had the Army, he had the weapons. And there was something else. Vargas was born in the state of Rio Grande do Sul, on the southern border of Argentina and Uruguay, which is heavily influenced by Germans and Italians. In Europe, Germans and Italians were moving in a very special direction. Germany with Hitler and Italy with Mussolini. Vargas was very sympathetic to the Germans. He let a Nazi party, a fascist party, be born in Brazil, the Acao Integralista Brasiliera party, the AIB. They didn't say they were fascist, but they were. They wore green shirts and black pants. Green shirts instead of brown shirts."

"Was that Vargas's party?"

"No, no, his party was the Liberal Alliance, I think. But there was also a Communist party that he hated, but he allowed it to function because he thought Germany would destroy Russia, and the Communist Party would go away on its own. He didn't anticipate that the United States eventually would get into the war."

"But we're still talking the early 30s—"

"Yes, I'm talking about how the situation was formed. There was already that nationalist populist movement in Germany and Italy, and Vargas was trying to do the same thing in Brazil. In Belém, in the north, we had a governor, a general, by the name of Joaquim Cardoso Barata, appointed by Vargas. Governador Barata. He was a very violent man. He persecuted his political enemies. He killed many of them. In 1935, there was a movement, a kind of counter-revolution, organized by students and law professors and journalists—"

"The intellectual class."

"Yes, to topple the government because it was almost impossible to live there. I joined the movement."

"Wait a minute. You joined a counter-revolutionary movement?"

"Yes."

I had not heard any of this before. "Was it a local movement or national?"

"National. And local. Led by a man named Luis Carlos Prestes. A Communist, very charismatic, but the counterrevolution included many people who were not Communist. You see the country was divided. The intellectuals on one side and the popular masses and the armed forces for Vargas on the other."

"Were you a Communist?" I had to ask.

"No. No. But I was against Vargas. This effort mostly took place in Recife and Rio de Janeiro. Prestes sought to get conspirators from the Army to join him. In Belém one night, when we had all these things set up, we attacked the fire department, we attacked the police department, we attacked two ammunition depots that belonged to the Army. We took over. We seized those places."

"You did?" I was shocked and thrilled imagining him as a revolutionary.

"I had a rifle. We used rifles, and we took over. I was very animated. Shouting. Taking orders. Following the plan. We took the ammunition we found there. We took over all those buildings. But not for too long. Maybe for twelve or fourteen hours. But eventually we lost. The government had more weapons. And some of my friends were shot. Some were killed. Others were expelled from school. Intellectuals were thrown in prison."

"How old were you?"

"I was eighteen."

"Were you arrested?"

"Yes, I was arrested for five days. They took my picture. But since I was young and not the head of the movement, they let me go. The government decided only to have criminal trials against the leaders and collaborators. They kept the working class, the masses, on their side. I had to stay away from school for about one month."

"This is very impressive. What did your father think?"

"Well, my father didn't like it. He didn't approve of it. He didn't like Vargas either, but he was a conservative man. The law is the law, the government is the government, the authority is the authority, right or wrong. And as a Jew he didn't like to act against the established government because he felt it is counterproductive, that there are reprisals. And Jews always pay a very high price."

"Did anything happen to you at home?"

"My actions created a problem in the family because my mother didn't like violence. Young people killed, students killed, that was a terrible thing. My father was upset, but my mother was very cordial with me. She was very good. I could talk with her because she was a very calm person and liked to listen. Finally, you would agree with her, because of the way she talked to you, and advised you, in a very affectionate way, and you went along."

"What happened with the revolt?"

"We were enthusiastic patriotic dreamers, and we paid a heavy price. But finally, the government, the federal government, removed that general and named a law professor as the new governor and things stabilized. José Malcher was the new governor. He was a practicing lawyer. But he was a man of good name, so he became governor of the state. So, in a way, we prevailed."

"I'm still trying to imagine you carrying a rifle. I had no idea that you were part of a counterrevolution. That is so cool."

"You think so?"

"I do. Did you stay active in politics?"

"Well, after this I was asked to announce on the radio. It was the first radio station founded in Belém. I remember the station. PRC5 Radio Clube do Para. The Radio Club of Para. We were 'The Voice of Para. The voice that speaks and sings for the plains.' This radio station still exists, founded by three people, one was a professor of mine, a professor of Portuguese, the other was a journalist. Another man too, who liked fútbol. Soccer. It was an association. Radio was a new thing, a novelty, a new technology that young people engaged in. We broadcast from a house. The station played records of samba music borrowed from business owners and listeners. Listeners would bring their records to the station to play. They asked writers from the newspapers and students from school to contribute. I was invited to read a paper every week on whatever I wanted to talk about."

"Papers you wrote?"

"Yes. I remember that my turn was Friday night. The radio closed at 10 p.m. every night. After that time, no more radio. So, every week I went there on Friday night, the best time, when everyone listened, and read my commentary, but my father didn't like it because it was Friday."

"You mean because of the Sabbath?"

"Yes. Sabbath begins after sundown Friday, but he was also worried about what I might say. But anyway, I didn't care, I went and talked to whoever listened deep into the state. I read things about politics, literature, everything, and spoke into the microphone. It doesn't mean what I did had high literary value, but I spoke the language very well, I had a nice voice, and I said interesting things, and it gave me the chance to be known. At that time everybody knew me."

"Really?"

"Yes. Why are you surprised? But my father told me, listen, just don't attack the politicians. As a matter of fact, he told me two things. Don't talk about politics and don't talk about religion. I understood that reprisals and the idea of anti-Semitism were on his mind, always. What could I say?"

"Did you limit what you said?"

"I started talking more about literature, culture, music, history, poetry. And there were other guys on the radio too. Musicians. Singers. We got together. One was a student of medicine, the other was a law student, the other one was an accountant, and we organized a club of our own. This was about ten or twelve people."

I was all about clubs. Every group I joined it seemed eventually someone would ask me to lead it. I formed the Presidents' Club at Rollins College. I was the president of the Presidents' Club. "What kind of club?"

"A club where we went to one home one night and another home another night and we talked about literature and medicine and the law. We would talk late into the night.

I talked about Portuguese literature because that's what I was interested in. I had a very good memory. I had books and poetry memorized. And it was a beautiful atmosphere talking with these friends and talking to people through the radio . . . but I gave it all up."

"Why did you give it all up?"

"I was in the last year of high school. And I started thinking about leaving Belém and going to Sao Paulo. The most important city in the country. The biggest city in South America. My dream was to become a lawyer and then to become a teacher. And I wanted to go to the best school. The Faculdade de Direito Univeridade do Sao Paulo. The Law School of the University of Sao Paulo. Just like going to Yale school or Harvard school."

"I didn't know that. Your parents must have been thrilled."

"My father didn't want me to do it."

"You're kidding? Isn't that the life your father wanted for you, like your older brothers, like your Uncle David?"

"You see, this is how things go. My father thought I should stay in Belém, close to the family, because things were going well for me, I was achieving, and I might get distracted in Sao Paulo. The problem was my father was very strict. He didn't give me a chance to explain, to show him my ideas, and my plans. However, he was a very loving father. He wanted me to be somebody. And he felt that if I stayed in Belém I would go on with my studies without interruption. I would have more of a chance to succeed with family support. He worried that I would be disappointed in Sao Paulo. But I insisted and insisted. I didn't want to stay in Belém. I thought I must go. I must start my new life."

"And you left?"

"Yes, and my father paid for it all. I depended on him one hundred percent. I didn't have a job. Until then I never worked in my life. He bought tickets for me to go by vessel from Belém to Rio and by train from Rio to Sao Paulo. I had never been on these things before. I had my luggage with me. I had my hat with me with these big dreams."

"You were nineteen?"

"Yes, and when I arrived, it was not what I expected. I didn't like it at all. My father was right. What happened next was very different from my hopes."

CHAPTER FIVE

WE TOOK ANOTHER break. I poured myself a tall glass of Coke. It must have been years since my father had shared any of these memories. Maybe years since he had thought of them at all. How he could remember the details was beyond me. His usual steady voice had quickened. I pressed on.

"What happened when you arrived in Sao Paulo?"

"I was at the train station with my luggage, and I looked up and the buildings were so big. And the temperature was cold. The southern climate of Brazil is very different than the north. The skies were gray. Everything was gray when I was used to the colors and warmth of the north. I had the address of my brother. My brother José, who was fifteen years older than me. He was the second oldest after Leon. José was thirty-four and a lawyer. That's what I knew about him. We didn't grow up together. When I arrived at his apartment, I was very, very surprised."

"Why were you surprised?"

"I thought he was living one way, but he was living another."

"How so?"

"You see, when he opened the door, he was in his pajamas. I had not seen him in many years, and he looked older than his pictures. The apartment had books and food all over the place. I'm standing at the door in a suit and a hat. I wore a hat then. He said he had one question for me. He said, 'Is our father responsible for your expenses here in Sao Paolo?' I said, 'Yes, why?' He said, 'Because I'm broke. You can stay here, you can sleep here, it's no problem, but I'm not able help you.' He went on and on. I was very surprised."

"Were you expecting him to help you?"

"I wasn't expecting what I heard from him. I walked in and sat down with my luggage. He said that I should know that he was a member of the Communist Party. That he was a believer in that thing. He was very enthusiastic about Communism. He had a tremendous admiration for Leon Trotsky. He said he had been arrested, and that he had spent six months in jail, and his law license was canceled."

"Wow."

"Yes, very nice welcome."

"Did anybody in your family know that he was a Communist and lost his license?"

"No. Nobody. He hid it all from my father. He was trying to make a living translating books because he had a very good knowledge of four or five languages. Not that he could speak those languages, but he could read and write and translate. He had a very good knowledge of Latin, and at that time he was translating Spinoza from Latin to Portuguese. He spent all his time in his pajamas, reading books, eating food, and he was restricted where he could go in the city."

"He couldn't show you around."

"No, he just stayed home. And because of that situation, his wife left him. His first wife."

"What did you say to him?"

"I said, 'Listen, I feel bad for you, but now I'm here. I don't know the city, it's a big city, a very strange city. Everybody speaks Portuguese with a very strong Italian accent. It hurts my ears. The weather is terrible. People move so fast. I don't like it. I'm a fish out of the pond. So, what now?'"

"Did you stay with him?"

"I stayed with him for six or seven months. My father sent me money every month. José asked for some of my money because I was living with him. He said I was increasing his expenses. I was very sad. I didn't like Sao Paulo. It was a European city. Dark, rainy, cold. I was not used to that thing. I came from tropical weather. I was depressed, but I would not admit this to my father. I hid from him just like José hid from him."

"Did you go to law school?"

"I had to prepare myself for law school. You had to pass a test, the Exame Vestibular, which is very tough, to get into law school. I didn't know what was going on in the city, the intellectual life, the social life of the city. For the first time, I wasn't part of it. I became unsure of myself. I started thinking I was from a very small town. I decided to go to a private school, an intermediary school, and make a revision of a few things, to prepare for the test. Meanwhile, José asked me to help him translate. This is what I did. I went to this school, started studying, helped my brother translate, and we spent my father's money."

"José stayed in his pajamas?"

"Yes. Talking all the time about Lenin and Trotsky. He didn't leave me alone. I started reading about Communism, which I never did before, just to get him to stop talking. He had a beautiful library about Communism, and I think I read most of the books there. But, of course, my brother was a man of much deeper learning and culture. He understood that thing better than I did."

"Did you get active in the movement?"

"No. No way. The Party was outlawed anyway. Out of business. It took about two or three years for José to regain his license, but during that time he lost his enthusiasm for the profession. No client and no law office would hire him. He stayed in his apartment, using the money my father gave me that I gave him. So that was the situation I was in."

"Did you think about going back to Belém?"

"I thought on many occasions about going back, but at the same time I thought I could not. I said, 'I'm staying here.' So, I don't remember the date, but anyway after six or seven months, I had my exam, my test, and I passed."

"That's great, Daddy."

"Yes, so I went to law school, the one I dreamed about, and started going to classes."

"How was it?"

"Beautiful. Beautiful. A beautiful time in my life. The professors sounded very important. They showed an interest in me. I started to make friends. I moved into my own apartment. I wrote letters to my parents about law school. My mother and father encouraged me, they were proud of me, and I felt good about myself. I was building my future. On my way to becoming a lawyer and teacher. Learning. Studying. Reading. Talking to classmates about what was happening in the world. I would walk to the Metropolitan Cathedral in Sao Paulo. To the square in the center of the city. To the Palace of Justice. I had coffee in bookstores. Beautiful time."

I imagined my dad in law school. Young. Tall. Well spoken. A Jew from the Amazon. Strikingly different from his Latin Catholic classmates, talking politics, history, legal precedent, world affairs, commanding a room with his insight and education. The scholar within him was his most essential self, a person immersed in books, conversation, and learning. I knew that feeling. I knew the sense that the wisdom of the ages was mine to access, that language yielded to my will, that creation was at my fingertips, that the future was mine to bend. I'm sure my dad felt it, the stars aligning, the earned optimism, the muses at his call. But then the Fates, always the Fates, spinning the thread of life, measuring the length, and giving it a sudden twist.

"What happened?"

"I was drafted into the Army."

I heard a lecture once about Fortune, Chance, and Luck. The speaker drew distinctions between the three, something about randomness, agency, and intention that I can't remember. Just the exhortations: *Expose yourself to opportunities. Say yes to as many things as you can. Assume you can learn from anyone.* Everything I knew about my father was that he carried on against the most difficult odds. He fought to make things happen and resigned himself to what did. What would Seneca and Epictetus and Marcus Aurelius say? Didn't they know about ask, believe, and receive? Wasn't it about virtue for them? Didn't they say only our own actions and attitudes are within our power?

"What year were you drafted?"

"1937. I was twenty years old. My father received the draft letter addressed to me in Belém. He sent me a telegram. I remember opening it. I had to go to the Army recruitment office in Sao Paulo."

"How did you feel about it?"

"Bad. Terrible. I asked my father if he could interfere, if he could use his influence, so I didn't have to go into the Army, but he said, 'No, the law is the law. The authority is the authority. You're not any better than your neighbor or anybody else. You are a Brazilian, yes, so that's it. You must go.'"

"Wow, Daddy. I'm so sorry."

"He was very strict about these things. Very proper. So that was it. I was angry at my father for not helping me. I was disappointed and sad. I left school. I remember walking out of my classes for the last time. Walking out of the building. Let me tell you something. There is a famous student of the law school, a poet from the nineteenth century, Manuel Alvarez de Azevedo. He was a Romantic. The Romantic period. Very famous in Brazil. I used to read his poetry. He wrote about love and death. Sentimentalism. Being a dreamer. He died young like Byron. That's who I was thinking about, Azevedo, as I left the building. I would not let myself look back."

"I'll have to read his poetry."

"Yes, there is one you should read called 'Se eu morresse amanha!' 'If I died tomorrow.' That is how I felt. That is one you should read."

"Do you know it?"

"I know some lines. 'Quanta gloria pressinto em meu futuro!/Que aurora de porvir e que amanha!/Eu perdera chorando essas coroas/Se eu morresse amanha!'"

"What does that mean?"

"It means 'How much glory I foresee in my future!/What a dawn to come and what a tomorrow!/I would lose those crowns crying/If I died tomorrow!"

"You lost your crowns."

"Yes."

Crowns I knew I had. I waited. I tried to think of a poem I might recite. None came to mind. "What happened next for you?"

"What happened next was the Army."

"Could you have gone in as an officer with your education?"

"Maybe I could, but I said the less responsibility the better. I didn't want to have anything to do with that thing. Every day I hated it. Marching. Learning how to kill people. And it was a very lousy army. The food was lousy. The people were lousy. Everyone telling you what to do. And what do you learn there? How to fight someone who is stealing your boots. How to steal food from the officer's canteen. How to play cards and get drunk."

"It doesn't sound like you were a model soldier."

"No. You see, my spirit was taken away from me. My ideals were taken away. My dream and future were taken away. I went from poetry and law and politics to shooting guns that didn't shoot straight. So, I stopped caring, it was a very difficult time for me, and I reacted."

"What did you do?"

"Let me tell you a story. One day there was a sergeant who was stealing from the Army, he was a man responsible for payments to soldiers, and he made up a list with names that never existed and kept the money, and he was put in jail. Then he was released and ordered to pay back the money. So, this sergeant comes to me and asks, 'Is your father rich?' He asked me this because I was different. I looked different. I could read and write. Most people in that Army then could not read or write. I said, 'Why?' He said he needed a loan. I said, 'I can help you, but to do so I have to leave the camp, I have to contact people, and it might take two or three weeks, and somebody has to answer for me and say I am still here.' He agreed to this plan, and I left."

"You went AWOL?"

"Yes. I thought, so what? I ran away. I took off my uniform. I went to good restaurants. I went dancing. About two or three weeks later he realized I wasn't coming back with the money, so he sent a notice to his friends in the city, and these men found me. I was in a nightclub. These two men entered and asked the host if I was there. The host pointed at me. I was at a table. They came to me and stood over me as I was having a drink. One man asked me if I was Ambrosio Peres. I said, 'Who's asking?' The man said, 'It doesn't matter who's asking. The sergeant wants your money. If you don't come back, we'll find you again and kill you.' Everyone in the club was watching. I said, 'I'll come back but I don't have any money for him.' They left the club after knocking a drink over at my table. So, that was it. I had no choice. The next day I went back to the camp, and when I got there, I was arrested."

"Wow."

"And a very funny situation happened. I was there in jail, military jail, and I started talking to another soldier who also was in jail with me. We were smoking cigarettes. You see, I was in the dirt now, explaining what happened to me, and he mentioned the name of an officer at the camp that sounded familiar to me. I remembered an important family from Manaus by that name. I asked the soldier if he knew if the officer was from Manaus and he said yes. So, I wrote a letter to that officer at the camp, a general, saying that I knew he was from Manaus, that I had lived in Manaus, and I mentioned my father's name in the letter. This was a very important thing to mention my father. That same day a guard came to my jail cell and told me I had been called to the general's office. They took me to see the general in this big office with a big desk. The general said he knew my father, that my father was a great man, and he asked me why I was in jail. I didn't tell him about the sergeant because it might make matters worse, so I just said I missed one or two days of roll call. The general said, 'You wait, and you will hear from me.' The next day I was released, but this sergeant, he found out and never left me in peace. Never."

"Things really changed for you."

"Yes, my whole life changed. After the Army I was on my own. I had to start a new life. I had to make my own money."

"You began working."

"Yes, but things got a little worse before they got better. I was diagnosed with tuberculosis and sent to a sanitorium."

We left it on that note. A week went by. I asked my dad to come my way again to continue our conversation. He said he didn't want to take the bus and would drive. I told him where to park. He said he would follow the signs. We met for lunch again at Puerto Sagua. This time I paid. When we went to his car to get his notebook, his car wasn't there. He stood on the corner of Collins Avenue and 8th Street dumbfounded.

"I know I parked here."

"I'm sure you did."

I would have bet the house that if any car had been towed in the entirety of Miami Beach, it would have been my dad's car. Trying to park illegally on the beach was the world's worst gamble. I knew it was going to happen to my dad.

Miami Beach was a city of sharks, and towing trucks were the Great Whites. They circled the streets, looking for any car they could devour. Residents and tourists and anyone passing through ran the risk of their car being bitten and taken away. Off the cars would go to one of two shivers – Tremont Towing or Beach Towing Services – one block apart in a heartless dark enclave north of the Venetian Causeway.

My dad and I crossed the street and walked back to my apartment not saying a word to one another. We climbed the staircase to the second floor, my dad two steps behind me pulling on the rail. When we went inside, it took me a minute to find my cordless phone. I called the phone number on the Tow-Away sign I had written on my hand. The number rang and rang. Finally, a voice. The voice put me on hold. After fifteen minutes, the voice again. *$300. Bring cash.*

"We have to find an ATM," I said to my dad.

"I will pay you back."

That meant it would be my cash from my account. After giving my dad water from the faucet, we walked out of my apartment, down the hall and down the stairs, to my Nissan Sentra parked in a spot safely reserved for residents of my building. My dad looked tired. He was wearing white slip-on sneakers. I didn't like seeing him in sneakers. I preferred seeing him in his familiar black shoes. He got into the passenger seat. I took the wheel.

I drove to the nearest Barnett Bank drive-through, which, of course, was out of order. We headed north along Washington Avenue to find another ATM. I withdrew $300 worth of twenty-dollar bills from the next machine we found. I gave the money to my dad to count, which he didn't do. He just held the cash loosely. I had written down directions to Beach Towing Services. I reversed direction, driving south. I knew my dad felt bad, but I didn't make it any easier on him. Instead of air conditioning, I turned the windows down in the car for the heat to come in. My dad held onto the assist grip above him as we turned corners and caught every red light on the way. We parked in a jammed lot, in front of a one-story stucco building, with a garish 24 hours/7 days-a-week sign warning us.

I expected a rough-looking man behind a metal desk in a stupid-looking office, but it was worse. We had to stand outside in the sun in a line of angry people who also had their cars towed to get to a small double-paned window with a round hole in it to shout through and pass papers to a rough-looking man sitting on a metal stool in a stupid-looking office. We stood in line for thirty minutes as the man in front of us became increasingly upset as the man behind the window said he would not release his car unless he had a notarized letter from his rental company. This went on and on as the man in front of us cursed and yelled at the impossibility of getting a letter faxed to the towing company on a Sunday afternoon and threatened every possible lawsuit to the man behind the window. It didn't matter. The man in front of us didn't get his car.

Finally, we were at the window.

We read every sign stuck on the walls. YOU MUST BE THE REGISTERED OWNER OF THE VEHICLE. YOUR DRIVER LICENSE INFORMATION MUST MATCH YOUR VEHICLE REGISTRATION. YOU MUST SHOW TWO (2) FORMS OF IDENTIFICATION (ONE OF WHICH SHALL BE A PICTURE IDENTIFI-CATION). We read the Towing Bill of Rights, printed in letters so small we could hardly make sense of it, and the AS OF AUGUST 1ST 1991 CITY OF MIAMI BEACH TOW RATES that listed the Class A through D Tow Hook-Up Fees, Administrative Fee, Outdoor Storage Fee, Waiting Time and Labor Fee, City Permit Fees, Fuel Surcharge Fee (when appli-cable), and Every 15 Minute Fee.

It was an even bet that my dad was driving with an expired license and that he let his insurance lapse. By some grace from the universe, he had a current license in his wallet and a AAA insurance card. We waited as a man in a soiled uniform in the impound lot retrieved my dad's registration from the car. That lasted another twenty minutes. My dad tried joking with the man behind the window. Did you hear the story about the barmaid? It didn't go well. In ten more minutes, as the line behind us grew, out from behind the fortress gate came my dad's beat-up Chevy Impala.

My dad drove his car slowly back to my apartment, following me on West Avenue to Alton Road, right on 9th Street, then left on Collins Avenue, back to the front of my building, as I kept him in my rearview mirror. We circled my block twice before I signaled to him to take a spot that opened. He accelerated. I closed my eyes as he almost hit the car in front of him.

"Daddy, when we last talked, you said that you got tuberculosis. What year was it? What happened?"

We were safely back in my apartment. I had turned down the air conditioning to give my dad a breather. I opened a Coke for each of us. It was four o'clock in the afternoon, and we were three hours behind schedule. We could have rescheduled our talk for another day, but we were in it, and listening to my dad, recording his life, would salvage something from the day. I had a copy of Martin Amis' new book, *Time's Arrow*, on my coffee table, a story told backward, and the book, and my dad, the tourists outside and the tides of the ocean a block away, somehow made continuing our conversation the only call. I pushed the record button. The Maxell tape began to turn.

"I think it was 1940 when I got sick. I remember it was a year, maybe a year and a half, after I left the Army."

"Were you working?"

"Yes, I had to find something. Anything. I worked in the office of this textile company in Sao Paulo, doing paperwork, and one morning I got up, I had a cold, I kept coughing and I spit blood. I told my boss what happened to me, and he said I should go see the doctor. The company had a doctor paid by the company. So, I went to see this doctor, and he took me to the hospital to have an X-ray taken, and a few days later he called me and said I had TB."

"Did you suspect you had it?"

"No. But it was a common disease in Brazil, especially in Sao Paulo because of the weather and lack of comfort. We didn't have heating systems, and sometimes we had four seasons in one day. So, my boss told me that I lost my job, and he wanted me to go to a city with a sanitarium—"

"Wait a minute. You came back from the doctor, he said you have TB, and you lost your job?"

"Yes. Well, they let me go because they thought I shouldn't stay there with the other guys. The company had fifteen or twenty employees in the office, and tuberculosis is very contagious. So, they fired me."

"Well, that makes perfect sense. Were you upset?"

"Was I upset? Yes. But you get sick, and you must go. Out of the company. This is the way it was, but I had a very funny feeling. I was upset but at the same time I didn't believe I had TB. So, I went to see my brother. I had to talk to him through a door. This is what my brother was like. He said I should go to his doctor. His doctor, after examining me, said, 'No, you don't have it. What you have is a very bad cold.' I said, 'What about the blood?' He said, 'Well, maybe what you have is a very serious throat irritation. It is not a big problem.'"

"Did you believe him?"

"I wasn't sure what to believe. It was my brother's doctor. I was in very serious doubt. So, I let my father know. I didn't want to let him know but I did. I called him long-distance in Manaus and told him I had tuberculosis. He really got upset. He contacted a friend of his whom he had business within Sao Paulo and authorized him to send me to Switzerland for treatment. This man called on me and told me he would arrange it on behalf of my father. I said I wouldn't go."

"Why not?"

"Because I didn't want to cause more problems for my father, more expenses, and things like that. I thought what he had done for me so far was good enough."

"So, no to Switzerland?"

"No, no. I told the man I wouldn't go. I would try to get some treatment in Sao Paulo. So, I went to a third doctor and this third doctor said I had it. And he advised me to go to a sanitarium. You see, it was very difficult to treat TB at that time. No antibiotics."

"Was tuberculosis considered terminal?"

"Yes. Definitely. Once you got it, you got it. Maybe you live five, six, seven years. It depends on each case."

"How old were you then?"

"Twenty-three, twenty-four years old."

"When you asked the doctor how much time you had, what did he say?"

"No, I didn't ask him that question. He said that I had to go, that it would be the best thing for me to do. So, I decided to go. I got on a bus and went to this city, Sao José dos Campos, on a high elevation, good climate, and I went there and rented a room in a house, a boarding house, and I was shaken.

Especially when I saw the city and I saw so many sick people walking around on the streets."

"This was a place for TB people?"

"Yes, a place for TB people. But then I got so nervous, so upset, so shaken, about that thing, that I decided to leave that place and go back to Sao Paulo."

"How long were you there?"

"About three weeks. Three, four weeks."

"What were you doing there?"

"Nothing. You cannot do anything. Just stay there and count the time. I could not take it."

"So, you go there to prolong your life but also to die?"

"That's right. Exactly. One day I said, 'No, I'm not going die here. I'm going die on the streets of Sao Paulo.'"

"Did you think you were going to die?"

"I did not know. One afternoon in Sao Paulo it was very misty, a little rain, a light rain, and I walked into a movie palace just to kill time. And I was very nervous because I was under the idea that I was sick. So, I walked into that movie and stayed there, in the dark, and it was a movie with Bette Davis. And in that movie, she had a brain tumor, and she had brain surgery. And that made me so nervous, so excited when I saw that thing, that I had to leave the movie. I was without any control, I didn't feel the ground, I didn't feel anything. I was walking down the street in Sao Paulo, walking fast, and after six or seven blocks I was completely out of my mind. I looked up and saw a sign of a doctor, *Duensas Nervosas*, Nervous Disorders. In that time, they didn't call it psychiatry. And I walked into this office and insisted that the doctor see me, and he did. I was very, very nervous, so he gave me a vein shot to calm me down. I remember that because he said, 'I'm going to give this to you and you're going to feel very hot but don't worry about it.' When he started giving me that thing I saw a wave of heat on my head. Then he told me to stay there for about an hour or so. I did, then I left. And I went home. I lived by myself in those days, and I felt bad being by myself. I was scared. I thought anything could happen to me, day or night."

"*Dark Victory.*"

"What?"

"*Dark Victory.* The movie with Bette Davis."

"Yes . . . *Dark Victory.*"

We took a short break. I wasn't sure how to show sympathy to my father. I wasn't emotional around him. I was either quiet or distant or self-absorbed. My preferred way to engage him was to ask questions, to show interest, to listen, but avoid sharing anything about myself. He could be quiet and distant and self-absorbed too, unless asked to tell a story. He could also behave in ways completely foreign to me. I wanted to hear the stories that explained his life, and I didn't want to offer comments that would keep him from telling me more. I could read moments when he wanted me to express my understanding or affection, to be a demonstrative son, but I played it straight, most of the time, and he played it straight too.

"What happened next, Daddy?"

"I went to another doctor, a suburban doctor, and he did what the other doctors did, but he asked me other questions that the other doctors did not ask me. He asked me if I was coughing. I said no. Do I have a fever? I said no. Do I feel very weak? I said no. So, he said, 'Well, this is very interesting. Probably there is a mix-up in X-rays in the hospital. Go to the hospital and get your X-rays and let me take a look at it.' So, I did. I took the first X-rays back to him, and he said, 'This is not your lung. This is somebody's else's lung."

"You mean a mix-up?"

"Yes. He even told me, 'Listen, maybe the sick guy is free on the street thinking he is in good shape.' Well, four doctors, four different opinions. I thought I'm going to forget about this thing. I'm going to live my life. In the meantime, my father helped me financially. I got another job, worked for four or five months, and I felt fine. One day I joined a weightlifting club because I was skinny. And I lifted weights for a few months and I felt fine, and that's when I got into the insurance business, which is a very active business, walking around, going from street to street, and I didn't feel tired. This insurance company transferred me to Rio, and it was a norm of the company to have everyone checked by doctors. So, I was checked by a doctor. He had X-rays taken, and he said, 'You had TB.' I said, 'Had?' He said, 'Exactly.' I said, 'Do you mean, I don't have it?' He said, 'Exactly.' I said, 'How is that possible?' He said, 'Well, these things happen. Sometimes the body heals itself. Can you walk three blocks?' I said, 'I can walk thirty blocks.' So, he told me to get it out of my mind."

"Did you?"

"Yes, then the war started."

CHAPTER SIX

I KNEW A few things about Brazil during the war, but not much. I studied history between the two world wars in college and perked up when my professors made one or two comments about Brazil. I knew the Vargas regime was sympathetic to fascism, but pragmatic about American investment in the country. Brazil was the only South American country to send troops to Europe to fight during the war. The Brazilian Expeditionary Force fought in the Battle of Monte Castello and other key battles in Italy in 1944. A fact I had never forgotten.

"What happened next?"

"Well, I began working in the insurance business. I was with this insurance company in Sao Paulo. I was good at it. I was independent. I was my own boss. I felt I had some qualities as a salesman. The company was happy with me."

"Were you selling to individuals?"

"Individuals, companies, everything. And I was handling accidents and life. And I was having a very good life, living in a nice apartment, my own car."

"This was during the war. What was the name of the company?"

"SulAmerica Seguros. Seguros means insurance. It was a large company. A Brazilian company, a very large company, maybe today it is the largest insurance company in South America. During that time, I began to travel in the country. Mostly between Sao Paulo, Rio, Spirito Santo, and Minas Gerais. I covered those territories. I was free to go to all of them."

"It seems things began to turn around for you."

"Yes, this was a very good time for me during the war. I had money in my pocket. A new lease on life. I got to know things I didn't have access to before. Women like crazy."

Here we go, I thought. I had been waiting for when he might bring it up. I knew my dad had his playboy years. I would broach it and see what he would say. "Tell me more."

"I went to clubs. I was young. In my twenties. Spending money. Dressing well. Like you now."

"Not exactly like me." I wasn't that way at all. I was sure of it.

"I liked to dance. I learned the tango. I was kind of an assimilated Jew. All my girlfriends were Catholic and my friends also. My father used to say, 'I don't care what religion you belong to as long as you are a good person.' And I was thinking that way. You see, if I come to like a Catholic woman, then I'll marry her and if, by accident, I come to like a Jewish woman, then that's it too."

"Well, you obviously liked being a bachelor at the time."

"Yes. Oh, that was the best thing. I could move freely, I had no obligations, fooling around, monkeying around, dancing around . . . but working. I never had problems with the law, I never had vices but smoking. I was not a drinker. I never saw a drug in my life."

Well, some of that sounded like me. Except for the dancing. My best dance was a very bad version of the Twist. I liked women, the conversation, I was good at seduction in my own way. I also liked to work. I was good at that too. I couldn't stand drinking beer. I would only have an occasional mixed drink. An Old Fashioned or fruity drink with an umbrella. I didn't smoke and never took a drug in my life. I imagined my dad in his twenties during the war years. Living life on his own terms. Living like I was living now. Full of promise. Putting the pieces together.

"Were you interested in the war?"

"I was, very much. I followed it very closely. You see, Vargas was a foxy politician. He was against the Americans, he didn't like the Americans, and he had that inclination toward Hitler. Naziism and fascism were mushrooming in the country with the government's blessing. But the Japanese made a mistake to attack the United States in Pearl Harbor, and the United States declared war on Japan and Italy and Germany, and Vargas did not have another choice but to join the United States."

"Why?"

"Because Vargas was in power already for about ten years because of loans from the United States. That money helped him pay his generals lavishly. Generals at that time were making a tremendous salary, and that's how the dictatorship stayed in power. When the United States got into the war, it was a chance for Brazil to receive more and more money. The Americans started building airports all over our country because Brazil was the shortest distance to Africa. Belém, Sao Luis, Recife became very important American bases. And millions and millions of American dollars and many Americans came into the country. In Belém we had about five thousand American soldiers."

"I didn't know that. Did any of this affect you?"

"It was good for me because it was good for Brazil. The country was modernizing very fast. In the meantime, there was a very strange situation going on in my family. My father, like I said before, his life was boring in Belém after he retired. He was not used to that thing. So, he started trying to get into some kind of business again. He was invited by two young fellows to join a new rubber venture in Manaus. My mother didn't want him to do it. But my father wanted it, and he got into that business, so he moved by himself to Manaus. His partners were two young brothers, Isaac and Jacob Sabba, who were also of Moroccan Jewish origin. They organized this company, Peres, Sabba & Company. It was a big deal. My father capitalized the company. The company financed factories and infrastructure and transportation facilities. My father made a lot of money. The United States was paying any price for rubber, and Brazil became the only market again for rubber because Japan controlled Indonesia. They were making a hell of a lot of money."

"Was this like his old company?"

"Much more modern. Much bigger. Up until that point Brazil was a country that exported commodities. The finishing

of products happened elsewhere. But now Brazil was indus-
trializing. This time my father and Sabba produced finished
products for international and domestic markets. They were
making the final products themselves. My father secured
financing and big loans from the Bank of London. But then
Sabba signed a sales agreement with a German company. That
was 1941, '42. And the United States and the allied countries,
England and everyone else, placed the firm on a blacklist."

"Sabba was selling to both sides?"

"Yes, because the Germans offered a higher price. When
my father found out that the firm was on this blacklist, a kind
of boycott, he got so upset, so angry with Sabba that he decided
to leave the company. He said I don't need these problems, this
aggravation. My father was very strict. His word was his word.
Period. And he said, 'Why should I help Germany? We are
Jews.' So, he left the company and went back to Belém."

"And that company today is?"

"The largest company operating in the Amazon. Very
large. They own a petroleum company. Many sawmills.
They're very wealthy people. They represent maybe seventy
percent of the Amazon economy. The last time I went to
Manaus I saw him, this Isaac Sabba. He lives in Rio now.
The business is run by his children. It is worth millions and
millions of dollars. And they had nothing. My father was
the one who supplied the money. Not only money, but also
credit. Because in that kind of business you need more credit
than money."

"Did your father ever ask you to join him in Manaus?"

"No. No. And I would not have gone. But my father did invite José."

"Your brother, José? You're kidding. He was such a screw-up."

"You see how things go. He invited José to go to Manaus to see him, and José went and asked for money when he was there, and my father gave it to him. At that time, it was a good amount of money. The Brazilian currency was almost on par with the dollar because the United States had poured so many millions of dollars into the country. My father gave José about $150,000."

"That's a lot of money."

"And my father told José to give some to me in Sao Paulo. So, when José came back to Sao Paulo, he sent a notice to me to go see him. This was many weeks after José had already been in Sao Paulo. He had taken his time. So, I went. And José was now in a nice apartment, a nice building, and he set up his own printing company to publish his translations. When I saw him, I found him a little . . . fat. He said that he had just come from Manaus, which was not true, and he was talking like a very, very important person. He said in this voice, 'Our father gave me this money to give to you, but before I hand this over to you, I want you to tell me what you are going to do with the money.' I was so upset. This stupid Communist. I wasn't going to take that. It was none of his business what I did. So, I said, 'Listen, I don't want the money. I don't want it. If you insist, I'll tear it up right here. Keep it for yourself.'"

"How much was it?"

"Maybe five thousand dollars. Out of $150,000. He had kept the rest. He was offering me a much smaller amount than he was supposed to give me. It was still a lot of money. I could use it. I said, 'You come back from Manaus with our father's money and now you think you're rich. Keep your money.' We were shouting. So, he told me, 'If you don't like what I'm telling you, the door is open, you can leave.' I said, 'Okay.' So, I left. I stayed three years without seeing him."

"I saw that coming."

"And then something else happened. My father died."

At the beginning of 1942, after a period of neutrality, Brazil broke diplomatic relations with the Axis countries. Germany and Italy responded with U-boat attacks against Brazilian merchant ships in the South Atlantic. In May, Brazilian aero-naval forces began to attack Axis submarines. Patriotic fervor stirred. Popular demonstrations demanded that the Brazilian government enter the war. Then in August, German submarine U-507 began hugging the coastline of the Brazilian coast searching for unescorted ships. On August 16, over the course of several hours, she sank the *Baependy*, 270 souls lost, the *Araraquara*, 131 souls lost, the *Annibal Benévolo*, 150 souls lost. The next day, the carnage continued. U-507 torpedoed the *Itagiba*, 36 souls lost, and the *Arará*, 20 souls lost. Two days later, U-507 struck again, sinking the sailing ship *Jacyra* and the Swedish cargo ship *Hammaren*, 31 souls lost. Political frenzy erupted. On August 22, President Getúlio Vargas declared war on Germany and Italy.

In rapid order Brazil became a logistical base for the Allies, with airfields and military bases opening along the coast. Thousands of Allied troops and supplies moved from Brazil across the Atlantic. The demands of the war effort spurred industrialization and modernization, leading to significant economic growth. Major corporations expanded: *Companhia Siderúrgica Nacional* (CSN) produced steel, *Companhia Vale do Rio Doce* (CVRD) extracted iron ore, *Fábrica Nacional de Motores* (FNM) produced aircraft engines. The United States War Department ordered hundreds of millions of dollars of goods from Brazil: bauxite, manganese, mica, copper, wool, rock crystal, and rubber. The Great Rubber Battle of the Amazon ensued. The Rubber Development Corporation (RDC), financed with American capital, ramped up production in the Amazon, hiring thousands of rubber tappers to harvest latex. Roads, ports, and rail lines were carved into the rainforest. Private rubber or *borracha* extraction companies surged, including *Companhia de Borracha da Amazônia* and *Companhia Geral de Borracha*. In the mix, were the investments Isaac José Peres had made.

"In 1942, my father decided to move to Rio because by then all my sisters were living in Rio and married, and he was by himself with my mother in Belém."

My father and I had taken another break before continuing our conversation. This time we changed seats. I was on the couch across from the white laminate entertainment console that fit exactly along the apartment wall. My dad sat in the café chair that had been my power seat. We were in rhythm. We were talking as if we had spent a lifetime in conversation.

"This was after he left the company in Manaus?" I asked.

"Yes. He left, he retired, he came back to Belém, and in the meantime my sisters started getting married. First Cota, then Clara, then Simi, then Mary, and they all moved to Rio. He took all his money, sold all his property in Belém, and moved to Rio. From Rio he went to Sao Paulo a few times because Sao Paulo was growing so fast, so dynamic a city, that he felt it was good for him to invest there, buying properties or undeveloped lots or things of this kind. He bought an apartment in Rio for himself and my mother, and then he bought two or three more apartments to rent, and then he bought three or four houses in Santos, a city on the Atlantic coast, and in Sao Paulo he bought several lots, but the main thing for him was to be with his children. He didn't understand life without them. So, he moved to Rio. That was in 1942. So, I decided to move to Rio also, leave Sao Paulo and go to Rio, and work for the same company. Rio was a different city, beaches, sunshine, more relaxed. I used to see my father every two days, every three days."

"How were you getting along with him at that point?"

"With my father? Very well. He had some regrets about me, but deep inside he loved me, and I loved him. We had some misunderstandings, I wanted to go my way, and he thought I was wrong, but he finally proved to be right, and I proved to be wrong. But I said, that's the way life is, and I'm going to live my life according to my personality, my ideas. But one thing I never did was to commit crimes or get into problems with the law. Somehow, I always went around those things. Sometimes I found myself in hot water, but I always got out of the problem."

That was my dad's defense. He did it his way. "What kind of problems?"

"Well, problems, you see, sometimes you owe money, and you don't pay. Only business problems, not personal problems, or moral problems. Sometimes you live beyond your means, and it creates problems. You buy what you don't need but only what you want."

"Was that happening to you?"

"Yes, it happened to me several times."

"Did you live lavishly?"

"No, no, I never did. But I liked to live like you do."

"Like me?"

"Yes. You like nice things."

"I do like nice things. But I pay for them." I said it, and instantly wished I didn't. My father flashed his eyes at me. One disrespectful comment from me could blow everything up. I braced for what he would say next. The two or three seconds of silence that followed seemed interminable. Maybe I had more room to challenge him. Maybe he had become far more invested in our conversation than I knew.

"Brazil had declared war," he said, in the same measured tone as before. "The country was progressing, and my father became sick."

He allowed me to escape. I softened my voice. "What happened with your dad?"

"He began having stomach problems. He couldn't eat. He was always vomiting and becoming weaker and weaker."

"Ulcers?"

"Yes, and he was advised by a doctor to go to a . . . how do you call it?"

"A spa?"

"Yes. A spa. So, he did, with my mother, and a few weeks later I got a call saying that I should go there and pick him up and bring him back to Rio because he was feeling very bad. So, I drove to the city and brought my parents back. The doctor saw him and decided to operate on him."

I regretted the comment I made. I still had it on my mind. "Were you worried?"

"I don't know that I was worried. They decided to operate on him, and the operation was not well performed. Or his care afterward did not go well. You see, let me explain this thing to you, which is very important. Today when they operate on you, they make you sit up immediately, or hours later walk around. That time they kept you in the same position in bed for days and days and days, that position in a man of advanced age congests the lungs. You became prone to a lung problem."

"Pneumonia?"

"Yes, and the doctors tried to get penicillin, already known in the country, but controlled by the Army. Because the United States during the war only supplied this antibiotic to the armies of the countries allied to the United States. It was available in the Army. Through connections my father was able to get some of this drug, but the doctors were not familiar with it. They treated him like this, every two hours one injection of ten or twenty thousand units. And it didn't do any good. After six or seven days of application, he died." My dad said it, not showing any emotion.

I paused, trying to read him. Should I ask him how he felt? What his father's death meant to him? Instead, I asked, "Did they administer it incorrectly?"

"Well, I don't say that it was administered incorrectly, but it was not in sufficient dosage. It was not enough. And due to his age and the fact that he was debilitated and very weak, the medicine did not work the way it should. Now this was proved months later when the inventor of penicillin, the British scientist by the name of Alexander Fleming, gave a lecture in Brazil to a school of medicine. He said penicillin had to be applied in very high dosages to give the right result. In the United States at that time, especially for pneumonia, and gonorrhea and those infectious diseases, they gave one high dosage shot. But in Brazil they were giving frequent small injections, hour-to-hour, hour-to-hour, day or night."

"Were you with him in the hospital?"

"Oh yes. All my sisters and my mother were there. I saw him die. I closed his eyes."

"Do you remember the day?"

"October 28, 1945. We buried him the next day. He was wrapped in a white linen shroud. I stepped into the grave and received his body. The great man was gone."

My dad turned twenty-nine one week after his father died in Rio de Janeiro in 1945. I was the same age as I sat across from him in Miami Beach. Hearing him talk about receiving his father's body in a grave, I imagined doing the same and receiving his body wrapped in a shroud one day. I wondered what it would be like to cradle his body in my arms. Would my child do the same with me one day in the twenty-first century? I knew I didn't have that much time left with my father. Even if he lived for many more years, I didn't see him that often. An afternoon here. A few remaining holidays there. One day I would receive a call that he was gone. What would I have left of him? Photographs? Cards and letters? Tapes of his voice in my desk drawer?

"How did your father's death affect you?" I asked the question calmly. I suspected the answer would break something open in him. Wasn't his father the measure by which my dad judged himself? *Virtue. Intelligence. Work.* Those were the words embedded on his father's tomb. The words on the Peres family crest, if we ever had one.

My dad reached for his water. "It affected my family, especially my mother. You see, at that time a wife was very dependent on the husband, one hundred percent. When my father died, my mother felt she was alone. She had no experience. She didn't know how to handle money or business or anything like that. All her life she was a housewife. She didn't worry about rents or bills or property. They had been married for fifty-five years. That's a long life together. And she became very sad, and the rest of the family did too. Simi felt it a lot, and Clarita also. But Esther and Mary were very busy raising a family, so I cannot say how it affected them."

Them. Not him. I would go with it. "What about José?"

"José? José was in Sao Paulo, he made it to Rio two days after the funeral. He was shocked because he didn't expect my father to die. The only thing I remember about José was that he had a lot of misunderstandings with my father, and one day he told me that he was sorry that those things happened. And I told him, 'Listen, you think that there is no death and life is eternal? You don't believe in death? You will find out one day.'"

"You were angry with him?"

"I was angry with him because he started fighting with my sisters about money."

There it was again. My dad's distaste for money. "Was there a will?"

"Yes, there was. As a matter of fact, there were two, but the last one was the one that was valid. It took a few years. Lawyers got involved."

"How was it all distributed?"

"Well, half of the money was for my mother. That's the law anyway. The other half was divided among the seven children.

And the share that should have been for Leon, already dead, had to be divided by seven. And the stipulation was that my mother would keep all the properties, which was worth some amount of money, and everybody else received only money."

"What was the estate worth at his death?" I wanted to know. I wanted to know what my father squandered.

"Well, I don't know, we had cruzeiros then. I don't remember the exchange rate, but I think it was a little over two million U.S. dollars at the time. So, half of it went to my mother represented by properties, the valuation of these properties was up to the courts."

"So, in today's dollars, about ten or fifteen million dollars?" I was trying to calculate fast in my head.

"Maybe. I don't know. My share was one-seventh of one half. About $120,000 or $130,000 dollars then. I don't know what that would be now. I gave almost sixty percent back to my mother because she needed it for the lawyers, and the other part, about $50,000 I used."

"That would probably be $400,000 today. In 1992 dollars. Wasn't that a tremendous amount of money to suddenly have?"

My dad paused. "Yes, it was. Yes."

"What did you do with the money?" I was prosecuting him. He sensed it.

"Well, I didn't have any plans, so I spent it like crazy."

"On what?"

"On women and trips and things like that. I never bought anything expensive for myself like jewelry. I never liked jewelry anyway, but I spent a lot on nightclubs . . . and books."

"Nightclubs and books?"

"Nightclubs and books. And women. That was my life, anyway, but it was a very well-oriented life. You see, this is very interesting, because, of course, I liked to have a good time with women, in cabaret, I liked to dance, I didn't drink a lot, but I liked to dance, and I went to the library every week, two or three times a week. I was always interested in politics, in history, I was always looking for acquaintances with writers or newspaper people, and people of this kind. That was my life. A very active life."

"You didn't invest any of that money, did you?"

"No, no. I didn't invest anything."

"What happened to the properties under your mother's name?" I was clearly annoying him, but he answered anyway.

"My mother sold some of the properties and other properties she kept. But she was not a good administrator, she failed to pay taxes on the properties and got legally very entangled. More lawyers got involved, and finally when she died, ten or twelve years later, the properties she had were sold to clear taxes. What she had left was divided again."

This time I reached for my glass. I was on my third Coke. I was off-track not pressing him on what his father's death meant to him and any grief he must have been feeling. Or maybe he had just answered the question saying he spent his inheritance. I shook my head to gather myself. I decided to ask directly again. "Daddy, you didn't say how your father's death affected you. How did it affect your life? Your approach to life?"

My dad paused for a long beat. "It was sad. I was sad. It is the saddest thing when you lose a very close parent, and that endures for many, many years. But you go on with your life, you get busy, you assume new responsibilities, and time takes care of these things. It is a very strange thing. You mourn. You grieve. But you also become your own person. You become free in a way. And this can help or hurt you. You no longer have guidance. But you make new decisions. You take chances that you would not take before."

I drew a Christian cross on my legal pad. I'm not sure why. "You loved him, but you were free from him."

"Yes."

"And did you? Take chances?"

"Yes. For a while I kept on doing the same thing, working and earning my living, but things were changing in Brazil. After years of dictatorship, we had a new president. Eurico Gaspar Dutra. There was a promise of democracy. Things became possible, and I wanted something new in my life. A new beginning. I had made mistakes, the war was over, my father was dead, and I could start again. I could be someone new."

"What did you do?"

"This is what happened: after the war, the United States began returning properties to Brazil, bases and airports along the Atlantic coast of Brazil. There was an airline, Aerovias Brasil, that flew cargo planes to the United States. And the main base was in Rio, but they used all the airports along the coast. And they had their own installations, towers, everything. After the war, the airline began passenger flights overseas. Then the company was put on the market. The new owners bought all the assets of the airline. DC-3 planes, large inventories of repair parts, radio towers. And one day I saw an ad in the paper, this ad was looking for a sales manager. I had good experience in sales, and I applied for the job. I heard later that there was fifty or sixty people interested in the job, but it was given to me on a trial basis."

"Why were you interested?"

"Because I could travel. I could move. I could be free."

"What were your responsibilities?"

"I was sent from Rio to Sao Paulo to sell stock to get more money for the company, and to open new offices throughout Brazil. To grow the company."

"That sounds exciting." I knew it must have excited him, being his own man, meeting new people.

"Yes. I was thirty years old. A good salary, commission on the sale of stock, and a bonus on the opening of each office, each agency. I opened offices in Belém in Para, Sao Luis in Maranhão, Teresina in Piaui, Fortaleza in Ceara, Ilheus in Bahia, Vitoria in Espirito Santo. I had a pass to fly. I could use any plane. I was traveling. Traveling. Four, five weeks in one city, then four, five weeks in another city, opening offices and training people. And I did a good job, and I made a lot of money. I bought a condominium for myself in Sao Paulo. I bought a lot in Sao Paulo, in a very prime area of the city. I bought a few lots in Santos. I bought an apartment in Rio."

"So, you were investing after all. Like your dad."

"I was spending money. Spending on a good automobile, I bought a car, an American car, a Ford, one in Sao Paulo, and another one in Rio. I was spending too much. I was going nuts. I thought I was a playboy."

"Were you?" I wanted him to tell me more.

"Well, in a way, in a way, yes. Good suits, expensive suits, Italian suits, things like that. But I was getting tired of that thing. Then one day, in 1949, the president of the company, he liked me very, very much, I used to write his speeches, he called me one day and said, 'Do you want to go to Miami?' I thought he wanted to transfer me, but he said no, I am sending you on vacation as a reward. I said, 'Okay, why not?' So, he gave me a ticket to go and come back, and he gave me $1000. To enjoy myself."

"For all the good work you were doing?"

"Yes. So, I went to Miami in February of 1949. The first time out of the country. And I found Miami very interesting, very bucolic, very romantic. I was ready to take my chance."

CHAPTER SEVEN

ON MY COFFEE table I had a book on Miami with photo-graphs of the city from the 1930s and 40s: with black and white pictures of seaplanes, dolphins, fishermen, tarpon, streets lined with palm trees, hotels, motels, and office buildings, and resi-dences in the Mediterranean Revival, Art Deco, and Miami Modern architecture that came to define the city. Buildings had breezy corridors, covered galleries, shady courtyards, and expansive lobbies to keep people cool before air conditioning. After the war, new year-round residents, seasonal visitors, and international travelers drove Buick Roadmasters, Ford Coups, and Cadillac LaSalles down Biscayne Boulevard and Collins Avenue. Boats from the Caribbean docked along the Miami River. Tourists and cargo filled the 36th Street Airport and Port of Miami. Restaurants, nightclubs, and department stores bustled with activity. People had money to spend, developers dreamed big, as promoters, then and now, billed Marvelous Miami a subtropical paradise. The gateway to the Americas.

I looked at my watch. It was early evening. My dad had arrived at a turning point in his story. Coming to America. I could drive him home now, or put in another cassette, and listen a little more. There was no chance I was going to work on Judge Fay's opinion. I decided we could keep talking for another half hour.

"Where did you stay when you arrived?"

"I stayed at the Everglades Hotel, which was my first hotel in Miami. It was a beautiful hotel, a first-class hotel. I stayed for about two months—"

"Two months? I barely can get a week off from work."

"Yes, two months, and I said, 'I'm going to go back to Brazil to get my visa and come back to Miami for good.' I went back to Brazil, I talked to the president of my company, and I told him that I was resigning because I'd decided to move to the United States."

"Was it because you were unhappy?"

"Listen, Miami was a dream. America was a dream. I could live in a more organized country, a more decent country, where politics were not corrupt, not like in Sao Paulo. Miami was small, but it was clean. It was beautiful and bright. I walked the streets. I went into stores. I saw things I had never seen before. People were optimistic. America was the envy of the world. I could create a life. So, this is what I did. I told the company that I was resigning, that I didn't want my job anymore. They told me that I was making a big mistake because the company was growing—"

"And you had a future in the company."

"Yes, a great future in the company. But I said, 'I don't want a future in the company or in Brazil, I want a future in America.' So, after returning to Brazil, I went to the American consulate and applied for my visa. At that time, Brazil, because of the war, was not in the quota system. There was goodwill between the two countries. Brazilians were free to come here. So, I applied for my residence in the United States."

"Your Green Card."

"Yes. Five or ten days later, the Consul called me and said, 'Yes, it has been approved, you can go any time.'"

"That was quick. You have to wait like ten years now."

"I packed up my bags. I sold all my properties, I sold everything, paid off other things, and put in my pocket $18,000 cash, and came back to Miami."

"And said goodbye to your family?"

"Yes, goodbye to my mother, goodbye to my sisters, goodbye to my brother. I told them what I was doing. José thought it was a good idea that I leave, that Brazil was really a rotten place."

"He thought that it was a good idea that you leave?"

"Yes."

"What was your brother doing at this time?"

"He tried four or five times to return to practicing law. He joined different law offices, then he applied for a job as a professor at the University of Sao Paulo, and decided to make his living as a writer, writing books about history, about the Jews, about philosophy, translating books from Spanish, or French, or Latin, into Portuguese. That's what he liked to do. It was not well paid because these things don't produce a lot of money, but he made a living. He had money from the inheritance. Then he got married a second time to a lawyer. She had a good job with a railroad company. I believe she helped him financially too. He never left Sao Paulo. He died there."

"So, he became a professor at a university, and you came here. You didn't have a job, did you?"

"No, no. I came here not knowing anyone. I went to school in Miami to learn English, to the Berlitz school first, then to a private school, and then to a vocational school."

"Where were you living?"

"I was living here on 27th Street and Biscayne Boulevard. The area was beautiful at that time. I had an apartment. I connected with a small Brazilian community, very nice people, who were here in Miami working for the Brazilian consulate and for Aerovias Brasil. I decided to get a job in Miami to be exposed to the English language because I was learning English in school. You learn a lot, you learn about grammar, you learn how to read and to understand what you read, but you don't talk. So, I got a job at the airport, I applied for a job at the airport, a very lousy and dirty job, cleaning the inside of planes."

"Cleaning the inside of planes?"

"Yes."

"That was the only job you could find?" I couldn't imagine him picking up cigarettes and soiled napkins that people left behind.

"Yes, because of my English. You could be a genius. You could know twenty other languages, but it doesn't make any difference in America if you don't speak English."

"How did you feel about the job?"

My dad looked at me as if I had lost my mind asking the question. "You do what you have to do. If I dropped you in China, what would you do? The job didn't bother me. I made the decision to come to America. I would start at four o'clock in the afternoon and work until 11 p.m. at night."

"Did you wear a uniform?" I have no idea why I asked that question.

"Yes. And a lot of good people did too, including American students from other states. The plane came, we got on the plane, we cleaned it up, and that's it. And then we would sit down there, smoke, and wait for the next plane. And go home. The salary was $45 a week. I worked there for six or seven months. And I learned to speak English."

"You learned to speak English cleaning planes?" I couldn't get past it. "Which airline?"

"No, it was not an airline, it was a company that gives service to airlines. And it was $45 a week. It was good money."

"It was?" At the law firm I would earn that in five minutes.

"Yes. I had this apartment, furnished, one bedroom, and it was in a new building. It had a stove, a refrigerator, everything. I spent $15 or $20 on food, so I still had $10 or $15 left every week. And I still had part of my money from Brazil . . . So, this is very funny. One day I was at the airport waiting for this Brazilian plane to arrive, Aerovias Brasil, the company I used to work for. And the president of the company that I knew from Brazil stepped out of the plane and he saw me, you know, ready to clean the plane, and he looked at me, and I looked at him, and he looked at me, and he said, 'I don't believe it.

I don't believe it. I don't believe my eyes.' He said, 'Peres, what the hell are you doing here cleaning this plane?' I said, 'Where are you staying tonight?' He said, 'The Everglades Hotel.' I said, 'Okay, I will call on you and let you know what I'm doing.' He said, 'Please do, because you look crazy to me.'"

"Were you embarrassed?"

"I was, a little. Because that's a kind of disappointment. Well, the next day I went to the hotel, and I saw him, I met him and talked to him, and he said, 'You're coming back with me to Brazil. I'm going to give you a ticket because you're not going to stay here cleaning planes.' He offered me my job back. Not the same job, but another position in the company. But I said, 'No, I'm staying here.'"

"Were you tempted by the offer?"

"I was in a way, yes, because I did not see my way clear here. After a few months the whole thing, coming to America, started looking like an adventure without any purpose."

I waited for a long beat. "You didn't have a plan."

"No. But sometimes you just live. I didn't go back. I stayed here."

I stayed silent, fidgeting. Then I asked, "Did you regret that decision?"

My dad took a long look at me. "Not immediately, but a few years later when I found out that one of the guys who worked with me at the company became governor of Sao Paulo, and another one became president of a different organization, I felt I missed the boat. But these are decisions you make, and I wanted to stay in America."

I flashed to my time after I graduated college. I had everything going for me. A stellar academic record. Recommendations. I could have applied to the best graduate programs in the country. Harvard. Yale. Princeton. I could have moved to the West Village and submitted stories to *The New Yorker.* But I didn't. I was completely unclear what I wanted to do or who I wanted to be. Instead, in the summer of 1985, I moved to Boston, stayed at my friend Adam's house in West Newton, put on a suit every day, took the Green Line into the city, tried to find a job in human resources with my history major, assessing human talent was the future, but to no avail. Then I moved to Houston, to the energy capital of the nation, and stayed with my brother in his home, sent out resumes to start a career in marketing and communications, but no responses. Houston was amid an oil glut and economic recession. Two months later I moved back to Orlando to rekindle a college romance that was an emotional mess and thank God it didn't rekindle, and took the only job I could find, selling Hawaiian Tropic suntan lotion and scrubbing slime from the edges of pools at Disney World. For six weeks I was a pool boy, sitting in a thatched hut, demonstrating to pasty Midwesterners how to put on aloe, feeling I had completely tanked my college education. I didn't have a plan and could not make sense of where I fit in the world. A few months later, I found a job selling financial software that ran on IBM and Burroughs mainframes to regional banks, applied to the CIA, then to law school at a state university as a way forward. Three years went by. Sometimes you just live.

"What did you do next?" I asked.

"After the job at the airport I applied for another job with a manufacturer of brassieres here in Coral Gables."

"Brassieres?" I raised my eyebrow.

"Yes."

"You're kidding."

"Called Deala."

"Dial-a-bra?"

"No, Deala. I applied for a job to sell in Cuba. I began selling lingerie in Havana. In 1951."

"You were thirty-four years old and single selling lingerie in Havana in 1951?"

"Yes, it was a good place, a place to enjoy life, good night-clubs, a lot of nightlife, a lot of women. I started going there, staying for two weeks, coming back here. Traveling between Havana and Coral Gables. Selling lingerie to women."

"Wow."

On that note, we called it a night.

The next day, on a Monday morning, I woke up early to head to the office. I had three opinions to draft for Judge Fay with three months left to go in my clerkship. I loved going into the office. All of it. Dressing in the morning. Turning on NPR. Putting on my security badge. Crossing the Causeway toward the city. Chatting with Ed, Ed, and Christine. Bantering with Mary Ann. Sitting across from Judge Fay as he explained a ruling and what he wanted drafted. Seeing his carved wooden block on the wall to *Write Fast,* a plea for us to believe in our convictions and stay on task. Sitting at my desk with law books and briefs and the trial record on either side of me. Typing with two fingers on each hand. Drafting an opinion with a summary, background, discussion, and finding that would serve as precedent in the circuit for years to come.

Judge Fay was two years away from senior status on the bench. He had a career that I marveled at and hoped to emulate. He attended Rollins College, a multi-sport athlete, earning letters in football, basketball, and crew. He co-founded the water-ski team, graduating at the top of his class in 1951. He served two years as a second lieutenant in the U.S. Air Force. While stationed in the Azores, his commanding officer recruited him to represent airmen in court-martial hearings. Assisted by the G.I. Bill, he attended the University of Florida College of Law, where he edited the Florida Law Review and graduated again at the top of his class in 1956. He went into private practice, quickly becoming a partner, before co-founding his own firm, Frates Fay Floyd & Pearson in 1961. He served on numerous professional associations, provided pro bono counsel, lectured, and represented clients in complex cases. He was a founding limited partner of the Miami Dolphins and negotiated the contract that brought Coach Don Shula to the team. In 1970, President Nixon nominated him to the U.S. District Court for the Southern District of Florida. In 1976, the U.S. Senate confirmed him to the U.S. Court of Appeals for the Fifth Circuit, which later became the Eleventh Circuit.

That's how to do it, I thought. *That's how to live a life that adds up.* I could be him. I could be the Hon. Mark F. Peres one day, an esteemed judge on the federal bench. I could take the same path he did. I attended Rollins College, excelled in the classroom, served as president of the ODK Honor Society, and received the Algernon Sydney Sullivan Medallion for character and service. I performed well enough at Florida State to secure a federal appellate clerkship. I had an offer pending from Jenner & Block, a top-tier national firm. I could become a partner, serve the community, consider politics. I could launch the Artist Studio-Law Firm I had in mind. I could develop a fine legal mind in constitutional law. I could be appointed to the federal bench. I could hear cases, render rulings, and mentor bright and eager young minds ready to make a difference. I could live a life of success and virtue. Just like the Hon. Peter T. Fay.

Against a deadline to complete a draft opinion, I worked into the night. One thing I could do was lock in when writing. I worked from 9 a.m. to 5 p.m. without leaving my chair, walked to Bayside to clear my mind, and returned to the office at 6:30 p.m. to write until midnight. I had the chambers to myself. The Duke vs. Michigan national championship game played on the small television in my office. Every sports fan in the country had the game on. The returning national champion Blue Devils (Thomas Hill, Bobby Hurley, Antonio Lang, Grant Hill and Christian Laettner) vs. the Wolverine Fab Five (Jimmy King, Jalen Rose, Chris Webber, Ray Jackson, and Juwan Howard). Jim Nantz and Billy Packer called the game. It was close at halftime with Michigan up by one. I wasn't sure who to root for: Duke, who in the previous game against Kentucky, defied odds when Christian Laettner caught a full-court pass with 2.1 seconds remaining, turned, dribbled, and put up a Hail Mary field goal to win the game, or Michigan, whose starting five were all freshman who wore black sneakers, black socks, baggy shorts, and were decidedly more dope and tight than the Blue Devils. As I kept writing, and drinking Coke to keep me up, Duke pulled away in the second half.

By midnight I had a complete first draft in hand of *United States vs. Kimmons*, in which the appellants, who had been convicted of conspiracy to affect commerce by robbery of armored car companies, and who had been sentenced to life in prison, challenged the district court's application of the U.S. Sentencing Guidelines. My draft opinion reviewed the facts of the case, discussed the appellants' various claims, considered case precedent and statutory law, and, in accordance with Judge Fay's instruction, affirmed the challenged convictions and sentences. I knew I would have to work a few more late nights to revise it, double-check citations, and finish footnotes, before giving it to Judge Fay, who would revise it again, pose questions in the margin, and have me complete the final draft before he would circulate it to the other judges on the panel.

I was proud of what I had written. I didn't shy away from a rhetorical flourish or a poetic turn of phrase. I had two more cases to go, one appealing an evidentiary ruling in a trial on offenses arising out of a conspiracy to launder illegal drug proceeds, and one on whether a magistrate judge misapplied a legal standard for partial takings under a comprehensive land use plan. The cases were typical of those that made it to the appellate court. Each case presented knotty issues of fact and law. Each case had multiple parties and amici briefs weighing in. Each case had oral arguments when counsel briefed the court and judges on the panel asked questions. As clerks we listened in on arguments, taking notes in the back of the courtroom. We were not privy to the discussion between the judges. They would decide the case between themselves and who would write the opinion. Nearly every case that Judge Fay shared with his clerks included a concurrence or a dissent. I found the debate between all the parties, with different stakes for everyone, involving civil and criminal law, state and federal considerations, procedural and constitutional issues, intellectually rigorous and rewarding.

I also knew I was in a bubble.

In three months, I would be outside the halls of the court and working in a law firm that operated under very different incentives. Lawyers trade time for money. The culture at most large firms expected young associates to work eighty-plus hours a week billing time in seven-and-a-half minute increments. Depending on the firm, and the nature of the cases, and the senior associates and partners who assigned the work, a junior associate could spend weeks buried in discovery. This meant opening boxes, tagging documents, writing interrogatories, responding to requests for production, then drafting motions, responding to orders, sitting in on depositions, and billing,

billing, billing. In complex cases, with multiple parties and causes of action, discovery could go on for years. Corporate clients would spend millions of dollars in litigation, seeking leverage, before settling. Whatever the case was about would become lost in the space-time warp of legal procedure.

Could I do it? Yes. Did I want to do it? No.

That was it. That was the choice in front of me. Could I manage my career and become Peter Fay one day? Did I take a job at the law firm and buck up and do the work that every other attorney did learning their trade? Or did I live on the edge and ride the rails, devoting myself entirely to the life of a writer? Could I do both? Would one life completely compromise the other?

Three days later I printed out the first draft of the opinion and put it on Judge Fay's desk. I had a busy weekend in front of me. I had been invited to my friend Bob's wedding in Tallahassee. Bob and I had gone to college together. We met freshman year in a history class, where both of us became history majors. He was high achieving, a great athlete, and president of the student body. He went to law school immediately after college, unlike me who was caught up in three years of unsettled drift before applying. He graduated with honors, then went to work for Floyd Pearson Richman Greer in Miami, once Frates Fay Richman & Greer, the firm that Judge Fay had co-founded. In 1989, at the age of twenty-six, Bob returned to Tallahassee to run for Congress. I was in my second year of law school. Bob asked me to join his campaign. I served as a friend and advisor, wrote letters and editorials on his behalf, traveled with him, coordinated events, and encouraged him. We were both centrist Democrats. I spent a summer in Washington, DC working for the Progressive Policy Institute, the think tank arm of the Democratic Leadership Council, that sought to shift the politics of the Democratic party to the right. Bill Clinton, Al Gore, Sam Nunn, Lawton Chiles, Chuck Robb, and Dick Gephardt were founding members of the DLC. Bob ran a terrific campaign, on the coattails of the centrist mood, but lost in the primary to a more established candidate. I admired Bob. I admired his confidence. His talent. His work ethic. We were pacesetters for each other. I had his wedding circled in my calendar and was looking forward to getting away.

I drove to Orlando after work, arrived in Casselberry, and stayed overnight with a friend I'd dated briefly during the time I was cleaning pools at Disney World. The next morning, I continued to Tallahassee, arriving in time for an afternoon Law Review party at the Rotunda. I caught up with Dave, Marjorie, and Rob, classmates from law school, with whom I had been exchanging letters about starting my own Artist Studio-Law Firm. Dave was beyond brilliant, seemed to understand the inner workings of the universe, and was sure to work in national intelligence one day. Marjorie and Rob were an item, artistic, sensitive, free-thinking. Each of them had independent and unconventional personalities, and if we didn't work together, each of us would one day work for ourselves. It was one shingle, or four shingles, and the more we talked about Tallahassee, Miami, Sarasota, and Jacksonville, civil and criminal practice, individual and corporate clients, writing novels and screenplays, trailblazing for art and justice, the more we began to laugh. The Artist Studio-Law Firm was not going to happen. It was a fanciful idea. We had to pay rent. Maybe someday.

That night I went to the rehearsal dinner at Annella's Restaurant, watching Bob in his element. Bob and his family were the Kennedys of Tallahassee. His dad was a founding partner at a highly regarded boutique firm with state government ties. His mom was active in community service. His sisters were lawyers and professionals. They were a highly accomplished All-American family. Bob and I were roommates during my third year at Florida State, while he served as Assistant General Counsel for the Florida Department of Education.

The next day, Saturday, April 11, the morning of Bob's wedding, he and I played basketball in the rain. He had a great outside shot, was taller than me, and could jump higher. He played varsity basketball in high school and intramural throughout college. He ran full court, could dribble, pass, and post. I never played on a team that wore a uniform. My game was half-court, defense, and rebounding. He would always win one-on-one, but I won my share when we played three out of five games of HORSE. We competed in all things.

The wedding was a beautiful affair under a tent at Bob's parents' home north of Tallahassee. The band played

Jamaican music. I mingled with friends from college and law school who shared news about offers from firms, graduate school, business plans, and appointments in Tampa, Jacksonville, Orlando, Miami, Boston, Chicago, New York, and Washington, DC. Everyone was on the move. Everyone compared notes. Everyone was making their way.

I drove back home on Sunday, seven hours straight, nearly five hundred miles, from the Panhandle through the heart of Florida along the turnpike to I-95 to Miami Beach. As I parked my car, I knew I would join Jenner & Block. How could I not?

I didn't talk about my sex life with my dad, and I didn't expect him to talk about his sex life with me. That's not something we did, and I didn't know any fathers and sons who did either. He had his secrets. I had mine. One way something that happened never happened was never to speak of it again. We make up our past by remembering what we want. I could imagine his life before he met my mom. We were not unalike. He loved books. He enjoyed working hard. He enjoyed the company of women. I did too. Here is how I imagined his life in Havana: a briefcase full of black lace bras. Calling on stores. Dating models. Taking them to the Tropicana. Buying a Presidente cocktail. Watching the showgirls in feathered headdresses. His hair slicked back. Women in garters and halter tops. Guitars, horns, and bongo drums. Dancing the mambo under the

Arcos de Cristal. Then a room at the Hotel Nacional over-looking the Malecon.

I imagined my dad playing the cards dealt to him, which is what men on the make do. He could speak Portuguese and Spanish fluently, and his English was getting better by the day. He was tall and slim. He had money in his pocket. He could charm. He could dance. He knew the ways of the world. But there are two tragedies in life: one is not getting what you want, and the other is getting it. It was a quote I knew by Oscar Wilde.

"Did you enjoy Havana?"

"Yes, boy."

"I bet you did."

"Sometimes I would stay for four months at a time. It was too much. I started knowing Cuba too well. Fights. Murder. Affairs. It was as rotten as Brazil. Corruption all over the place. I said, 'What the hell am I doing here? What is there to stay here for? I didn't run away from my country for this. There is no point in staying here.'"

There is going and there is leaving. My father had his reasons for going everywhere he went. He also had reasons for leaving. I sensed there was more to the story about why he left Brazil. I decided to probe.

"Before we move on, I just wanted to ask you a couple of questions about the time we covered. When you first left Brazil and moved to Miami in 1949, it just doesn't make sense to me why you would leave everything in Brazil so quickly to begin with nothing in Miami. Was there something in Brazil that compelled you to leave?"

"No, no, no, no. It was just an impulsive move. I was doing quite well, working for a very large company, well liked, with no reason whatsoever to leave the country. But it was one of those things. They offered me a free ticket, I came, and I liked the country, maybe because it was new and foreign to me, and I decided to stay. I envisioned a new life. It was a pure adventure."

"What was the name of the president of the airline? The person who saw you on the plane and asked you to return to Brazil?"

"José Alfredo de Almeida, known as Zeze de Almeida. A famous businessman. He was president of a group, this group consisted of a bank, three textile plants, a steel corporation, and the airline. The bank through the years became one of the largest commercial banks in South America. Banco Bradesco."

"So, there was no personal reason why you wanted to leave?"

"Well, I lived with a woman for many years. In Sao Paulo and Rio, sometimes in Minas and Belo Horizonte, a married woman who was separated. She had four children, and I was getting fed up with that thing. She had a very bad temper. When I came to Miami, I thought it was a good excuse to stay thousands and thousands of miles away from her. At that time a trip from Brazil to the United States was a very difficult trip, a DC-3 flying three-and-a-half days to get here. Long waits in airports. Planes that broke down. You had to think twice, three times, ten times, before you got on one of those planes. So, I thought it was a good way to get out of that relationship."

I had never heard of this person. I was curious who she was and what hold she might have had in his life. "What was her name?"

"Who?"

"The woman you left behind."

"Maria."

That's all my father said. I waited for him to tell me more. Finally, I followed up. "Were you ever interested in marrying her?"

"Me? No, no. Because at that time we could not do it. There was no divorce in Brazil. Divorce in Brazil was instituted many, many, many years later. She had four children, two sons, one was epileptic, very sick. One day she came with him to the United States to get him treatment."

That was more than I expected. "While you were here?"

"Yes, and they stayed here for about two months. With me in my apartment. And I took the boy to the Children's Hospital here in Miami. I think it was the Variety Children's Hospital. Then they left and that was it. This was 1951. And I never saw her again."

"Never again?"

"No."

"Okay, I was just curious what compelled you to leave Brazil. Anything else?"

"That was it. I realize that I made a very serious mistake leaving the company. It was not the right time for me to do it. But maybe it was predestined. You know, maybe God had told me to come."

We had picked up the conversation two weeks after I had last talked to him. After Bob's wedding, I began working on two more opinions for Judge Fay, went to see *Leibestraum*, an indie movie at the Coconut Grove Playhouse, and hosted Linda, a girl I once dated who was down from New York, for the weekend in my apartment. Linda and I had dinner at Ruen Thai on Washington Avenue. We were joined by Suzanne, who brought along Mimi, a sales engineer at IBM. Mimi was bright and conversational and caught my eye.

My dad and I were in my apartment. This time he'd taken the bus. We decided to meet on a Wednesday night because my dad had a sales call with a jewelry vendor on the beach. My dad secured a small order for a few semiprecious stones from Brazil and was in a good mood. We drank a mix of orange, apple, and papaya juice I had in my refrigerator.

"In 1953, I was tired of Cuba, I was tired of Miami. I decided to move to New York. It was the center of the world. A beautiful city. A fantastic city. I sold what I had in Miami and went to New York with a suitcase in my hand. I started walking around Manhattan. I didn't know anybody. Times Square was beautiful at the time. I got into a hotel, the Hotel Edison on 47th Street. And I said, 'I'm going to work for myself. I'm not going to try to get a job. There must be an opportunity here for me. The thing is to find it.' So, I opened the yellow pages, and I looked for companies involved in Brazil nuts, hides and skins, vegetable fibers, vegetable oils, and things of this kind. And I called them. I asked them if they were importers of those things. They asked me if I had something to offer. I said no, because I didn't have anything, but I said I was surveying the market."

"You were pretending."

"Yes, I was pretending to represent companies in Brazil as a sales agent. If I could get an order, then I could take that order to real companies and represent them. I could be an independent agent representing Brazilian companies in New York. Working for myself."

"Did it work?"

"Yes, it worked. I called an importer on Hudson Street. They were buyers of Brazil nuts. I told them I represented companies that could sell Brazil nuts at a good price. This wasn't true, but I had to look legitimate. So, I went to one of those answering services on Fifth Avenue, 550 Fifth Avenue, a very distinguished address, and rented a PO box there, put my name on the board, went to City Hall, registered my company, and tried to get orders. Once I got an order, I would have to find a supplier. Then I got on a plane to Brazil. I went to Manaus, Belém, Sao Luis, Piaui, Ceara, Recife, to all these companies in Brazil that produced raw materials. And I told them I could be their agent in New York. On a commission basis, you see. So, they authorized me, gave me offers I could bring back, and I came back to New York. I rented an office in the same building on Fifth Avenue. And I got into the market, started calling on people. Very hard, very tough, difficult to break the ice, very, very shrewd people, and sometimes I got very discouraged and thought I would never make it."

"Where were you living?"

"I was living on Fifty-First Street between Seventh and Eighth. It took me some time, but I started selling. I sold cashew nuts, hides and skins, and Brazil nuts, and I started making money again. I was not very versed in those items, I had to learn, and I learned by selling. And you must become known in the market. If you are not known in the market, buyers don't trust you. They don't even listen to you. But I kept working. I made several trips to Brazil to get more lines and represented more items and companies."

"What was the name of your company?"

"It was Itamar Trading Company. My first company. I learned how to deal with American buyers, I got to know their idiosyncrasies, and it was very good for me. And I made a good living, I had my own apartment, I paid my own expenses, and I was happy. It was 1955. I was thirty-eight years old. This is when I decided I wanted to get married. This is when I met your mother."

And this is when the going and the leaving and the chaos of my family began.

CHAPTER EIGHT

I HEARD THE story many times, or at least pieces of it that my sisters and brother and I could summarize in a few sentences. Every child can tell a version of how their parents met: at school, on a blind date, at a coffee shop. I knew the headline that my father met my mom at a Carnival party in Brazil. I knew that she was much younger than him. I knew that she was the belle of the ball. I didn't know all the details, I'm not sure anyone but them truly knew, but I had this chance to know more.

It was 7:00 p.m. I figured my dad would stay at my apartment for two to three hours before I would drive him home. He always made a point of looking at what I was reading. I had the latest issue of *Time* magazine with Bill Clinton on the cover, a book on the science of the brain, and *Damage*, a banger of a psychosexual novel by Josephine Hart, to inspire my own relationship thriller that I had begun to write, on my coffee table. My dad lingered in front of my bookshelf, pulling a copy of *The Revolt of the Masses* by José Ortega y Gassett I had from college, flipping through it before returning it to my shelf.

"Why were you suddenly interested in getting married?" I asked.

"Well, I'll tell you a very strange thing. One day a lawyer from Maranhão, the state in Brazil that your mother is from, came to see me in New York. He was a member of the Lions Club, representing Brazil at an international convention in New York. He brought a letter from one of the companies I represented, so he came to see me to deliver the letter, and we began spending time together."

"What was his name?"

"His name was – let me see if I can remember – his name was Perdigao. Antonio Perdigao. He was also a law professor in a small law school in Sao Luis. We got very friendly, we went to lunch and dinner, and went to my apartment, and we walked around New York. It was all very agreeable between us. Then one day he told me, 'Listen Peres, I think you are a very intelligent man, your conversation is good, your Portuguese language is beautiful, but you have a very empty life here, living without any objective. You should not be alone.' I was taken back by this, and I tried to explain, I said, 'Listen, doctor,' we call lawyers in Brazil 'doctor,' so I said, 'A few years ago I came out of a situation which was not very pleasant for me, and I am very much afraid to get into another one.' He said, 'Well, that situation was completely different. I'm talking about a family girl, from a good family, with very good principles like we have in the northern part of Brazil. In Sao Luis, in Maranhão, there are beautiful girls from very nice families with the best habits and customs in the world. You're not going to find them here.'"

"Had you found anybody in New York?"

"Well, I met some women, but they were too liberal for me. Too much freedom and I was scared that it wouldn't work out, you know."

"Did you feel that he was right when he said your life was empty?"

"Well, yes. Yes, I did. So, he said, 'When you go back there, I'm going to introduce you to some beautiful girls there, people that I know, families that I know.' I said, 'Okay, doctor.' And I began to have this in my mind. I began to think he was right. That was in 1955, in January. By the end of February, I made a trip to Brazil. It was Carnival time, and I was getting into the habit of going to Carnival in Brazil every year, just to have a good time. So, I went to Belém first, and from there to Sao Luis in Maranhão."

"With the idea of meeting someone?"

"Yes, yes, yes. I was invited to a Carnival Ball in Sao Luis. I remember that I did not have a costume, so someone gave me a shirt that was red and black and yellow. I put it on and went to a social club, a private membership club. The music started, people started dancing, and I saw this girl dancing, and looking at me, maybe because I was the tallest man there, with a foreign face, I never looked Brazilian anyway. And I started looking at her and said, 'Well, maybe something's here.'"

"What did you think about her when you saw her?"

"I thought she was beautiful. She was with her family by a table, and I came by, and I said, 'Would you like to dance?' She said, 'Yes.' So, we started dancing, I asked her name, and she said, 'Lourdes.' She gave me her card, a calling card. Maria de Lourdes da Silva Frias. With her address on it. Very formal. Her family called her Lourdinha. She asked where I was from, and at that time it was very important to say that I came from the United States. So about one or two o'clock in the morning, the party was over, and I said goodnight, and I asked her if I could see her again."

"What was your impression of her?"

"She was a very high-class person. I had that thing in my mind to find a wife. To start a family. The next day I went to see Antonio, the lawyer who I'd met in New York who was back in Sao Luis. I told him who I met. He said, 'Beautiful! I know the family, the father is a Portuguese man, he's very honorable, very decent man, and he's rich. Do you want me to talk to them about you?' I said, 'No, not necessary. I just wanted you to know that I met this girl.' From there I went to see a company I represented, and I told them who I met, and they said, 'Oh boy, you marry her, you are the luckiest guy in the world.'"

"So, people knew Lourdes?"

"Oh yes, yes, and they knew her family, mostly her father. Her father owned a bakery that was very popular, and he owned the building too. So, I had this plan of going to Sao Luis on the first night of Carnival, the second night in Fortaleza, and the third night in Rio. I stayed with my plan, but before I left for Fortaleza, I went to her home to say goodbye. The family lived above the bakery. A very nice building on Rua Godofredo Viana with blue and white tiles and five balconies that overlooked the street. I met her father, her mother, her sister, and two brothers. They treated me very nicely, very elegantly. I told Lourdes I would write to her from Rio."

"You were thirty-eight and she was twenty. Was there any concern about the age difference?"

"No, no. No one talked about that. From Rio I wrote her a letter telling her that I was very impressed, that I would like to maintain some kind of communication with her. I gave her my address in New York and from Rio flew back to New York. And she answered my letter. I got her answer in New York."

"What did she say?"

"She said she liked meeting me and she would like to see me again. Three months later, in May, I went back to Brazil, to Sao Luis, and I went to her home, and went out with her. I remember getting on a bus to go around town. The people on the bus were like chaperones. We talked for a long time on the bus as it went around and around the city. I stayed there about three or four days, and I asked her to marry me."

"You were there for three or four days, and you asked her to marry you?" I knew the answer but every time I was no less impressed.

"Yes, and she said yes."

"Did that surprise you?"

"Yes and no. It surprised me because I was unknown. She was taking a risk. However, I had local recommendations, my lawyer friend, the companies I represented. They all knew me. And it didn't surprise me because there was a scarcity of men in that city, men in a position to marry nice girls from nice families. That was my impression. I was different. Educated. From the United States. Your mother had this vision for herself. She rejected every man in that city. She wanted this much bigger life. And I came along."

"So, there was no courtship?"

"I was not in love with her, and she was not in love with me. I married her because she was the right person. I said, 'Love will come later.'"

"That's certainly an approach. Do you think she made up her mind the same way?"

"Maybe she did. I returned to New York, then returned to Brazil in July. I told her family I was ready to get married, and they prepared the whole thing, the whole party, the cake and everything."

"So, you spent less than two weeks together before you got married?"

"Yes, no more than that. So, on 20 July 1955, we got married. As a matter of fact, I was very sick that day. I went to a restaurant there and the food didn't suit me, and I got very sick. I married that way anyway."

"Maybe a sign." I said it quietly.

"What?"

"Were you nervous?"

"I was thirty-eight years old. I was not a baby."

"I understand, but you had been a bachelor a long time, and getting married is a big deal."

"Well, I made up my mind and that was it. You see, I was very selfish about the whole thing. I didn't try to find out too much about how she was feeling. I was willing. She was willing. I thought I had found the right person, a person of good character, from a good family, a decent person . . . and I didn't want to fool around anymore with divorced women, women I found in nightclubs, in bars, in restaurants. I didn't want to marry that way. I said, 'Not me.'"

"Were you accustomed to being with women of her character?" I knew it was an oddly phrased question, but I thought at the root of much of their problems and why they stayed together.

"Well, I came from a family that was very strict, that had high expectations, but I was not strict at all. But I thought, 'Why should I get married to a woman I met at a bar? That's not going to work.' My plan was to marry a person with very decent moral habits who is well educated. Lourdes was very bright, very well raised, and she was very beautiful too."

"She was the complete package." I knew my mom certainly thought so.

"Yes, so I said, 'Well I found what I was looking for.' But I didn't know anything about her temper."

"And she didn't know anything about yours."

I held my breath again.

"No, she didn't know anything about me either. Maybe if she knew a few things about me, she wouldn't marry me. Maybe if she knew I had that womanizing syndrome, she would not marry. Maybe I wouldn't have married her if I knew she had a very hot temper. Nobody told me that. So, if we made a mistake, we both made the same mistake."

Another defense.

"Well, you two set a lot in motion," I said.

"Yes, but we did not know about any of that then. My intention was to build up a family. I was very honest about that, and very serious about it. To forget all my past and start a new life on a decent basis with the purpose of building up a family."

"So, the leopard was going to change his spots?"

"That's right, exactly."

We left that hanging in the air.

On my bookshelf is a photograph of my mother the night she met my father. Her family had professional photographs taken of her that night. My mom looks stunning. It's a profile shot. She is wearing a pearl earring and a pearl necklace. Her dress is off her shoulders. She is looking to her right. Her skin is flawless. Her eyes, nose, lips, and chin are in perfect proportion. It's the photograph that everyone looked at when they came to my apartment. It's the photograph that reminded me of goodness and beauty. Youth and dreams and promise. Of a life of esteem and grace she expected to live.

My dad and I took a break. He had gone to the bathroom three times since we started talking. He had a slight pained look on his face. When he came back to his chair, he opened his notebook, looked at something he had written down, then closed it.

I continued, "After the wedding did you go on a honeymoon?"

My dad put his notebook to the side. I wished my dad had a similar accomplishment, that he was a man of letters, that he shared scholarship with the world.

"Did you go on a honeymoon?"

My dad gave me a surprised, almost hurt look for not following up on what he just shared. "No."

"Why not?"

"Because I had to work. My plan was to take Lourdes back to America. That would be the adventure."

"Did you introduce her to your family?"

"I told my mother. I told my sisters. They lived in Rio and did not come to the wedding. Lourdes never met my mother because we came immediately to the United States. My mother was pleased. She wanted me to get married. She thought I shouldn't go on like this, as a single man, from city to city, from country to country, as a wandering Jew. She thought I should have a family like everyone else, like my sisters did, like my brother did, and everyone in her family."

"Did Mommy know you were Jewish when you got married?"

"Yes, I looked different from everyone else, green eyes, big nose, but this was not a problem. We had a civil marriage in her home."

"Mommy is very Catholic. She prays to saints."

'Yes, she is Catholic. Sometimes she is too Catholic and sometimes she is not too Catholic. As a matter of fact, in

San Francisco, she asked me to marry her in the Christian religion and I did."

"You mean a second wedding?"

"Yes, and I stood there, and I married her again."

"Huh. I did not know that. So, when you got married, the first time, in 1955, you took her to America. She must have been excited."

"Well, I had to do some business first. I took your mom to Belém where she stayed with a Portuguese family friendly with her father while I went to Manaus for business for three or four days—"

"Wait a minute. You just got married, and you dropped her off so you could go to another city for business?"

"Yes. Then I came back to Belém, picked her up, and we went to Recife because Manaus, Belém, and Sao Paulo did not have American consulates. I applied for her permanent visa for residence in the United States. I came prepared for that. I took proof of my business, of my American bank account, and several letters of recommendation from American buyers. The Consul immediately gave her a permanent visa. It took two or three more days, and we flew to New York."

"It sounds like marrying Mommy was a business deal. You saw what you wanted. You closed the sale and brought her back."

"Listen, this is how your mother and I married. She was very excited to come to America. She would be special in her family. The first to live in the United States. A big deal. She knew what she was doing. She packed a lot of suitcases. But she was also young. Romantic. New York made a big impression on her."

"I imagine it did."

"We walked the streets. Rockefeller Center. St. Patrick's. Central Park. All along Fifth Avenue. It was a wonderful time in New York. We went to see a movie. *Love is a Many Splendored Thing*. She was excited about her new life."

"And you were excited to have her in your life, weren't you?"

"Yes, I introduced her to people as my new wife. People saw that she was much younger than me. But your mother was very confident. Very social. Very polished. She could talk to anybody. She attracted attention."

"But didn't everything change suddenly? Didn't the balloon pop?" I knew the answer.

"Well, this is a complexity. This is how things are. A month before I went to Brazil I met a man, a Brazilian in New York, who wanted to be my partner in my business. I must explain what happened."

"Go ahead." I put my pen down.

"His name was Avelino Santos. He started to use my office, my telephone and everything else. He put money into the business, and we made some deals together. In the meantime, I was in Brazil. Then I came back to New York. He came to my apartment, he met Lourdes, and then started talking, and said he wanted out of the business."

"Why?"

"He changed his mind. He said, 'I want to go back to Brazil, I don't want to stay here, I've changed my mind, so let me have the money back I invested.' And I said, 'Wait a minute. I just got back from Brazil, I just got married, a brand-new wife, I cannot give you your money back.' He said, 'No, no, no. I want to go. I want my money back.'"

"How much money are we talking about?"

"About four or five thousand dollars. This was a lot of money in 1955. I could not give him the money back because it was invested in deals. I had some money, but I had a wife now. Why should I give him my last penny? I felt very bad about it. It was a big embarrassment for Lourdes. She was watching us argue."

"And it escalated."

"Yes. I didn't know what to do. I told him, 'Listen, I don't have the money to give you.' He said, 'You get it. Take care of your young wife and give me my money.' Very threatening."

"He was threatening Lourdes."

"Yes. That was his way of threatening her in front of me. I told him, 'You are not going to get it. You are acting in bad faith. You are trying to throw me against the wall and I'm not going to take it.' If I was by myself, he would not threaten me, I would solve the problem right there, but I was with Lourdes. What could I do? The next day I went to my office building, I closed the office, I came back to the apartment, I packed up our clothes, and we got on a bus to New Orleans. I didn't want to stay there, get into that fight, have him hurt Lourdes. It was a terrible thing."

"How did you explain this to her?"

"Well, I tried to explain, but she was twenty years old. She was dreaming about this new life in Manhattan. It was a shock."

"Did you have any money?"

"I had what I had. About two or three thousand dollars."

"And you walked away from your business entirely?"

"That's right. I left the business, I left my brand-new car, I left the furniture and everything in the apartment. We took what we could carry on the bus. And we went to New Orleans. I did this to save her further embarrassment. We could start our marriage someplace new. Away from everything in New York."

"And why New Orleans?"

"Because of the port. Because of the import-export business which is very important in New Orleans. Not every city has a port."

"Did you know anybody?"

"I did not know anybody. I had never been there before."

"I can only imagine that bus ride. The conversation the two of you were having. She must have been overwhelmed."

My dad didn't acknowledge my mom on the bus at all. Not what she must have felt. Not traveling through miles of lonely roads and highways. Not wondering about the man she married. Not that they were suddenly on the run.

"We went to the French Quarter," he said. "The Roosevelt Hotel. This is how our marriage began."

How to begin the perfect relationship.

CHAPTER NINE

THE PHONE RANG in my apartment. I heard my mother's voice on the answering machine. Her accent always made me smile. She had trouble with the 'th' sound and mispronounced words like 'cookie' that cracked me up. I picked up the phone.

"Hi Mamae." "Mommy" in Portuguese.

"Hello, my son. Is your father there?"

"Yep, he's here." I turned to my father. He shook his head to tell me he didn't want to talk to her. "I'll be bringing him home soon. What are you doing?"

"I'm watching *Murder, She Wrote*."

"How appropriate." She must have wanted to murder my dad a dozen times. "We'll be home in an hour." My mom and I talked a bit more. My mother had the same knack as Jessica Fletcher from the show figuring out who-done-it. About twenty minutes into any episode, my mom would identify the killer. She always got it right. Impeccable instincts honed over years of being with my dad.

After finishing the call, I put in a new cassette tape.

"What is your mother doing?" my dad asked.

"She's watching TV. Identifying the morally compromised and impulsive antagonists."

"What?"

"Nothing. I just want to circle back for a moment. This man who threatened you, did he want his money back because he found out things about your business? He was working at your desk while you were away. Was there something not right about your business?"

"No, no, no, no. When this happened, I wanted to get out of New York. I did not want to take any chances. And I wanted to start this new life with your mother. To start a family. That was my goal. That was the most important thing. And this would have been very difficult in New York."

"But your entire business was there. And you left it all behind."

"Yes, it was a shock. But sometimes these things happen."

I looked at my bookshelf over his shoulder, frustrated. I knew my dad's life was one misadventure after another. He had a reason for everything.

"Was anyone after you?"

"What do you mean?"

"Was anyone after you? Were you in trouble? Unpaid bills?"

"Listen, business can be tough. I was protecting your mother. When you start something new, you start something new. You don't mess around."

I let it go, suspicious. "Okay. So, what happened next?"

"I rented an apartment in New Orleans and started looking for a job. I saw an ad in the paper: an import-export company looking for a sales manager. I applied, met the president, his name was Rafael Ordorica, a Mexican guy. He asked me where I was from, and I said from Brazil. He smiled. He said, 'Don't tell me! I lived in your country, I was bureau chief for United Press International, and I know a lot of people in your country. You've got the job.'"

"Some good luck."

"Yes."

"What was the name of the business?"

"Hemisphere International Corporation. The company was producing lubricating oils and distributing to South America."

"What did you know about lubricating oils?"

"Nothing. You learn on the job. My job was to control the sales in every market and report to him every week. A good job, but very small pay. I needed to earn more. About three or four months later he called me into his office, and said 'Peres, I'm sorry I cannot raise your salary, I cannot give you a better position in the company, but I am going to recommend you to a very important company here in New Orleans.' So, two days later he gave me a letter and I went to this company, Frieberg Mahogany Company. A big company. The president, Mr. Harry Freiberg, read the letter and offered me a job on a thirty-day trial basis. He said, 'You're going to buy tools and equipment for the plant.'"

"What did you know about tools and equipment?"

"Nothing. You learn on the job. I started working the next day and meeting people, a very large office, many, many people, about two thousand people in the plant. I had to replace someone who was old in the company, a purchasing agent. At the end of thirty days, I went to see Mr. Frieberg, and he said, 'We are going to give you the job for another six months. I have a report from the Comptroller that you are doing well.' I stayed three years."

"Wow. So, a steady career?"

"Well, not exactly, but it was good for me to start a marriage on a steady basis. I gave up having my own business and said 'This is my job. I have a salary every week.' And Lourdes got pregnant. And we had three children in three years. Your sister Rachael, named after my mother, in 1956, your sister Arlene, named after the actress Arlene Dahl, in 1957, and your brother Edison, named after Thomas Edison, in 1958. All born in New Orleans."

"So, things were going well?" I was certain he would say yes.

"Yes, very well. We lived in a nice neighborhood. I had my car, and we were very happy. I had a private chauffeur to take me downtown to call on suppliers, and my reputation was very high in the company. I could be bribed at any moment and make a lot of money, but I never accepted anything. I learned the business. I bought equipment, very heavy equipment, I bought all the tools the plant needed, and then materials for the office, and after a while had two guys under my supervision."

"And Mommy was happy?"

"Yes, we had problems, but this was a very good time for us. She was young. At home. With the children. We had nice neighbors. We were not rich but living very nicely. Living like Americans. The American dream."

"And then what?"

"Well, you see, things happen."

We were getting near the time I'd promised my mother that I would drive my dad home. It was also a Wednesday night, which meant the Eleventh Circuit judges were down from Atlanta and Jacksonville. Panels were hearing oral arguments all week. Mornings began in chambers with Judge Fay. He would brief us on the cases on the docket for argument, and what to listen for from counsel and what issues the judges wanted to explore. He expected us to have summaries of case law cited in the briefs ready in the event the judges wanted holdings as they deliberated. I had the next morning on my mind as my dad got a second wind.

"What I'm going to tell you now is a very interesting situation. At the time the company had operations in British Honduras and Chetumal in the Yucatan Peninsula. This is where our mahogany came from. One day, Mr. Harry Frieberg's brother, Mr. John Frieberg, the vice president, called me to his office and said, 'I have a diplomatic mission for you.' He said it with a sarcastic voice. He said, 'We are having two problems in Central America, one in Belize, British Honduras, and one in Chetumal, Mexico. You are used to dealing with Latin crooks, aren't you?' I said, 'What's the problem?' He said, 'One wants more money, and the other one wants a bribe, and they won't release the logs we need to fulfill our orders.' I said, 'Why did you pick me?' He said, 'You're Latin, aren't you?' "I said, 'Yes, but I'm not from Honduras or from Mexico. I'm from Brazil. We speak a different language.' He said, 'Same thing. You can do it.'

"So, two or three days later I got on a plane, and I went to Belize first and went to see this company, and I introduced myself, asking to speak to the general manager. A big Englishman, very tall, very strong, and very polite in the English way, came out to meet me. He said, 'Mr. Peres?' I said, 'Yes.' He invited me into his office. Very polite. He said, 'You are not American.' I said, 'No, I am not.' He said, 'Where are you from?' I said, 'From Brazil.' He said, 'Where in Brazil?' I said, 'From the north of Brazil.' He said, 'Where in the north of Brazil?' I said, 'From the Amazon.' He said, 'Where in the Amazon?' I said, 'From Manaus.' And he said, 'Your name is Peres, right?' I said, 'Yes.' He then offers me coffee. And he said, 'I have something to show you.' He goes to his bookshelf, and he comes back with a picture of my father."

"Your father?" I did not see that coming.

"Yes, and a wave of emotion came over me. Boy, I felt 'What is happening?' He then said, 'Let's talk in Portuguese.' He begins to talk in perfect Portuguese. He said, 'How is Rachel, your mother? How are your sisters?' I said, 'Fine, fine.' And I started to cry."

"Oh my gosh."

"It was very emotional for me."

I never saw my dad cry, but I saw him more than once fight back tears. How he responded to the memory of his father moved me. "What was his name?"

"His name was Mr. Hore. A British name. He said, 'I lived in Manaus for thirty-five years. I owned a sawmill in Manaus. I was born in London, my wife also, but my children were born in Brazil. I met your father. He was a very important man. A very good man. This is why I have his picture.' He mentioned other people from my family. Boy, he knew everybody. He picked up the phone and called his wife and gave instructions to have the luggage from my hotel sent to his home. It was unbelievable. Just unbelievable. And I stayed with him for two or three days. We talked about the problem with Mr. Frieberg. He said, 'I'm going to solve this problem for you. I hope they give you a promotion because I don't like your company. This is the best I can do and I'm going to do it for you.' I asked him about Chetumal and whether he had any advice. He said, 'The man in Chetumal is a crook, but he's a general. The best way to deal with him is to tell him he's a great man.'"

"Is that what you did?"

"Yes, after staying in Belize and saying goodbye to Mr. Hore, I went to Chetumal, met this general, a very important guy in the middle of the jungle with those big stars on his shoulders. He began complaining about the gringos, that the gringos are thieves, that they are the enemy of Latin America, and why am I working with gringos. I said, 'This is just a job for me, and I would like to solve this problem to your advantage. The logs are in the bay for months and months and we need them. We have contracts in Europe and in the United States that we must supply, we must fulfill these contracts, and we need you to release these logs.' He said, 'Taxes have to be paid.' This was his way of asking for a bribe. I said, 'You tell me how much the taxes are, and I will let the company know and you will hear from us.' That night I stayed in his home, he told me the amount he wanted, and the next day I flew back to Belize and then New Orleans. I told John Frieberg everything that happened in Belize and he was very happy. He said, 'What about that crook in Chetumal?' I said, 'This is his proposition. Now it's up to you to decide.' He said, 'Can I counter?' I said, 'I don't think you should. You don't like this general, and he doesn't like you. You think these Latin people are crooks and they think you are exploiters. You need the logs, they have the logs, see what you can do.' In a few weeks they settled all the matters."

"You were a hero."

"Yes, I was a hero. Then at the end of 1958, the company was sold. And the new owners, people from Texas, came into the office, big boots, big hats, firing people, and replacing them with people they brought from Texas."

"They let you go."

"They asked me to stay for two months. But I said no. I had plans to start my own business again. And your mother was unhappy. And this is when things got very difficult."

"Daddy, it's getting late. I should get you home."

"Yes, we can talk in the car."

That's not what I hoped to do. Usually when we were in the car, we didn't say much. He might make a comment about what building used to be on what corner or he would ask me a question about my plans, and I would deflect. I thought our drive would be much of the same. Plus, I was getting tired. But my father was talkative. We had a thirty-five-minute drive north along Collins Avenue to Sunny Isles if I made most of the lights. I could slow it down with the tape recorder running between us. We walked to my car. South Beach had its own energy at night. Even at 11 p.m. on a Wednesday, people were walking to shops and clubs on Washington Avenue and to cafes and hotels on Ocean Drive. We settled into the cocoon of the car, and I turned the recorder on.

"I must tell you about Harold Gorman," my father said. "He was a vice president at Freiberg. His wife divorced him to marry the president of the company. And he felt very bad about it. He didn't want to give up his job because it was a very good job. He was a lumber expert. He was very unhappy about the situation seeing his former wife in the same dining room at the company. He liked to talk, and he told me how sad he was, and I would give him advice to find someone new. I told him to do what I did and find a woman of decent moral principles. I would talk to him about import-export and opportunities to buy and sell commodities. He didn't know anything about import-export. All he knew was lumber. Then the company was sold, and Mr. Gorman was fired. This got him nervous and excited, and he said to me, 'Let's set up a business. You put up your knowledge and work about import-export, and I'll put up the money.' I was a little skeptical about having him as a partner, but I said okay."

"I see trouble coming," I said.

"This was 1959. We started a company. Overseas Resources Corporation. We opened a nice office in New Orleans. Mr. Gorman, me, and a secretary. And I began organizing everything. I started traveling to Central America, to different countries, to see what we could buy and sell. I went to El Salvador, Nicaragua, Peru, and Guatemala, and came back with a plan to sell paraffin wax to the candle industry, and chemicals to the soap industry. I made a trip to New York to get sources of supply, went back to Central America to name sales representatives."

"You're building a whole new business."

"Yes. Traveling. Traveling. Building it from nothing. Meanwhile your mother is at home alone with the children. Then one day I met a man in a hotel in New Orleans who was vice president of a very large chemical company in the United States by the name of the Wyandotte Chemical Corporation. Based in Michigan. This company, among other things, produced some chemicals for the sugar industry. He was familiar with the sugar production in Cuba, Mexico, and Central America, but not in other countries. I told him about the large sugar production in Brazil. He was a little skeptical about it. But then he asked me, 'If it is true what you are saying, will you accept selling for us in Brazil?' I immediately said yes in the lobby of the hotel."

We stopped at a red light across from the Eden Roc and Fontainebleau. The hotels had their heydays at the same time as my father's story: 1959. The days of Sinatra and Garland and Gleason. There was a legendary dispute between the hotels. The Fontainebleau had been built first, the vision of hotelier Ben Novack, its sweeping curves, grand lobby with its "stairway to nowhere," and expansive pool and cabanas attracting celebrities and world attention. The Eden Roc was built the following year next door, by hotelier Harry Mufson, former partner of Novack. The two men became infuriated with each other, suing over the interference of sight lines and the casting of shadows. The dispute went on for years.

In the glow of the car and Miami Beach at night, my dad continued.

"The man went back to Michigan and then called me on the phone and said, 'The information you gave me is correct. We checked with the Department of Commerce in Washington and our embassy in Brazil. We were very surprised with the information that Brazil is the second largest producer of sugar in the world. What surprised us is that Brazil is not exporting sugar.' I said, 'Of course not. Cuba only has six million people. Brazil has one hundred twenty million people who consume the sugar the country produces.' He said, 'If you want to come to Michigan then we can start a relationship.' So, I told Mr. Gorman, and he got very excited about the opportunity."

"What was Mr. Gorman doing?"

"Nothing. Sitting in the office. Being a big shot because he financed the company. But he didn't know anything. He just looked at the money. He was very shrewd. And emotional. He was a big man. A lumber man. Very strong physically."

"Did you go to Michigan?"

"Yes, I spent three weeks in Wyandotte. They gave me two big notebooks to translate into Portuguese. I translated these two books, learned their processes, and we planned for me to move to Brazil."

"Permanently?"

"Yes, and I told Lourdes. And this made her happy. You see, she was missing Brazil. She was used to a different life. When Rachael was born, your mother's mother, your grandmother, and your uncle Mario, your mother's brother, came to New Orleans. They stayed with us for two months. I forgot to mention that in 1955, two or three months after we married, your mother's father died. This was a blow to Lourdes. Her mother inherited the business and didn't know how to run it. It began going down very fast. Meanwhile, I was traveling, leaving Lourdes alone. So, when I told Lourdes that we could move back to Brazil, she thought she could be back with her family. Back with her mother and raise the children in Brazil. She was twenty-four years old."

"Did you have a plan?"

"The plan was for me to go to Central America first, call on customers and agents, close deals, I closed a very important deal on caustic soda for the soap industry with a very large company in Guatemala, and secured arrangements for Wyandotte. I told Lourdes to pack up our things, to end the lease on the house, and to bring the kids and meet me in Guatemala. Then as a family we would move to Brazil."

We came up to North Beach on the right. Traffic on either side of us. "It sounds like this was all happening very fast."

"Yes. Very fast. When I got to Guatemala, one of my agents, a local man who knew the market well, Lorenzo was his name, a man with fourteen children, a very hard worker, very humble, very good, told me that one of his children was sick, and he asked me if I could advance him some commission. I asked him how much he needed. He said, '$500.' This was a good amount of money. I said, 'Okay, it's no problem.' I could sign for the company. I went to the bank with Lorenzo and explained to the banker about the corporate account in New Orleans, and I would like to have $500 transferred to Guatemala. He made some calls to our bank in New Orleans, the transaction was authorized, and I gave the money to Lorenzo."

"I see what's about to happen."

"Meanwhile, Lourdes had made all the arrangements and came to Guatemala. She packed up the house. Gave things away. Broke the lease. She took long flights with two little children and a baby with her. I picked everyone up at the airport. We went to stay in a Spanish hotel in Guatemala City. In the historical center. All of us in one room. One day I go to the patio in the middle of the hotel, and Mr. Gorman is standing there."

"You were not expecting to see him."

"No. This was a shock. He never left the office. I said, 'What are you doing here in Guatemala?' He said, 'I want my $500. The $500 you gave to somebody. I want my money back.' I was so fed up with him. He flew down from New

Orleans to confront me. I said, 'I'll have something for you in one hour.' I went to the hotel office and typed a resignation letter and met Mr. Gorman an hour later. I said, 'Here is your $500.' Mr. Gorman began yelling in the hotel. He said, 'I don't want your resignation. I want my money. I want my money!' I said, 'Earn it yourself.' He got very angry. He said, 'It's not going to end this way!' I said, 'Yes, it is. I am leaving. I don't want to work with you anymore. I don't care what the consequences are.'"

"Why do you think he reacted that way?"

"Because he wanted to impose his will. He wanted to assert his control. He looked at me as if I was inferior to him. I was Brazilian. I was Jewish. And it was very common at the time in the United States for people like him to look down on other people. I wouldn't take it. I walked out of the hotel and went to Lorenzo's home and told him what happened. He said he was so sorry, that he felt bad, that he didn't want to cause any trouble. I told him not to worry about it. That I would never work with Mr. Gorman again."

"So, there you are in Guatemala with Mommy and three kids with no company or home?"

"That's right. And no money. I told Lourdes what happened, and she was very upset, and the children were crying. We had reservations to go from Guatemala to El Salvador and then to Brazil. The next day I went to Pan American Airways to get our tickets, and I see Mr. Gorman. He is at the counter trying to cancel my flights, saying that his company bought the tickets, and he wanted the tickets voided.

The manager said, 'I don't see any reason to void the tickets. It doesn't matter who paid for them. The tickets were issued to Mr. Peres, and he is the only person who can cancel them.' Mr. Gorman started screaming, 'You're not going! I'm going to stop you one way or another!' So, I decided to take Lourdes and the children to the Brazilian embassy for protection."

"Wow."

"The next day a man from the consulate took us to the airport in an embassy car. Mr. Gorman was standing there at the counter staring at me as I approached the counter. He was a big man. I got my tickets, presented my luggage, and went back to sit with Lourdes. He didn't say a word. Then he left the airport. I went back to the counter, and the manager said, 'Enjoy your flight. I told the gentleman that you and your family are under the protection of the Consular authority.'"

"What do you think he was planning on doing?"

"I don't know, but in my mind, if he did anything, I was ready to kill him. If I didn't kill him in Guatemala, I'd kill him in New Orleans."

I believed my dad. I had seen him when he lost control: when he threw clothes across the room, when he screamed at my mom, when he would slam the phone down. But he was also tender and protective. We had driven to the front of my parents' building. It was midnight. I parked the car.

"Daddy, you never made it to Brazil, did you?"

"When we arrived in El Salvador, I told your mother the whole plan to live in Brazil was no good anymore. I wanted to go back to the United States. Your mother was upset. She was scared. Rachael was two-and-a-half years old. Arlene was one-and-a-half years old. Edison was eight months old. And your mother was pregnant. I called my local agent in San Salvador, who arranged for me and Lourdes and the children to fly to Mexico City. In Mexico City I contacted a representative of Wyandotte and explained the situation. He said, 'What do you want to do?' I said, 'I want to go to Los Angeles.' He got us discounted tickets and I used the last money I had."

"Why Los Angeles?"

"Because it wasn't New Orleans."

"Had you ever been to Los Angeles?"

"Never. Always a trip into the unknown."

CHAPTER TEN

THE NEXT NIGHT I sat in the back of the News Café drinking coffee, my Toshiba laptop open, halfway through a letter to my friend Adam while jotting down ideas into a notebook for the novel on my mind. During the day, under green umbrellas, Germans in sandals and white socks, Colombians in yellow shirts, and Italians behind gray sunglasses, sipped cappuccino between bites of chicken Waldorf salad, reading international newspapers and magazines from the newsstand inside. Along the street, beachgoers weaved their way between palm trees and crowds in front of the latest renovated hotels. Harley Davidsons roared. At night, inside the café, the music varied, from Mahler to Morphine. Above mahogany wainscoting, the walls were covered with photographs of scenes from old movies and celebrities. The News Café was the first place I showed people when someone visited me and where I went to write in the red loveseats in the back.

"More coffee?"

The waitress was my type. Working the room with sass, holding my gaze the one second longer in which a universe of possibilities existed.

"More coffee would be great," I said with a half-smile.

She gave it a long pour.

"New to the city?" I added.

"Just got here with my girlfriend." She said it with matter-of-fact timing as if she had said it a hundred times, luring and deflecting a hundred guys like me.

"Got it." Of course, that made her that much more enticing. Miami Beach teemed with every imaginable sexual combination. In clubs, back alleys, apartments, hotel rooms. In the sand and surf. I liked her.

"What are you working on?" She refilled the cup of cream on my table. I think she liked me.

"An erotic thriller."

"Oh, really?"

"I swear. It's not a line. Right now, it's just therapy." I could banter too. I showed her my notes. "I'm working through a relationship that ended a couple of years ago, and basically, I don't know what to do with my life."

"Well, that's probably true for half the people in the restaurant."

I laughed. "What's your name?"

"Jen. And yours?"

"My name? Mark."

"Hello Mark."

"Hello Jen. What do you do when you're not here?" What a perfect leading line, I thought.

"I play guitar. I ride the waves. I look at the stars. I trust my heart."

Not what I expected, but I loved it. She held my gaze again. I really did like her. Then she turned to the next customer and held his gaze too. Boy, she could work a room. I lowered my chin into my hands. I wanted to be like her. To live freely, artistically, idealistically, on the edge. I wanted to twist and spin and pour emotions. I wanted to speak to what was deep and great. I wanted to feel the planets and the notes of songs. Trusting my heart that the universe would provide. The next Rumi. The next Dylan. And I wanted to be someone else too. To live responsibly, conventionally, realistically, at the center of events. I wanted to lead meetings. I wanted to invest in the markets. I wanted to influence policy. The next Averell Harriman. The next James Baker. I wanted both lives. I wanted to merge worlds together. To experience the transcendence that comes from opposing forces. Entirely on my own terms.

The curser on my laptop beckoned. I was two paragraphs into my letter to Adam. I met Adam in sixth grade at Miami Shores Elementary when I showed up as the new kid. We played touch football on the streets. He was faster and quicker than me and went out for passes. I played quarterback, calling the routes. We had long discussions during our teenage years. He went to the University of Michigan. After he graduated, he started his own business selling crystals and river rocks in Ann Arbor. I thought I might stay with him after my clerkship to write my novel. I could walk the campus, have my own space in the library, listen to musicians play in town. We exchanged letters about how it might work, and who would take care of what in his home. It was clear after a few letters that I was reaching for a solution and shifting the weight of my choices to him. He was gracious and wise about it. We dropped the idea. I had to work out my life here in Miami.

I finished my letter to Adam: a couple of pages about my week listening to oral arguments and the upcoming NFL draft. We were both Miami Dolphins fans and the team had the seventh and twelfth picks. I couldn't wait to watch the draft on Sunday on ESPN.

Not the stuff of Rumi and Dylan and Harriman and Baker.

When I looked up, Jen circled back to me. She sat across from me in my booth and ate a French fry off my plate. A classic move that worked every time by every woman in the world. And incredibly daring as a waitress. She could get fired, and she didn't care.

"I want you to write this down in your notebook," she said. "I want to see you write it. Ready?"

I held my pen in my hand. "I'm ready."

"You can be busy, or you can be adventurous." Then she got up.

I wrote it down.

The next day was Friday, pay day. I had asked Mimi, Suzanne's friend, if she wanted to join me for lunch in Coral Gables. It wasn't quite a first date. It was more a get-to-know-you conversation that could lead to something. After the exchange with Jen, I was on the hunt. Mimi was conservative and refined. Cuban American. Well-dressed. A wry sense of humor. We met for chips and salsa on Coral Way. We were there for two hours. We talked about her work at IBM, about personal computers and networking and how people would be able to send electronic brochures through phone lines one day. We talked politics, and how she leaned Republican, but she hadn't decided on the upcoming election. And we talked about family, hers, mine, staying close, breaking away. I told her that I had been interviewing my dad. We were having the kind of conversation where everything is new about the other person and your best self is on display. Her soft brown hair fell to her shoulders, and her dark brown eyes drew me in.

"It's such a wonderful thing that you are doing. Interviewing your father," she said.

"I know it means a lot to my dad right now, and it will mean a lot more to me as time goes by. It's incredible the stories he tells. I don't know how he remembers it all. I don't know what to believe."

"What do you mean?"

"You choose what to remember, right? And you choose what to forget. What you remember lives on and what you forget fades away as if it never happened. We make up our lives in the telling of it."

"In what we keep secret too."

"Right." I wondered what secrets she had.

"What is he telling you?"

"My dad? He's explaining his life. He's explaining who he is today. I know he's felt judgment his whole life. From his father and brother. From his wife. From his children. This is his defense."

"Sounds like he's making his case."

"I think he is. He's near the end of his life. He has great talents that he squandered. He could have been someone else. He could have been a scholar. He could have made a hundred other decisions."

Mimi leaned back in her chair, considering me. "That probably weighs on him more than it weighs on you," she said. "You have your whole life in front of you."

"You think I'm being too hard on him."

"He's your father. Sons judge their father. You are going to see things differently than someone else who is on the outside looking in. What you might not like about him, someone else might admire. We all make choices, and we live with regrets. Aren't you deciding what to do next? Don't you think your choices might weigh on you in the years to come?"

"I hope not. I hope I get it right." I gave her my best smile.

That night I rented two movies to watch. I didn't want to be alone on a Friday night, and wanting company, and not quite there yet with Mimi, I invited Amanda, a friend whom I had briefly dated the previous year, to the apartment. Single life was dressing and undressing. It was women I once loved, women who were friends, and women who were more than friends. Trial and error. Loss and gain. Amanda was in the same mood I was in.

"These are weird movies." Amanda read the back of the VHS tapes I had stacked on my coffee table.

"That's me. Mr. Art House." I poured her a glass of wine. Amanda was fun. She was blonde, fit, and very sexy. She didn't waste time. She was at Miami-Dade Community College and wanted to go to law school. I was sure she would win every case.

Amanda took a VHS cassette out from her overnight bag and popped in a tape into the recorder. "Let's watch *The Player*. This one is better than the ones you have. Tim Robbins plays a Hollywood executive being sent death threats from a writer."

"I don't think it's a better movie than the ones I rented."

"Don't argue. You'll lose." Amanda curled up beside me. We finished the bottle of wine. We didn't finish the movie, caught up in what we both wanted that night. As we sat afterward cross legged on the couch, eating pasta I had warmed up in the microwave, she tossed back her hair. I knew an interrogation was coming.

"You're going to take the job, aren't you?"

"If I did, I could spend a lot more money on you." I said it in a teasing way.

"I have my own money. Or I will. But yes, you should spend money on me. I mean, look at me." She batted her eyes and uncrossed her legs. She knew how to flirt.

"Yes, you are spectacular." I gave her the compliment she wanted to hear. "And yes, I mean, it would be crazy for me not to accept that job."

"Why even think about it? You've worked hard. You've earned it. They like you. You could become a partner. You could have a house on Fisher Island."

"Well, that decides it then."

"I'm serious. I don't know why you're hesitating. Do you know how many people would love to have the opportunity?"

"To wear nice suits and drive nice cars?"

"Exactly."

"I do. I just don't want to screw up my life."

"You won't, if you hang out with me."

When Amanda fell asleep, I watched *Hamlet* with Mel Gibson, the movie I had rented, considering every word of the soliloquy.

My dad was in the hospital. He had been having prostate issues for some time. He hadn't told me. He kept health matters to himself. My mom said he needed tests. She didn't say what kind of tests. She said I shouldn't worry. He would just be in the hospital overnight.

"I'll go see him."

"He doesn't want you there, my son."

"Okay, I'll call him."

North Shore Hospital connected me to his room. My dad kept the conversation short. He said he had been having discomfort and the doctor wanted him to take some tests, and he would be fine, but we might have to delay our next recorded session until he felt better. I told him that would give me time to transcribe everything we had discussed so far. I had gotten into the habit of spending an hour at the end of the workday in chambers wearing headphones playing back the cassettes and typing out our conversations into WordPerfect. I told him to use the time ahead to jot down memories and we would get back at it soon.

It sounded like my dad would be okay. I couldn't imagine him other than healthy, determined to live forever, although he had his scares in the past.

"I have some news. I passed the bar." I received my letter that day. Earlier in the year, after weeks of studying for the Multistate and Florida portions of the bar exam, I answered countless questions and wrote essays over two days beside hundreds of other candidates in the Tampa Civic Center. I got it on the first go.

"That's great, Mark. I knew you would do well."

"There is a reception tomorrow night for people who passed the bar. Big event with partners from different firms."

"You see, you're on your way."

"I suppose I am."

My dad had his tests in the hospital on April 29. The month of May was a blur. I had my one night with Amanda and had begun dating Mimi. We played tennis in Crandon Park in Key Biscayne. I loved driving over the Rickenbacker Causeway, over the blue waters of Biscayne Bay, past Virgina Key and the Miami Seaquarium, and seeing the "Welcome to Key Biscayne" sign. Mimi was good at tennis. She liked winning. She had a strong serve and backhand, unlike my ridiculous way of swinging a racket. We played three-hour marathon matches. Later in the week we celebrated her birthday with Suzanne and a group of their friends at Negroni's Bistro, ordering champagne, before ending the night at the Clevelander on Ocean Drive. Then I flew to Tallahassee to attend Rob and Marjorie's wedding, still with distant thoughts of an Artist Studio-Law Firm. In the days that followed I watched *Star Trek: The Next Generation* with Mimi on Monday nights, sat in the sun at Dolphins minicamp at St. Thomas University (all eyes on first-round draft choices Troy Vincent and Marco Coleman), attended Mimi's MBA graduation ceremony at the University of Miami, met her mom at the celebration in her home afterward, was sworn in as a member of the bar and had a congratulatory lunch afterward with Judge Fay and Ed, Ed, and Christine at Los Ranchos, enjoyed arroz con pollo that Mimi made after more tennis, and spent a weekend with Mimi and college friends in Winter Park. In between, I put in long hours in chambers as two months remained in my clerkship.

On May 26, my dad went back into the hospital for a transurethral resection of the prostate. The doctor said it was a common surgical procedure for benign prostate disease. My father had a catheter inserted in him to relieve urinary pressure. Just hearing the word "catheter" made me squeamish. If I ever had to have the same procedure done, I would shoot myself first. The next day after work I drove to North Shore and visited my dad. He was propped up in bed in a recovery room with another patient on the other side of a drawn curtain.

"How are you feeling?" I asked.

"I'm okay. I want to get out of here."

"I know. You have to stay until tomorrow."

"What's going on with you?"

"Me? I'm fine. I just came back from Winter Park. I like being on campus."

"You should be a professor."

"Maybe one day."

"I have this joke to tell you."

"Okay."

"Joachim Nabuco goes to the United Nations."

"Him again." Joachim Nabuco was a real Brazilian historical figure that my father made the protagonist of many of his jokes. We had been hearing Joachim Nabuco jokes our entire lives.

"The United Nations decided to conduct a world survey. They asked every country this question: 'Please, with all honesty, give your opinion on the scarcity of food in the rest of the world.' The survey was a huge failure. None of the European countries knew the meaning of the word 'scarcity.' The African countries did not know the word 'food.' The Russians were puzzled about giving their opinion. The Argentinians were not familiar with the word 'please.' North Americans had no idea about the 'rest of the world.' And the Brazilians, to this day, are debating what is 'honesty.'"

"That's pretty good."

It went on that way for twenty minutes. My dad didn't want to talk about the surgery or what he was feeling or what medicine he needed or protocols he had to follow. Throughout our conversation, I stood leaning beside the door.

"I'm going to get going now, Daddy."

"Yes, you do that."

"How about if I come by this weekend? We'll set a date to keep talking. I want to know what happened when you moved to Los Angeles."

"That would be good."

I left the hospital room. My mother was sitting in a chair in the hallway. She had given me time to talk to my father alone. I told her I would come by their apartment on Saturday. She said she would make lunch. Carne asada with the roasted yellow potatoes I liked. I kissed her, wondering what held people together. Probably really good food, to start. I drove back to South Beach, not focusing on much of anything along the way.

CHAPTER ELEVEN

MY DAD STOOD over the stove in his apartment pushing a minute steak and caramelized onions on a frying pan with a fork. He had already made white rice and warmed a can of Goya black beans. My dad was good with these kinds of meals. Likely all the way back to his bachelor days. He had a roll of paper towels beside him to wipe grease that splattered out of the pan.

It was Saturday, June 13. I had set aside the afternoon to begin my sessions again with my dad. It had been six weeks since we had recorded a conversation. He looked better. There was color in his face. He was wearing a patterned button-down short-sleeved shirt for the summer months and dark pants with his familiar black shoes. When I walked into the apartment, my dad had the television on. His go-to programming was *Meet the Press*, Larry King, any reports from Mike Wallace or Morley Safer, *Crossfire*, and commentary by David Brinkley. He was following the election closely, rooting one day for Clinton, another day for Bush, another day for Ross Perot. If it wasn't the news, he would put on Spanish television to watch boxing. He would shout and make noises at jabs and left hooks and hurried combinations. He could tell you about middleweight fighters back to the 1950s when he would go to the Gillette Cavalcade Friday Night Fights in Madison Square Garden. He saw Willy Pep, Sugar Ray Robinson, and Archie Moore in person. He followed every fight and television appearance by Muhammed Ali. He got a kick out of Howard Cosell.

We had lunch, cleared the table, and settled into recording. My mom had gone to Publix and K-Mart. My dad and I had the apartment to ourselves.

"When did you arrive in Los Angeles?"

"March 1959. I didn't want to go back to New Orleans because Mr. Gorman was there. Los Angeles was also the cheapest flight."

"What was on your mind?"

"I was worried, disappointed, anxious. I had been working very hard to build a business in Central America, especially with the chemical products for the sugar industry. And it was over. Wyandotte wouldn't take me if I wasn't in Brazil. I had to forget about it. I was worried because of the family. You see, it is very hard on a man with three small children and a wife going to an unknown place without money. I had nothing when we got off the plane. No home. No work. No prospects. Nothing."

"What did you do?"

"When we landed, your mother had enough American money she kept in her purse for a taxi. I told the driver to take us to a modest neighborhood and to drive around to see if I could find a room to rent. The driver took us to Echo Park between Hollywood and downtown. At the time Echo Park was very poor, many immigrants. I saw a sign that said, 'Room for Rent.' I told the driver to wait for me. It was about 7 p.m. at night. I talked to the night manager and told him I had my wife and three children in a taxi, and that I did not have any money because I was waiting for a bank transfer in two or three days. This was not true, but I said it, and that I had my luggage with me, and we needed a place to stay. He went outside and looked inside the taxi, he looked at Lourdes and the children, and he said, 'Okay, come on in.' We got a room, very filthy, very bad, with fleas, but I couldn't complain. I said, 'This is it.'"

"How was Mommy?"

"Listen, this is not the life she expected. But she had no place to go. We had small children. I started cleaning the bathroom on my hands and knees with rags because your mother did not want to use it. Too many fleas. Dirty. A terrible place. But we slept there. The next morning, I got up, and started walking around, looking at the environment, trying to think. I had to find a way to feed the children. Then it came to me. I remembered that I knew someone in Los Angeles. Mr. William O'Brien."

"Who was he?"

"He was a man who came into the office at Frieberg Mahogany. He owned a sawmill in Belize. I helped him buy some tools for his sawmill and he gave me his card. I remember very well that it said Los Angeles. So, I went to a phone booth and looked up his name in the phone book. Five cents a call at the time. I called all the William O'Brien's. On the eighth call

I hit the jackpot. He remembered me. I asked if I could see him. He said to come over anytime. He gave me his address. I asked someone on the street corner how to get to the address. I did not know the city. They told me to go to Sunset Boulevard and take a bus downtown. Ten cents. I found his building, a very big building, a beautiful building, and I said, 'Oh boy.' I went inside, took the elevator, and he had a beautiful office. The secretary told me to wait, and then he came out. He said, 'Oh, Mr. Peres, so glad to see you, come on in.' He was the president of an oil company. He said, 'Are you on vacation here?' I said, 'Not exactly.' And I told him what happened to me."

"All of it?"

"All of it. I had to be completely honest with him. He thought I was a little desperate to leave the way that I did, but I said, 'I can lose everything, but I cannot lose my self-esteem. Then I have nothing left.' He looked at me, then he said, 'Okay, Mr. Peres.' He gave me a check for $250 and said, 'Take this to my bank. If you have any trouble, ask the manager to call me.' I said, 'Thank you very much, but I didn't come here for money. I need a job.' He said, 'You need money right now. I'll get you a job. Where are you staying?' I gave him my address. Well, I went to the bank, got the money, went back to the apartment, told Lourdes what happened, paid two weeks of rent, and bought food for the children."

"Did he get you a job?"

"Yes, but not at his company. Two days later a man shows up that Mr. O'Brien sent. He arrived in a big Cadillac. He knocked on the door and he saw Lourdes. He saw the children.

He looked around. And he said, 'Mr. O'Brien has arranged a job for you. Can you come with me?' I said yes, I put on a jacket and tie, and we got in his car, and we started driving and driving. I'm in the back of the Cadillac, and we went to the San Fernando Valley. We went to a construction site, and he introduced me to the foreman."

"What did you think was happening?"

"I did not know. The foreman, a tough man, looked at me, and he didn't like what he saw. He said, 'Are you ready?' I said yes, I wasn't sure what I was saying yes to, but I said yes. He said, 'Do you have a hammer? Do you have boots?' I said no. They took me to the Army/Navy supply store, and they got me a pair of boots and overalls and a hammer. I put my tie and jacket on a hanger. The man who brought me in the Cadillac said, 'Good luck, Mr. Peres.' Then he drove away. I walked back out to the construction site in overalls. The foreman asked to see my hands. I showed him my hands. He was not happy. I said, 'I'm sorry, I've never done this before, but I'm going to do the best I can.' He said, 'Okay, come with me. I want you clean up these boards.' I said, 'I don't understand.' He said, 'You heard me, clean up these boards.' I didn't know what he meant. He got angry. He said, 'I'll show you what I mean!' He put a board on top of two sawhorses. The board had thousands of nails in it. He started taking all the nails off with a hammer. He was so fast and strong. PAH, PAH, PAH! The sound of the nails coming off. Then he gave me the hammer. I couldn't do it like him. But I did the best I could. By the end of the day, I was dead."

I had no idea about any of this. "What were you feeling?"

"Listen, I was not happy. But you must be humble in these situations. I took three buses home. The next day I got up at two o'clock in the morning to get there by 7 AM. I found out that Mr. O'Brien owned the construction company. The foreman had no choice but to take me on. Then I got my first check, we moved to another apartment in the building, and I kept on fighting. I did this for three months, wearing overalls and boots, pulling nails, hammering, getting on the bus, for three months, March, April, and May."

I imagined his hands calloused and bloody. I wondered if I could do it. If I could be so determined. "How were things at home?"

"Your mother was very, very unhappy, three children, pregnant. She was writing her mother and receiving letters every week. I was doing the best I could, fighting like a bull."

"Sounds like things were very tense." I felt for my dad. I felt for my mom. I was embarrassed about my own concerns.

"Yes. In the meantime, Mr. O'Brien heard reports of me working hard. He helped me get a used car for $20 a month that he guaranteed. One day he sent word that he got another job for me at another company, at Grant Tool & Oil, where I filled out orders at a warehouse. No more overalls. Then one day Mr. O'Brien called me to his office. He said, 'Mr. Peres, I am very pleased with you. You have shown that you really want to work.' I said, 'I don't have another choice.' Then I said, and I had been thinking about this for some time, I said, 'Mr. O'Brien, I can help you too.' I asked him if he would be interested in setting up an export business to sell petroleum products in Central America. If he financed it, I could establish the accounts. I explained to him how he could make a profit. He listened very carefully. He asked me a couple of questions. Then he said, 'That might be a very good idea, Mr. Peres, let me think about it.'"

"That was bold of you."

"For some reason, he was backing me. He had taken an interest in me. I did not want to disappoint him. And I had nothing to lose. Just as this was happening, Lourdes's mother sent her tickets to return to Brazil and bring the children."

"Did the tickets include you?"

"No. Her mother would never pay for me anyway and I would never accept. I was very upset. I said, 'Okay, you go.'"

"Was Mommy leaving you?"

"I don't know. She could not take the situation. Bad apartment. Bad neighborhood. Little money for anything. Seeing me in overalls. She wanted to leave for some time. She was eight months pregnant. I took her to the airport and from there she and the children flew to Miami, then to Belém, then to Sao Luis. I remember the children hugging my legs. I left the airport with a broken heart."

I grimaced. My dad was such a proud man, willing to debase himself to feed his family, and then to lose everything. "Did you think you would see her and the children again?"

"I didn't know. I went back to the apartment alone. My head was on fire. Do I let them leave for good, forget about them, start a new life, get rid of the burden of a family? At that same time, I had that deep sense of responsibility. I didn't want to lose the children, I didn't want to lose my wife. I thought I had a commitment to fulfill. I was in a very, very bad depression."

"What did you do?"

"I went to see Mr. O'Brien again. I told him what happened. He was surprised. He said, 'Do you want to join your family in Brazil?' I said yes. He said, 'Okay, I will help you.' He called his travel agency, and he paid for a ticket for me to go to Brazil. I told him I didn't know how I would be able to repay him. He said, 'Just be with your family and be happy.' The next day I resigned from the tool company, and in the beginning of July I left for Sao Luis."

"Why do you think he helped you so much? He was the president of an oil company."

"I don't know. There are bad people and there are good people. Maybe he saw something in me. That I would humble myself. I would work even if it killed me."

We took a break. I flipped the tape in the recorder. My dad was forty-two years old in 1959. He had already lived more lives by that time than anyone I knew. And in many ways the drama of his life had not even begun. "What happened next, Daddy?"

"I arrived in Sao Luis. Lourdes and the kids were staying with her mother. I knew I was going to have a tough time with her family. That I would face humiliation. I anticipated all these things. At that time her mother was declining in social status. There was a big fight going in the family about the loss of money after the father had died. Lourdes was actually very happy to see me."

"She was?"

"Yes, this is how things go. You see, I had come back for her. Two days later your mother gave birth to Dolores. On July 6."

"Mommy named Dolores after her mother."

"She did, yes. That was her mother's name. The next day, I remember this so well, Lourdes was still in the hospital, and I went to her mother's house with a gift, to patch things up, and her mother called me to sit at the table and she said she couldn't afford to support us, that I had to be responsible for my family. I thought, well, here is the beginning of the humiliation. I listened, but I thought I will never, never stay in Brazil. Even if I had to swim, I was coming back to the United States."

"This is when Dolores got sick."

"Yes, she was just born, and she contracted diarrhea in the hospital and the doctors couldn't do anything about it. She was very, very dehydrated. Very, very sick. She was about to die. She was just two or three days old. Lourdes was very upset. I had to do something. I was praying to God to give me some ideas. Then I remembered that there was a law in Brazil that allows Brazilian citizens living in the United States for two years the right to bring a brand-new American car into Brazil. I sold my rights to bring an American car into Brazil to an exporter friend I knew for $2500 and I bought tickets for the family to fly to New York."

I don't know how my father always thought of these things. "Did Mommy want to leave Sao Luis?"

"I told her we had to go. Who was going to support her and the children? She knew she couldn't stay there. You see, we both needed each other very, very badly, emotionally. She was happy that I came back for her. She said goodbye to her mother. We packed up and flew to New York. Three long flights. All the children. These flights could take days. Your mother carried Dolores in her arms. At Idlewild Airport in New York, I called Roosevelt Hospital. I told them I had a child that was dying. Then we took a taxi, all of us in the taxi, and we went to the Emergency Room. Dolores stayed in the hospital for twenty-one days, with tubes all over her body, and she survived. Meanwhile, we stayed in a hotel on 73rd Street and Broadway, before finding a place to live in Queens. And Lourdes and I started all over again in New York, the land of milk and honey, where our marriage first began in the United States."

My mom came home with groceries in a folding shopping cart she used to steady herself when she walked. She could walk just fine without the cart, but it gave her stability if she had to carry any weight as she managed the hallway and elevator. Using the cart also allowed her never to be seen using a walker if it ever came to that. She opened the door with her keys. My dad and I were at the table in midsentence. I got up to greet her and took the groceries out of the bag.

"Hello, my son," my mother said. "What is your father telling you?"

"How perfect you are for each other."

She made a face. "Don't believe everything he tells you."

"I would love to hear your side of the story."

"Let your father do the talking. I keep my memories private."

That was a point of contention between them. My father had remarked more than once that my mother remembered everything and would never let him forget anything.

On my legal pad, I scratched hashmarks. Between 1955 and 1959, my parents had already moved from Brazil to New York to New Orleans to Los Angeles to Brazil to New York. Over the next decade, the pace would quicken. After drinks and cheese sandwiches between white bread my mother made for my father and me, she went to her bedroom. I could hear soft music from behind her door.

I turned back to my dad. "You're in New York. It's 1959. It's Kennedy vs. Nixon. What did you do next?"

"I went to the Brazilian Trade Bureau because they published a bulletin with opportunities of business between Brazil and the United States. I knew a few people there at the Bureau. I overhead a man saying he was interested in rosewood oil. I told him that maybe I could help him. He gave me his card. Mr. Champon. Essential Oils. He had a French accent. He asked me to come see him in his office. The next day I went to see him. A beautiful office. I said, 'I was born in the Amazon, and rosewood oil comes from the Amazon. I have connections. I can help you.' He said,

'What can you do?' I said, 'Let me prepare a telegram and you send it over your telex machine.' So, I sent this telegram to Jacob Izagui, my cousin, who bought my father's business. The next day, Mr. Champon got a reply. He called me at the hotel. He said, 'Mr. Peres, we got an answer, and it's a very good answer. Can you come over?' I said yes, I took the subway and saw the message with greetings from my cousin and an offer for five drums of rosewood oil at a good price. Mr. Champon got very enthusiastic. He said, 'You know we are brokers of essential oils and buy and sell oils all over the world for perfumery. We have offices here in New York and in Paris and Madagascar. Why don't you join us?' And this is what I did. We negotiated a draw against commission, and we got underway."

"Did you know anything about rosewood oil?"

"Not really. But I knew how to sell."

"And you moved the family?"

"Yes, from the hotel to a place in Queens. One family was on the upper level, and we were on the first level. I signed a six-month lease."

"This took you to the end of 1959."

"Yes, then one day I got a letter from my sister Simita, saying that my mother was very, very sick. I put a call to Rio, and Simi told me she thought I should go to Brazil because my mother would not live long. I had not seen her in three or four years. She had a series of strokes. Her left arm was paralyzed. I decided to go to Rio via Belém, and the day I arrived in Belém, I was at the Grand Hotel, and I went around the corner to see my Uncle Samuca. And he said, 'I have bad news for you.' I said, 'My mother?' He said, 'Yes.'"

"She died on your way to Brazil?'

"Yes. And she was being buried that day in Rio. I missed it."

"How did you feel?"

"I felt bad. My mother was gone. I made that trip to see her, and I didn't see her. I stayed in Belém for three or four days, my uncle took me to the synagogue, he wanted to pray, then I flew to Rio. I went to see my sisters and stayed for two to three weeks and came back to New York. That was 1959. It was a tough year."

"Sounds like it."

"Unforgettable. But I think in the end I won. I won. And I felt good about it. I kept working for the company, Champon & Company, and living in New York. I remember we had a baby carriage with double seats. Lourdes and I would take the family to Central Park. Edison and Dolores in the little car, and Rachael and Arlene on the leash."

On the leash. I imagined my parents strolling the bridges of the park with my brother and sisters. "Did you go to other places? In New York?"

"More when I was single. I used to go to the library, the public library with the lions, and a few museums, and there were lectures in New York, and I went to a few of them. I had a friend in Greenwich Village who was a painter, a Bohemian, and he used to take me around the Village, and I saw these painters and artisans. Poets. They called the neighborhood the Montparnasse of New York."

"So, you were happy?"

"Yes, I had recovered. We were on our feet. I was doing okay. We had a place, I had a car, I had work to do, I was making money, paying my bills, we had food in the house."

"And then?"

"And then at the end of 1961, I made another terrible mistake. I took everybody back to Brazil."

I notched another hashmark.

"I know I'm asking this question a lot. Why?"

"Because of emotional problems. Your mother and her mother. Lourdes was worried about her mother because she was losing everything financially. Her situation was getting worse and worse. And Lourdes wanted to be with her. And Lourdes was worried that she might become sick, and she wouldn't see her like I didn't see my mother when she died. We always had arguments about going back to Brazil. Lourdes was very, very attached to her mother. Her mother came first, over and above her husband and children, whether she likes to hear this or not. And I gave in. We packed up and left for Belém."

"So, you blame Mommy?"

"No, I did not say that. I made the decision. I don't blame her for that. Family is one of those things. You're attached to your brother, you're attached to your sister, you're attached to your father, you're attached to your mother. This happens. I had a case in my family where two sons, two doctors, would not marry while their mother was alive because they didn't want to have any misunderstandings between their wives and their mother. They waited for their mother to die, and they were sixty-five when they got married."

"That's a diagnosis and prescription."

"Yes. Anyway, we left everything behind in New York, we went back to Belém, I rented an apartment in Belém, bought furniture, in Baptista Campos Square, and now the children had to go to school, so I put the children in a private Catholic school around the corner. And I said, 'What do I do now?' I opened an office in Belém, spending the money I had. People around there thought I was rich, but I was not. I opened this office, this brokerage office, to get offers from local exporters and send them to buyers in New York and make a commission. By that time, I was well acquainted with New York and well acquainted with Belém. I could make things happen faster."

"This is when you started traveling to Japan."

"Yes. But I must tell you this. I put an ad in the Brazilian bulletin in New York, also in *The New York Times*, and started getting replies from New York, and one of them was from a guy named Francis H. Devlin requesting an offer for cocoa beans."

"Cocoa beans. Okay, I'm keeping a list."

"And I helped fulfill his request with a supplier in Brazil. I started getting other replies from New York too, so I decided to go to New York to firm up contacts, and I was at the airport at the Pan Am counter in Belém, and I saw a man there at the counter asking to use the Pan Am telephone. A young fellow, blond, blue eyes, about my age at the time, early forties, an American, but he was speaking Portuguese. They gave him the telephone and he dialed and asked for Mr. Peres. And I said, 'Excuse me, sir, did you say Mr. Peres?' He said, 'Yes.' I said, 'I am Mr. Peres.' He hung up the phone and said, 'Are you the man who sent me this offer for cocoa beans?' I said, 'Yes!' He said, 'I'm on my way to Sao Paulo, but I thought I'd stop here in Belém to see you!' I said, 'I'm on my way to New York.' He said, 'Ah, I'm sorry to hear that. How long are you going to stay in New York?' I said, 'Maybe, two or three weeks.' And he said, 'Wait for me. I'll be back in New York in a few days, and we can talk then.' So, this is what happened. We met in New York. We had lunch together. We talked about business and our lives. He was an American who liked Brazil. I was a Brazilian who liked America. We were both importer-exporters. The same age. We liked each other. Two businessmen exploring possibilities. He said, 'If you ever come back to New York, we can work together.' I had this in the back of mind when I returned to Belém."

"So now Japan?"

"A tannery of alligator leather in Belém asked me to represent them."

"Hold on. I'm writing down 'alligator leather.'"

"This tannery wanted to sell in Japan. It was this new market. They paid my tickets to go to Tokyo and introduce exotic types of animal hides and skins to Japanese stores and customers. So, I decided to go to Japan. Very long flights. From Belém to Lima to Miami and then to Texas and to California and to Hawaii and then to Japan. This was one of the most successful things I ever did. An adventure. I loved Japan. The culture. The people. I learned words and phrases. I bowed and gave my business card with two hands. I was this tall Jewish Brazilian. The Japanese men were small. Very proper. I sold $300,000 worth of alligator leather. I came back thinking I was going to collect a huge commission, but the supplier in Brazil said it was too much. We argued about it, he gave me a much lower percentage, but everybody in Belém found out what I did and asked me to represent them."

"Still 1961, right?"

"I started taking these long trips from Brazil to Japan. On the next flight I went via New York. I had a letter from a supplier in Belém addressed to a company in New York by the name of Louis Denker & Company. Very large in the skin business. I took this letter to Mr. Denker which authorized him to give me $1000 for my expenses in Tokyo. He gave me the money and we had lunch together, and he asked if I planned on staying in Brazil forever. I said, 'No, I plan on coming back to America.' He said, 'If you do, if you would like to work for us, I have a job here for you.' I told him I was interested."

"So now you have two job offers, one from Devlin and one from Denker."

"Yes, I went to Tokyo via New York, I met more people, I remember selling another $100,000 of skins and leathers. I went to Osaka and Yokohama. On other trips I went to Hong Kong. I made sales there. I came back to Belém and got paid very well."

"Now, it's 1962, correct? The year I was born."

"Yes. Your mother is pregnant with you. And I told Lourdes, 'Listen, I don't want to stay in Belém. It's a waste of time. I don't have my heart here. Let's go back.'"

"What did she say?"

"When we were in America she wanted to be in Brazil. When we were in Brazil, she wanted to be back in the United States."

I laughed, knowing it was all too true. "So, she said yes."

"Yes. And we moved again. Back to New York. The whole family. Packed up everything. I connected with Devlin. We set up a corporation. Brazilian Products Company, Inc."

"I'm writing down all the names of your companies too."

"I became president. He was treasurer and secretary. Our business was hides and leathers. He kept his cocoa beans company separate. I rented this place month-to-month in New York for the family while I traveled again to Japan. After a few weeks, I told Devlin that I wanted to move to San Francisco. I had made a very good connection with one of the largest companies in the world, by the name of Marubeni Iida, which had a very large office in San Francisco. Living in California would make it easier for me to travel to Japan. So, Devlin and I decided on two offices; he would run New York, and I would run San Francisco. In the middle of 1962, we moved to California. Where you were born. And this was the best time in our lives."

CHAPTER TWELVE

MY STORY BEGAN on Sunday, November 18, 1962, at
1:11 AM at Mount Zion Hospital and Medical Center in San
Francisco. The fifth child of Mr. and Mrs. Ambrosio Peres.
My dad was forty-six years old. My mom was twenty-eight.
This was their time. The California sun shined on them.
They bought a home on Entrada Court in Ingleside Terrace
in San Francisco near Junipero Serra Boulevard. Their home
was in the inner ring of two concentric circles of mid-century
suburban one-and two-story homes that looked out on
a manicured park with a large twenty-eight foot marble and
concrete sundial where children played. To the left of their
home lived Mr. and Mrs. Hemnet, with whom my father
and mother socialized. Mr. Hemnet was a tugboat captain
and fire chief who became my godfather at a service at St.
Thomas More Catholic Church. To the right of their home
lived Mr. and Mrs. Humphrey, who hosted backyard cookouts.
My oldest sister Rachael was six, Arlene was five, Edison was
four, and Dolores was three when I was born. My brother and
older sisters attended Commodore Sloat Elementary School.
At home with us was Bendie, our sheepdog mix. My father

had his office on Market Street, in the heart of the city. When he wasn't traveling across the Pacific, on special weekends, he would take us to the Embarcadero and drive us across the Golden Gate Bridge.

"This was an incredible time for you," I said.

"Yes, for us. The best city in the world at the best time in the world. We lived very well. I had two cars. One for me. One for your mother. Very quiet life. Very beautiful. Everyone was in good health. We had made it."

Looking at the photo albums my mom kept, it was as if our time as a family began in San Francisco. My dad and mom look relaxed in a series of black and white photographs, my dad tall and lean in an open collar and wind breaker, my mom wearing a flattering skirt, leaning against their station wagon with the children sitting on the roof. Other photographs showed us in the backyard on a swing, my sisters holding dolls, my brother and sisters climbing trees, the family posing on the front lawn. There are two photographs that are my favorites: one of my dad in front of our home in swim trunks, in perfect physical health; the other of my mom in a casual white dress on a back porch, her hair windswept, looking like a stunning combination of Elizabeth Taylor and Sophia Loren.

My father continued, "My business was doing very well. I had made these wonderful contacts in Japan. I sold a lot. I started selling other commodities. I sold Brazil nuts. I sold black pepper. Hides and skins. Alligator. Leopard. Snake."

This is when my dad bought my mother a mink stole, diamonds and jewels, and exotic gifts from Asia. This is when we had a formal family portrait taken, my brother in a sailor suit, my sisters wearing matching dresses with lace collars. This is when my parents went to the movies, enjoyed their new Zenith stereo console, and hosted birthday parties for each of us at home.

"And life went on this way," my dad added.

I imagined life going on that way. Men still in jackets and ties, and women in skirts and gloves. I imagined elementary and high school, cable cars, Governor Reagan, Janice Joplin, Jefferson Airplane, Muir Woods, Stanford and Berkeley. I imagined growing up Californian, tanned girlfriends, chocolate and sour dough bread, writing for *Rolling Stone* magazine, playing guitar, meeting George Lucas and Steve Jobs, first and second rounds, optioning scripts and investing in Apple. I imagined stability and continuity and years on the West Coast adding up. It was an alternative, unled life that I imagined many times whenever I told someone I was born in San Francisco.

"This was everything you and Mommy wanted."

"Yes, we had a very good life. We were living a very good life. My business was the best it had ever been. Everyone was happy."

"What happened?"

"Life is not so simple. I met a man named Elder, a Palestinian man, an accountant, who worked for a brokerage company in New York dealing in sugar, and with the situation in Cuba at the time – this was after the Cuban missile crisis – his company closed. Elder needed work, and I asked Devlin

to give him a job in our New York office. One day I flew
to New York, and our receptionist, a Brazilian girl, said to
me, 'Mr. Peres, you need to get rid of Elder. He's not a good
accountant.'"

"Was he stealing money?"

"Well, he was deliberately confusing credits and debits and
not paying invoices. She said that Elder found out that I was
Jewish, and that he would never work for a Jewish person.
I told Devlin, who did not believe it. Devlin said he would
have lunch with him and confront him. Then we looked at
the books, and it became clear we had sold merchandise that
we had pledged to banks as security for loans that we should
not have sold. In other words, we no longer had inventory that
we should have had to sell to pay the banks. We owed a lot of
money. We let Elder go. Then Devlin said to me, 'You need to
come back to New York to help us get out of this mess.' I said,
'No, I have my life in San Francisco. I am doing well. My
family is happy. I don't want to move back to New York. You
let this happen.' He insisted. He said, 'You have to come. One
way or another, you are involved in this problem.'"

"This was in the middle of 1963."

"Yes, and I had to tell your mother. She loved San
Francisco. This was the life that she expected when we first
married. She liked it for many reasons, including that one of
her brothers and his family, had relocated from Brazil to San
Francisco. Your mother wanted me to help them, and I paid
for them to come to the United States. Our life was very good,
but I couldn't leave Devlin in that mess. It was my business too.

I was the president of the company. I told Lourdes that we had to go. We had to go back to New York.'"

"You couldn't continue to travel and try to make it work?"

"This is the decision we made. But I decided not to sell the house in San Francisco. Just to close it up. I called a broker in New York, and he found a house for us on Jewell Avenue in Forest Hills. A very nice house in one of the best neighborhoods in Queens. Beautiful street. Beautiful neighborhood. And I bought the house."

I was less than a year old when we moved to Jewell Avenue. I've heard my family talk about the house in Forest Hills many times in the same idyllic terms they talked about San Francisco. The pictures tell the story: a two-story home with bay windows and detached garage. My brother and sisters lining up from oldest to youngest playing dress-up in the kitchen. My brother standing on a stool wearing a Superman cape ready to fly. Everyone in winter coats and snow boots beside a snowman with buttons for eyes and a carrot for a nose on the front lawn. My dad in a hat shoveling snow. And the best photograph ever, one that I had framed in my apartment: my mom wearing pearls and my dad in a suit and overcoat holding hands by a silver tinseled Christmas tree with wrapped presents underneath with Bendie looking up at them. A suburban life in New York in the final months of the Kennedy years.

I could only guess what that house was worth now.

"Did you get out of the situation?"

"It took a while, but yes. It was difficult. We owed a lot of money to a company named A.J. Armstrong. Lawyers and accountants got involved. The company threatened that they would press charges for producing false documents. Devlin was very scared because his coffee business was doing very well. His lines of credit could be cut off. Everything got very contentious. One day I said I have to roll the dice. We had some unpledged merchandise in a warehouse, but it was not worth what we owed A.J. Armstrong. I went to the company and said I can go to Japan and sell off this merchandise at a high price, and pay off what we owe, but I want you to finance my trip. They thought I was crazy. They said we owed them, and they wouldn't give us one more dollar. I said, 'If it doesn't make sense to you, forget about what we owe you because the merchandise we have is not pledged to you. The only solution is for you to press charges or to pay for my trip to Japan.' I remember it was snowing like crazy that day in New York. I had a hell of a time walking the streets. After the meeting, instead of going to the office, I took the subway home. I was excited and nervous and crazy and angry. I had exchanged my life in San Francisco for that stupid thing in New York."

"I can imagine."

"A few days later I got a call from A. J. Armstrong. They agreed to finance my trip. I went to Tokyo. I went to Osaka. I went to Hong Kong. I sold everything. I sold more than I had. And I raised the money. When I got back, the letters of credit started coming in. I went to Staten Island every day, on the ferry, to our warehouse, to prepare shipments, reclassify goods, handle the transactions. Going from Queens to Manhattan to Staten Island. Back and forth. I worked night and day. And we paid everybody."

"Didn't you get sick?"

"Yes, I was scratching my arms and bleeding. The doctor told me I had a nervous disorder. He asked what I did for a living and how my business was doing. I told him. He said, 'Heal your business, and all this will go away.' On the way home from the doctor, I thought, 'I'm not going to stay here. There is no reason why I have to kill myself.' When I got home, I told Lourdes, 'Let's go back to San Francisco. We still have the house.' She said, 'When?' I said, 'Tomorrow. I can't stay here any longer.' And that's what we did.'"

"Back to San Francisco."

"Yes, back to California."

On the wall in my parents' apartment were five professionally taken black and white portraits of each of the children that my mom had commissioned when we were children in Forest Hills. One of Rachael, one of Arlene, one of Edison, and one of Dolores. The fifth one was of me just a few months old. What were the conversations that led to studio photographs? What did my mom spend? Isn't that what well-to-do parents did? The five framed portraits were the first items my mother put on the wall wherever she lived. The pictures of the five of us told us we were home. The five of us were her pride. We were her joy. The reason for every sacrifice and compromise and accommodation.

The moves from San Francisco to New York to San Francisco made no sense to me. My father had money. He had clients. We were in homes and neighborhoods that anyone would have said to stay in forever. Even a few years of stability would have secured our future. But always change. Always a reincarnation. My dad only hinted at regrets. If I ever found myself in the same situation, living in a good place where I could contribute my talents, carrying a cultural inheritance forward, I would plant roots. I would find some way of being both stable and bold. A lawyer and an artist. A citizen and a writer. Benefiting from compounding interest and smart risk-taking.

I headed to my apartment with the recorder in my hand.

The next day, on a Sunday afternoon, I balanced a hamburger and pasta salad on a paper plate, making small talk at the Jenner & Block firm picnic at Tropical Park. Attorneys and staff were all under the roof at Pavilion 12 avoiding the midday heat. The Miami branch office of Jenner had opened within the last three years. It started with two partners, one attorney from the main office in Chicago, and the other partner recruited from a local firm, who were slowly hiring to build a practice. There were a handful of associates who had come aboard, all of whom I met during the interview process. They were young, at the top of their class. The picnic was another step in the process. I had accepted their offer, but I was not one of them until my first day in the office. I said hello to the associates. I had a mitt and baseball that I had brought with me. It bothered me that in shorts and golf shirts, none of the lawyers looked the least athletic. They asked me about my clerkship and whether I was looking forward to starting at the firm while making inside jokes, that sounded like warnings, about working for the two partners. They also talked about recent commercial case law in a way that I could never imagine doing. I caught the eye of an attractive brunette my age who was helping manage the whole affair. One possible benefit, I thought.

Mimi and I had cooled. We enjoyed the same activities, had the same values and instincts, but the spark just wasn't there. Just two nights earlier, we had dinner at Big Fish on the Miami River and joined Suzanne and other friends at the Improv in the Grove. Mimi and I laughed through all the acts, drank sangria, then dialed down the relationship the next morning. It was the best of breakups, decided with a shrug and a smile. We resolved to remain friends with plans to hang out.

The picnic had started at noon. By 2 p.m., I wanted out. There was no one there I wanted to toss a baseball to or catch a Frisbee from. The two partners stood talking amongst themselves, away from the firm staff and the associates. Not a good sign. I couldn't imagine Judge Fay acting like them. He was the first to play volleyball and always made sure everyone was served first at chamber picnics. I shook hands with everyone I needed to shake hands with before heading to my car. I was two months away from starting with Jenner, unless I decided to walk away.

I didn't know what to do. I wanted a successful adult life script. Were the young attorneys happy with their lives? Wouldn't I be happy if I just got on with it? I wanted lessons from my dad's life to guide me. I had an opportunity to practice law that my father never did when his law school education was interrupted. He didn't go back to it and his life was one compromise after another in the world of sales and business. I could choose the law. I had a profession in front of me for the taking. Even if no one could catch a baseball at the firm. And yet little of the practice of litigation appealed to me.

When I got home, I ironed shirts for the week, then watched the Bulls blow out the Trailblazers. It wasn't close. Jordan raised the Larry O'Brien trophy. Two championships in a row.

The following Thursday night I met Suzanne at Johnny Rockets. The Grove was packed. People were moving briskly between Mayfair, CocoWalk, and Señor Frogs. It was opening weekend for *Batman Returns*. I had collected comics throughout law school, heading to Cosmic Cat Comics in Tallahassee across the tracks every few weeks to unplug my brain and buy Marvel and DC titles. I had the latest issues penned by Frank Miller and Alan Moore and Neil Gaiman. I had the run of *The Dark Knight* and *Watchmen* and *Sandman*. I had *V for Vendetta*, *Black Orchid*, and

The Rocketeer. I had two hundred comics – including *Beautiful Stories for Ugly Children* – in chronological order in two boxes protected with cardboard and wrapped in Mylar by the time I earned my degree. Each issue inviting me to heroes and myth and story. Suzanne didn't have any interest in Batman but said she would go to the movie with me. At Johnny Rockets, we ordered Original Burgers and strawberry shakes.

We talked about her residency. She had the temperament to be a great doctor. Deliberate. Precise. Compassionate. We talked about my clerkship. And then we talked about my conversations with my dad.

"My dad said after the worst year in his life that he won. He lost his business. His hands bled as a construction worker. He almost lost his marriage. He had nothing in his pocket. His mother died. And he said he won."

"Why do you think he said he won?"

"Because he fought through it. He didn't quit. He found a way."

"Do you admire that in him?"

"I do. But what I don't admire is that he puts himself in one situation after another where he has to fight his way through it."

"You think he brings it on himself." She slurped on her milkshake.

"Yes, it's as if he continually punishes himself for not being the person he hoped to be. And then he has to extract himself with skills that remind him of his gifts and talents. He sabotages himself to prove that he can persevere."

"That's pretty good, Mark. What would he say about you?"

"What do you mean?" I had been looking out at the crowd of people wearing flannel shirts and ripped jeans becoming more congested and turned back to her.

"Do you think he admires you?" She swiveled on her stool.

"Me? I think he respects what I created for myself and my work ethic and values."

"The life he made possible for you."

"Yes, the life he made possible for me."

"You see, he did win, didn't he?"

Nice, I thought. *She'd make a fine attorney.* "My mom made it possible too. She raised five children. Under constant pressure. She taught us to tell the truth. She was our moral center. My father wanted to marry a good woman, and he has to deal with it."

"You should interview her."

"She won't do it. She keeps it between the two of them."

"She might want to share her story one day."

"I hope I'm thoughtful enough to hear it then."

"What's next with your dad?"

"I know what's coming. I know he's about to tell me an incredible story. I don't know how he and my mom got through it."

We went to the movies and watched Bruce Wayne and Selina Kyle and Oswald Cobblepot, and the entire complicated crew put on their masks.

CHAPTER THIRTEEN

MY DAD AND I met again to record on Wednesday, July 1. I'd spent long hours since our last session in chambers, writing and mailing letters to friends, getting new contact lenses, attending a Father's Day celebration at my sister Dolores's home where my dad told Joachim Nabuco jokes, spent time with my sister Arlene and her family who had just moved back to Florida from Texas, and watching the start of the Summer Olympics in Barcelona. The Dream Team crushed Cuba 136-57.

My dad and I sat on his balcony just as we had during our first recording. It was a warm, clear night. I was wearing my Rollins T-shirt and torn jeans. My dad in his usual button-down half-sleeved shirt and dark pants. We began our conversation at 7 p.m. surrounded by blue skies.

"When we last talked, you and Mommy had moved back to San Francisco. It's 1964. Is there anything about that time you want to mention before we continue?"

"Yes. I want to reference Mr. Louis Denker. As I said before, Mr. Denker offered me a job in his company if I ever returned to New York. And I said I was interested. I said this casually over lunch with him. But I didn't do it. I decided to work with Devlin. Well, one day a court messenger walked into Devlin's office and served me with papers. Mr. Denker was suing me for $100,000 in damages for breach of contract. He alleged that he relied on me working for him, that he did not hire anybody else pending me joining him, and he suffered sales losses."

"Really?" And suddenly I didn't want to practice law again.

"Devlin and I had to hire an attorney. This went on for months. Denker would not settle. We went to trial. My lawyer did not want me to testify, but I took the stand. Denker's lawyer asked me if I had made the promise. I said, 'Yes, I did.' He said, 'Why didn't you fulfill your promise?' On the stand, I had this thought, I said, 'I agreed to work with Mr. Denker on hides and skins, but I didn't get into that business, I got into the leather business. If you read the invoices I sent in my business with Mr. Devlin, they say "Reptile leather," which is a narrow line. I didn't break my promise to him.' The judge looked at me a little confused, then his face brightened, and he called the lawyers to the bench, they talked, and my lawyer smiled and Mr. Denker's lawyer was very mad. They proposed a settlement where each party would pay their own attorney fees. I said no, because the law was on my side, and I wanted a determination. Devlin got angry with me because he did not want to risk a verdict. He said, 'For three days I have been sitting here without working and this is costing me thousands of dollars. Don't be stubborn. Let's settle.' I said, 'If you want to pay the attorney fees, that's your business. But I'm not going to pay.' Devlin said, 'Be an American. Don't be Brazilian.' Well, Devlin eventually paid the attorney fees. This caused a strain in our relationship. Plus, I was still upset about the Elder incident, how Devlin did not watch the books and forced me to leave San Francisco. So, we broke up the business. We cut things off. We stopped talking. When I returned to San Francisco, I was on my own. Independent."

"You preferred it that way, didn't you?"

"Yes, I prefer making my own decisions, and the consequences are my own."

"Well, not always your own. How was life when you returned?"

"Very good. We were back in our house. Back in San Francisco. Your mother was back to socializing with Mrs. Hemnet and Mrs. Humphrey. The children were back in school. I was weightlifting. I weighed about 185 pounds, the strongest in my life. I would go to the gym after work and on Saturday mornings. And I was back in business. I started to expand my lines, selling alligator and snake leather to the cowboy boot industry. I traveled to Texas and New Mexico. I was selling spices. I traveled to Japan again via Hawaii but also via Alaska. Let me tell you more about Japan."

"Okay."

"I was very lucky doing business in Japan, especially with Marubeni Iida, which was one of the three M's of Japan: Mitsui, Mitsubishi, and Marubeni. The difference between the three was that Marubeni did not manufacture anything. They financed the manufacturing from beginning to end and bought and sold every kind of product. It was a company with about eighty-five thousand to ninety thousand employees all over the world."

"You really liked Japan, didn't you?" I had a distant memory of a photograph of my father in a restaurant in Tokyo holding chopsticks.

"Oh, yes, and the Japanese liked me. They treated me very, very well. Brazilians had a very good reputation in Japan because Brazil was one of the few countries that accepted large immigration of Japanese after the war and allowed them to get into agriculture, business, and banking. In fact, the largest population of Japanese people outside of Japan is in Brazil. There are many Brazilian people with Japanese names. I walked the streets of Tokyo and Kyoto. I went to the temples. I went to museums. I learned words and phrases. I found that they were extraordinary people. Very hard workers. I found their sense of fatalism very interesting. They understood life and death as the same thing. It is a very orderly society. A very honorable society. I felt my soul was Japanese. The women are very respectful. They walk two feet behind their husbands."

"Did you have any close friends in Japan?"

"I did. His name was Takauchi. I remember one night he took me to his home on the outskirts of Tokyo. We drank tea. We looked out at the lights of the city. We talked about our lives. It was a special night."

"Didn't you have a past life reading that you were once Japanese?"

"Yes. I was told that I lived many years in the Orient before this actual incarnation. I believe this is true."

I liked that my dad was open to these ideas, even if I found them fanciful. I wondered what my past life reading would say. I had a relationship in law school where I was certain we had met in a previous life. I liked that my dad had a mysterious view of the universe, that we travelled through time.

"You also went to Hong Kong," I said.

"Yes, I went to Hong Kong three times. A completely different culture. The Chinese are less formal, more liberal, more democratic, more outspoken. Chinese food is very good. I have a joke for you."

"I'm ready."

"What is the secret of happiness?"

"I would very much like to know."

"An American house, a Chinese cook, and a Japanese wife."

We took a quick break. All of this led to the story that I knew would be difficult for my father to tell.

"You also traveled through Europe, didn't you?"

"Yes, always on the road. The last time I went to Japan I kept traveling west in that direction. I went to Hong Kong, then to Vietnam and to Cambodia, this was during the war, staying at the airports, then I went to New Delhi in India, and from there I went to Beirut, I stayed two days there, then

Istanbul about two days, from there I flew to Frankfurt, then London. I stayed in London for two weeks."

"What were you doing?"

"I was selling alligator leather. A quick story about London. I was with Japanese Marubeni agents in London, and they wanted to take me to their bankers. It's traditional in England to tell people where you bank. He met me at the Cumberland Hotel, and drove me downtown, and we got to the bank, the Marubeni man said, 'Where is your hat?' I said, 'I don't wear a hat.' He said, 'You cannot go into the bank unless you have a hat. You must show you have a hat.' I said, 'We are a block away. Is it really important to have a hat?' He said, 'We must get you a hat.' So, we walked blocks and blocks in the other direction until we found a store that measured me and sold me a Derby hat. It cost me twenty pounds. We went back to the bank. As soon as I walk in, I hang up my hat. No one wears a hat indoors. After the meeting, I walked out. My Japanese friend said, 'Ambrosio, you forgot your hat!' I went back for it. When I got to the United States, I wore the Derby hat for Lourdes and the children."

"All right, Daddy. I want to talk about something. You have this wonderful life in San Francisco. You're traveling the world. You're making money. You're living in a beautiful home. Your family is thriving. It's everything you've taken risks and worked hard to achieve. It's now 1966. You are forty-nine years old. And you are about to give it all up. Why?"

The expression on my father's face shifted. Both of us knew we were going to get here. There was a long pause.

"This is tough. I don't think I should tell the story of my life because it is not a beautiful thing. The atmosphere at home was kind of heavy and I thought we should move."

"Why was the atmosphere at home heavy?"

"This I cannot say."

"Should I ask Mommy?"

"You can ask her, but I cannot say. The situation was a little tough and we had to leave San Francisco."

I waited as long as I could. I tapped my fingers at his refusal to answer. I drew a large zero on my legal pad. "And you decided on Miami?"

"Yes. I thought that things were happening in Miami. I thought I could sell alligator leather to the Cuban people. The Cubans had started coming in after the revolution. The city was spending money on infrastructure. Building highways through the city. I came to look at the city. Lourdes came down too. We made the decision together. We went back to San Francisco, and I closed the business. We came to Miami as a family and rented a house in the Southwest section of Miami near Bird Road. It was a very good house. It did not have air conditioning. We kept the windows open. Miami was different then."

"That's where I had my accident."

"Yes, you were four years old. You fell off your bed and your head hit the sharp corner of a dresser. You split your head open between your eyes. There was a storm at midnight. Your mother took you to the hospital on her lap in her car following the police driving through the rain. I was not there. I was on a trip to Brazil. You survived."

Good enough. *I survived.* With a scar between my eyes. "That's also when I was taken to a speech therapist."

"Yes, you never spoke. You were silent. You just pointed at things. The speech therapist said that you were behind developmentally. She said your cooperation was poor, you didn't follow directions, and you were attached to your mother. She said your attitude was extremely negative."

"Maybe it was because my head had just been split open."

"Yes, well, you caught up."

Yes, well, I did. "And what was happening with you?"

"I opened a new business on 8th Street. Interseas Trading Company. Starting a new business in Miami was very difficult. I sold leather handbags and purses. I put merchandise in my car and drove from Miami to Ft. Lauderdale on U.S.1, and called on stores, selling door to door. That's the way it was. It was very, very difficult. I lost the money I brought from San Francisco. I began to lose it all."

"Why couldn't you continue the same business you had in San Francisco in Miami?"

"I cannot say."

Ugh, I thought. He was holding something back. I had gotten him to this point, and it just didn't add up. I knew it had to do with my mom, reasons between them, something at the heart of the marriage that he wouldn't broach. Not yet at least. We would get to it, either directly or indirectly. It would come out. I was sure of it. "Alright. Well, it didn't work out, did it?" I wasn't sympathetic in the way I said it.

"No. At the end of 1966, after just a few months, I had to do something. Your mother wanted to go back to Brazil. Aways back and forth. And I thought I might have a chance in Rio. I had some connections there. So, we moved to Rio."

"I'm keeping track."

"But you see, when we lived in Brazil, we always had to live better than the money we had. Your mother never accepted the idea of being poor in Brazil. She would not lower her standards while she was there. In the United States, yes, because we were foreigners, and no one knew us. But not in Brazil. She would not accept that. We had to keep up appearances. Her reputation was very important. So, in Rio we had to live in a very good apartment on Copacabana Avenue. The name of the building was the Menascal Building. A first-class building and large apartment. We sent the children to an American school, a private school. This was now 1967. I was spending money I didn't have."

"This is when you saw your brother for the last time."

"Yes, José. I received a call from my sister Simi. She said, 'Listen, you better go to Sao Paulo and see José because his wife called and he's in very, very bad shape and he's not going to last too long.'"

"What happened to him?"

"He ate a carton of figs that poisoned him."

"A carton of figs?"

"Yes, that was what I was told. I went to see him, and he was in very bad shape, very skinny. He had been separated from his wife, but she took him back when he became sick. We talked about a lot of things. Our mother and father. Growing up in the Amazon. Fights we used to have. Decisions we made. Regrets."

"Did you see him over the years?"

"Yes, whenever I traveled to Brazil, and came through Sao Paulo, I tried to see him. I had lunch and dinner with him. We talked about his activities as an intellectual. He was a man obsessed with books. He spent every penny he had on books. His failure in life was due mainly to his books."

"Maybe that was his success as well."

"Yes, maybe, but he went overboard. He forgot his obligations to his family. Anyway, he died. He was fifty-nine years old. Because of the figs."

"Did you go to his funeral?"

"No. I missed his funeral. I missed my mother's funeral. I missed my sister Cota's funeral. I missed them all. Sad. Just sad. But like my mother used to say, 'The older you get, the more your eyes are on the infinite.' That's just a part of life. Sometimes I lie down on my bed, and I think about the dear people gone. My father, my mother, my brothers, my sister, my friends. Until my time comes."

"I'm sorry, Daddy." I wanted to reach for his hand but didn't.

My father paused. "I tried working things out in Rio, calling on a few customers and friends, but nothing worked out. Nothing. I couldn't put things together. I talked to Lourdes about leaving

Copacabana and moving to a small house in the suburbs of Rio. She didn't accept that. That's a matter of pride. But I don't blame her because it is very unpleasant to leave your country and then to come back worse off than you left. You understand? I could do what everybody else does when the money is low, find a job, change our circumstances, live in a very humble house. Millions of people do this in Brazil. But we were not ready for that. We didn't accept that. Imagine taking American children out of a very high-class American school and putting them in a public school in Rio. If we were going to live within our means, we would have to move again. Back to Miami."

"Why Miami? You were just there."

"Because we were seven people in the family, and the tickets were cheaper. And Miami was cheaper. It was a mistake. I should have gone back to New York, but we came to Miami."

"I do remember some moments in Rio. I was five years old. I remember that you took me to Maracanã Stadium to watch soccer. I remember drinking Orange Fanta on the beach."

"I'm glad you remember." He said it as if I was uncaring.

"What happened when we arrived in Miami?"

"Well, this is when things went from bad to worse. This is the part I do not like to talk about."

The sun had set. We had our drinks on the balcony. My mother had come out to check on us and went back in. My father said he was ready to continue. I put a new Maxell cassette into the recorder. We lost eye contact. My father began to talk straight ahead into the night.

"When we arrived in Miami, I had nothing. No prospects. No lines of credit. I owed money. People were after me. I had to find something. We had to live somewhere. We stayed at a very low-cost motel on Biscayne Boulevard. I had a friend named Jaime Gutierrez who said he could get me a job at the airport."

"Back to the airport?" Apparently, it was where immigrants down on their luck went for a job.

"Yes. The company at the airport was overhauling warplanes that had been damaged in the Vietnam War. This is late 1967. Many American soldiers were dying. I went to this company at the airport to apply for a job and they called me to take a test. I went in for the test in a room with about twenty people. A very simple test. Simple math. Stupid questions like, 'How many legs does a horse have?' I answered all the questions in two minutes. Then I left. Two days later they contacted me and said, 'Mr. Peres, you passed the test with high marks. Please see this foreman at the company.' I went to see the foreman, and he asked me, 'Are you a mechanic, Mr. Peres?' I said, 'No sir, I am not.' He said, 'Are you an electrician?'' I said, 'No sir.' He called the office and came back five minutes later, and said to me, 'You're going to be an inspector.' I said, 'An inspector of what?' He said, 'Aircraft engines.' I said, 'How can I inspect aircraft engines? I don't know anything.' He said, 'Well, apparently the test you took said you would be an excellent aircraft engine inspector.' I said, 'I have never seen an aircraft engine in my life. If you want me to translate English into Portuguese or read a prayer in Hebrew, I can do that.' He said, 'Don't worry, Mr. Peres, I'll show you.' He brought me to a conveyor belt, he gave me a manufacturer's specification book, and a plastic ruler. He said, 'All you have to do, Mr. Peres, is when you see a part on the conveyor belt, pick it up, look at the name and number of the part, and measure it to check whether it is exactly according to the book. If it is not, send it back.'"

"Did you do this job?" I asked, sad for him and amazed.

"Yes, I did this job for three months. I went out of my mind, but I had to feed the family. I got a small check every week. Then they started laying people off because they weren't getting as many damaged engines from Vietnam. So, I lost the job. I couldn't find another one. We had no food at home. Things got so bad that I went to the government, the federal government, for help. They gave me a card that said 'Needy.' And every week I would go to a certain place and pick up dry food, like potatoes and powdered milk, and bring it back to Lourdes and the children. We ate liver and sardines."

"Where were we living?"

"In a terrible place. In the Northwest section of Miami. It was a lousy house. A shack on cinder blocks with no running water. There was a well in the back of the yard. Your mother and the girls would get water from a spigot from a nearby store. Tiny rooms. Rachael and Arlene slept on an old twin mattress. Edison and Dolores slept on the couch. You slept on a cot. I bought a used car because you need a car in Miami. It was falling apart. There was a rusty hole in the bottom of the car.

I could see the street under my feet. Your mother would drive the car. It would break down everywhere we went."

"This is when Mommy pawned her jewelry."

"Yes, she pawned what I had given her, one at a time."

I imagined my mother staring down at her rings and necklaces, parsing them out, on the edge of town. "How were you feeling?"

"Terrible. Awful. Bottom of the barrel. I wanted to commit . . . well, I don't say the word. I was so desperate. I kept thinking about it. I could not sleep at night. I do not like to talk about this."

My dad drew back. I looked at him, then looked down. I didn't want to see his face. I wasn't sure what to say to him or how to give him comfort.

"Why do you think your life had gotten to this point?" I asked. It was the first question that came to mind. I wanted some admission about how our lives had gotten so bad.

"What do you mean?"

"Why do you think it got to a point where you were suicidal?" Oops. I said it.

"That's a hell of a question." My father turned quickly to me.

I was in the stew now. "I mean, why do you think these things kept happening to you?" I grimaced as I said it.

"Listen, Mark, too many trips, too many things done without any good purpose, lack of good judgment."

"But why?" I couldn't believe I was pressing the point. I braced for the emotions I had hoped to avoid as my father crossed his arms.

"Well, we are now getting to the heart of the matter. This is what you want to discuss so I will tell you. It was not a matter of being unable to do things or to perform duties. I was a very hardworking man. I did what I proposed to do, but in the end, I failed because of things done in a very stupid way, without any common sense. Five trips to Brazil with my family, that's a lot of money, thousands and thousands and thousands of dollars thrown in the garbage. Interruption of business. It's very bad when you are doing well to cut it off and to go to another country without any reason, without any purpose, without a plan, spend all your money on rent and when you are broke you start all over again, and when the business starts picking up, you cut if off again and do the same mistake over and over again."

"Well, we just didn't move between the United States and Brazil, we also moved within the United States as well, from city to city, from neighborhood to neighborhood—"

"This is a different thing. This is different. When you are doing very well in New York or in Chicago or San Francisco or in New Orleans, you have your house, you have your apartment, you have your furniture, you have your business, you have your line of credit, and you are working, and you have your children in school, and then for no reason, no good reason whatsoever, you cut this off, you forget about this whole thing, you throw everything in the garbage, and then you go to Brazil and to do what? I don't know. To do whatever happens. In the meantime, you are using your money because you must eat every day, you must pay rent, you must pay expenses. And then you try to do something in that country, and you don't do it. You cannot do it. And then you come back to the United States without a penny. Then you start all over again. And then you build up another business. And you start feeling better. You put your children in school and one year later, I go back to Brazil? What am I going to do in Brazil? I don't know. Whatever. And you destroy your life five times. That's self-destruction. And why, why? Because of emotional reasons. Because your family expects you to perform miracles. They say, 'If we live here, we can live there, whatever you do here, you can do there.' But this is not true because the circumstances are different, the economics are different, the opportunities are different. You try it in your life."

I felt pinned. "I appreciate everything that you are saying—"

"I want you to imagine that you are established in your law practice here in Miami. You have your office, your customers, you have everything. Then you stop. You close it down. And you go to Brazil. And there you try to be a lawyer. You don't know the language. You don't know the culture. Then you come back but this time you come to New York to start again. And you build up another clientele and after hard work you are doing well, and you stop again. And you keep doing that. Now, if you do this in the United States, if you go from Miami to New York to San Francisco, you are still under the same law and culture. The country is the same, the language is the same, you take your assets with you. But when you do what we did, with young children, the emotional impact is severe. Take you, Mark. Let me talk about you. When we took you to Belém, you didn't want to talk. You hid in corners. One day you had a contraction of the muscles in your body. You could not breathe. I had to take you to a doctor in Brazil for immediate attention. They gave you shots to relax your muscles so you could talk. And why is that? You were what? Nine, ten years old? Because we kept moving you from one environment to another."

"I just think—"

"You might say that it is a character issue, my character, that I like to move around, that I can't settle down and cause my own problems. That might be a factor, that might be a factor, but when you feel that the people around you keep encouraging you to make the same mistake, and you are trying to solve problems, it is not a factor of your personality, it is collective bad judgment. If you don't learn from the past, your future is going to be very tough."

My father gave me a hard look and got up from his chair. He slid open the balcony door and went inside the apartment. All of it had come out. All of what was pent up inside him. I could see him talking to my mother. My mother glanced at me concerned through the glass door as I stayed seated outside. Then my dad went to the kitchen. I imagined him looking vacantly at the cabinets, alone.

CHAPTER FOURTEEN

MY MOTHER CAME out to the balcony. She replaced my drink. I could see all her years of struggle and understanding with my father on her face. She spoke to me in Portuguese.

"My son, your father is upset."

"I know. I upset him."

Then in English. "He is sharing everything with you."

"I don't know that he is. Why did we leave San Francisco?"

"This is between your father and me. Some things are private in a marriage."

My mother sat beside me in the plastic chair my dad had been sitting in. There was a crescent moon in the sky. My mother could sit for hours looking at the moon. She would play Brazilian music inside the apartment. These were moments of retreat and renewal for her. Moments of *saudade*, the Portuguese word for profound melancholic longing for an absent beloved that one might never encounter again. My mom was filled with *saudade* for the Brazil of her youth. For her father, mother, and sister, and brothers in Sao Luis. For the *sabrado* home she grew up in over the bakery. For the days when she protected and cared for her five children as a young mom.

"Why didn't you leave him in Miami?"

"I left your father many times, but I would not leave him then. Not when he needed me the most."

"Does he want me to go?" I was certain it was over between my father and me.

"Let me talk to him."

My father and I reconvened inside the apartment at the dinner table. He kept me waiting for twenty minutes before coming out of his bedroom with his hair wet and combed back. He sat stiffly at the head of the table. He didn't make any comment, other than to continue the interview. I stayed still. This is how our family moved on. We internalized hurt that created space for forgiveness. Even if it took a while.

"I know this was a very difficult time for you and the family. I appreciate you telling me about it." I said it sincerely. I wanted our conversation to continue. I knew my dad did too. We could never come back to this moment again. "Just to reset the stage, we are in Miami in 1967. And things are not good."

"No. Things are not good." My dad paused for a long beat. "But I will tell you this, in the meantime, I met this guy who said he wanted to get into business with me. He wanted to sell aircraft parts in Brazil. When you are desperate, you attract people who take advantage of you, and this is what happened. I told him I would work with him. He put up money to rent an office on Northeast Third Street and Flagler. He bought two desks and a file cabinet and a typewriter. We got two phones. I told him I had nothing. All I could do was work and try to get customers and sources of supply. One day he didn't show up at the office. Five days go by. I called up his home and his wife answered and said, 'I don't know where he is.' I was starting to get nervous. I did not really know this man. The whole arrangement was a grasp at hope."

"What happened?"

"Several days later, at eleven o'clock at night, I hear a knock at my door. We were in that terrible shack. It was the police with a warrant for my arrest."

"Wow." Another story I had never heard.

"Your mother was right there with me at the door in her dressing gown. We had both been sleeping. I got dressed, got into the police car, they took me to the police department, and told me I could make a telephone call."

"What did they charge you with?"

"Petty larceny. They said this man said I took his money. But I did not. I did not commit any crime. I called my friend Jaime, the one who got me the job at the airport, and he came immediately at twelve or one o'clock in the morning, and he put up the bond, and I left the jail cell. Jaime took me back home. I got home about four o'clock in the morning. And I was so desperate. I was thinking this is the end of the world. Why do these things keep happening to me? One million things went through my mind. But at the same time, I saw the children sleeping. Five innocent people who had nothing to do with my mistakes. Your mother had stayed up, waiting for me.

She was quiet. Asking me questions. We had coffee and let the time go by, one hour, two hours, and about 9:30 AM, I called Devlin in New York."

"When was the last time you had talked to him?"

"We had not spoken in four years. Not since 1963 when I went back to San Francisco."

"What did you say to him?"

"I said, 'Devlin, it's Ambrosio.' He said, 'Ambrosio!' in a very good way, which was a hopeful sign. I said, 'Devlin, I'm in Miami. I'm in the pit here. I'm in bad shape with my family. In very bad shape. I need your help to get out of Miami, whatever you do, if you want to help me, please do it today. I want you to know what has happened to me, but I will tell you the details as soon as I get out of here.' And he did not ask me any questions, he just said, 'Wait a couple of hours and call Eastern Airlines and there will be a ticket waiting for you.'"

"That was a good friend."

"Yes. That same day I flew to New York. I went to see him in his office in Manhattan. He looked the same. He explained that he was out of the leather business, he went back entirely to his coffee business. I told him that I had lost the business in San Francisco, I tried Miami and then Brazil, I was back in Miami, and I lost everything. I had to bring my family back to New York. He said, 'What are you suggesting?' I said, 'Frank, this is very painful for me to suggest, are you open to going back to the leather business? This is the only thing I can do right now if you want to do it. If you don't want to do this, I understand, I will have to look around New York and try to find work.'"

"You wanted him to finance you."

"Listen, I believe he had some guilt that it was his negligence that destroyed our business the first time. I said, 'Frank, you know me, and I know you. We can make this work if you stay in the coffee side of the business, and you let me handle the leather side.'"

"And he said yes?"

"Yes, he did. He said, 'Okay, Ambrosio, this time I won't intervene. I'll put up the money.' And I started to use his office and his telephone. I wrote letters to old customers I had in San Francisco. I wrote to Texas, to the cowboy boot people, and they started sending orders. And we got underway. Then Devlin purchased the tickets for the family to move up from Miami. This was 1968. And we found a place in Queens. We moved to LeFrak City, a new apartment complex in Corona, a very nice place. Devlin provided a personal guarantee for the rent. Your mother arranged for all of you to go to school. The public schools were very good. And we started again."

"What about your arrest in Miami?" I wondered if my dad had stolen money to feed the family.

"This was dropped. There was no proof that I did anything."

I was six years old when we lived in Lefrak City. I have my kindergarten class photo. P.S. 206 Annex – The Horace Harding School. Mrs. Ceruti. I'm in the first row, on the far left, in a white turtleneck and red sweater, looking earnest. A respectful child of an immigrant family. My hair is combed wet. My hands are prayerful between my knees. Clearly dressed for the day. The other boys wore ties. In kindergarten! The girls wore jumpsuits and white tights. My mom wrote a comment in the Chester Studios keepsake folder: "Mark has a special friend named Alexis. She is a nice little girl and they play a lot." *Why would my mom point out my special friend? Was I more interested in Alexis than crayons? And which one of the kindergarten girls in the photograph was Alexis?* I suspected the blonde in the back row. Good that I had game as a six-year-old. I have several pictures of my brother and sisters and I playing on monkey bars and swings in Lefrak City. There is one photograph of the five of us, all standing together, an apartment building the size of a universe behind us. My sister Rachael is tallest in the back, twelve years old at the time, then Arlene at eleven, Edison at ten, Dolores at nine, and me, in front, in blue shorts and a half-tucked shirt. It was definitely 1968. My sister Arlene had the strangest outfit: white pants, a blue shirt, a scarf around her neck, and red flowers in her hair.

It was getting late at my parents' apartment. My mother was tired. She had come out of the bedroom to get water from the kitchen. I set a ten-minute deadline with my dad.

"How were we doing as a family?"

"Well, the family was, I think, very well organized to a certain point. To a certain point. You see, we were all together, which was my main purpose, to keep the family together. Always. Regardless of circumstances or difficulties. I always thought that if we stayed together, we could solve any problem, one way or another."

"Mommy must have done a very good job keeping us together." She was the one with us every single day.

"Oh, yes. Definitely. You see, I have said this and will keep saying this, she was a very good mother. She was very good, very strict, she was very honest, and very decent. She set a very good example. Her behavior was always very good with each of you. But our life was always up and down, up and down, with problems that we created for ourselves. And of course, like in any marriage, other factors come into play. I do not speak of these things. I do believe that many of these things could have been avoided, that life in the family could have been better. We could be better parents in a few respects."

"How so?"

"We could be closer to the children. We could be more friendly with the children. More involved in their lives. We could give the children more opportunities to come to us, to be with us, and share their problems with us. You see, it was always a desire of mine to be very, very close to them. For instance, there was a time I wanted to talk to them every night, to study with them, to open books and read and teach them, and hear from them. These are things I did when I started having children and enjoying them, playing with them, but it was not enough. It was not enough because our marital life was very tense. Your mother and I had many fights. Too much violence, too much verbal abuse. And this wasn't good for the children. Our life, our family life could have been better, have a better quality. This is what I mean. And maybe if we were more understanding of each other, maybe many of our problems would not have come out."

"Don't you think one good thing that came out of our experience as children is that all of us persevere through our problems?" I offered a silver lining.

"We will see. Each of you is different. I have seen many people destroyed because their family environment is bad. That's very natural, you see, because Mark, everybody is born to become. We are all becoming. And you become according to the environment you live in, according to the education you receive, according to the social atmosphere you move around in. That's the way. That's how a personality is formed."

"Don't you think all of us value our family even more, having survived all this?" I meant it.

"This is my hope. This is the good part of all this. Imagine if it was the other way around. Our family could have been destroyed. Which was a possibility. Bad people come from broken homes, they see bad examples, they see violence, they see abuse, disrespect. That's their baggage, and they carry it along. When they have their own families, they do the same thing. But some people don't. Why? I don't know. This is our case here. All of you are good. It could be sheer luck. It could be your nature. Like the Bible says, good fruits come from good trees."

"I think so too." The mystery at the heart of our lives.

"But I sincerely believe that many problems we had could have been avoided. You see, it is hard to imagine that you go to Brazil, you live in a nice apartment, you live in Copacabana, you live it up. And three months later you are starving. How can you explain that? It's very tough. It's very difficult to understand. One day I walked from the Southwest all the way to downtown Miami on these two feet because I didn't have the money for the bus. I had holes in my shoes. But three months later I had thousands of dollars. How? But here we are. I am grateful to God and to heaven that we are together, that we are a nice family, everybody is responsible, everybody is decent. We are very proud of each of you."

"Daddy, just to wrap up, we made another move."

"Yes, I was doing business. I was selling, opening accounts, buying from two or three suppliers, but the business was small. I needed more money from Devlin to expand the business, but he was scared because of our first experience. His coffee business was also going down, getting very bad. He had a twenty-million-dollar business in coffee, selling to Coca Cola Company and Chock Full O'Nuts and other big buyers, then his suppliers in Brazil opened their own offices in New York, cutting Devlin out. He traveled to Haiti, Colombia, and El Salvador to get other suppliers, but it was not easy. So, his business started going down very fast, affecting my business."

"What did you decide to do?"

"By this time, I knew almost everybody in the hides and skins business. One day a friend of mine, Emil Buschoff, a big player in the business, said to me, 'Listen, Peres, why don't you go back to Brazil, open your office there, and ship hides and skins to New York. I'll buy from you. Whatever you have, I'll buy.' I went around to other big players, and I told them the quantity that Buschoff would buy from me. Another buyer told me that he would finance it. He said, 'You know how we work here, you know how to classify the skins, in Brazil they are always cheating, shipping second quality skins and labeling them premium quality, and when the merchandise arrived, there is no way to return it.' I got very enthusiastic about it."

"Weren't you wary about going back to Brazil?"

"I told myself this time was different because I had the support of these people, I had the market, I had the knowledge, and I had the suppliers. Business runs on this type of hopeful thinking. I decided to go back."

"This is 1969."

"Yes, back to Belém. We got a nice apartment, put you in American schools, and we did it again."

"But not for too long."

"No. There was a military government in Brazil after a coup d'etat. And all the laws began to change, including restrictions on the export business, making things very difficult. And this time the children were older and not happy. You were not happy. This is when you were hiding in corners, not talking, and having muscle spasms. You became a kind of recluse. I thought, 'My life is what it is. I'm fifty-three, but what about these children? Do we have to bring them up in Belém? They must learn the language. They must be reborn in Brazil to survive.' This became my preoccupation."

"How long did we last that time?"

"A few months. These federal officers would come to my business to inspect my inventory of hides and skins. Since the country had no constitution, we had no constitutional rights; we had to accept police intimidation. I didn't like it because my entire life, since I was young when I was politically active, I was very conscious of my personal freedoms. I was arrested and taken to the headquarters of the federal police. They said my inventory was not correct. I told a friend about these inspectors, and he said, 'Peres, you don't understand what's going on. They don't care about your inventory. They want a bribe. But you come down here with an American mentality.' And I thought, 'This is crazy. In America, I'm too Brazilian. In Brazil, I'm too American.' I got fed up. I sold my inventory for a third of the price. I came back to New York first. Then your mother sold all our furniture in public auction in Belém and used the money to buy tickets for her and you and your brother and sisters."

"And started again."

"In Forest Hills."

CHAPTER FIFTEEN

FIREWORKS EXPLODED ABOVE Biscayne Bay. Red, white, and blue reflected off the water at Bayfront Park. Fourth of July celebrations were underway throughout the city. Thousands of people in shorts and sneakers and sandals gathered at Lummus Park in South Beach, at the bandshell at 76th and Collins, and along boatyards in Coconut Grove listening to outdoor concerts and eating burgers and hot dogs with daiquiris and pina coladas. Hundreds more viewed the fireworks and the Miami skyline from condominium balconies on Claughton Island, from Hobie Island Park off the Ricken-backer Causeway, and from the deck of the Rusty Pelican in Virginia Key. Miami was beautiful at night. A postcard of romance and wealth and shimmering liquid glow.

"We're just like Miami, aren't we?" Mimi said.

"Tonight, we are."

Mimi and I had spent the day together. As friends. I was her guest at a wedding at St. Michael the Archangel Church. Standing and kneeling and admiring the bride. Mimi and I changed afterward at her place and went to dinner at Loggerheads. The fireworks started at 9:00 p.m. Under the exploding aerials and trailing brocades, we talked about consulting and her ambitions. The market in semiconductors was booming. Small company stocks had skyrocketed and were just now pausing with investors taking profits. She was sure to stake a claim to entrepreneurial life. She had that air that the world was hers to take. I told her I planned on joining Jenner. I could do anything after working a few years at the firm. I could advocate for causes. I could be a public servant. I could write the Great American Novel. I could be John Grisham.

"That doesn't sound like you really want to be a lawyer."

I didn't answer, raising my eyebrow instead.

Then she added, "How much do you think moving as much as you did affected you?"

"Interesting segue there, Mimi." A barrage of fireworks burst in the sky. "Why do you ask?"

"Maybe you need constant change in your life."

"Maybe I need stability." I wasn't sure whether she was probing for what kind of partner I would be if we were more than friends. "At times, the world never held still."

"Do you want it to hold still now?"

"No. I like variety. Here's how I think it affected me. I adapt. I compartmentalize quickly. I take good and bad news the same and I move on. I take chances. I don't mind risk. I control what I can."

"It could have been different. You could be different."

Mimi was as good a tennis player in conversation as she was on the court.

"My dad said the same thing. We could be broken and damaged and insecure. But I also know I was the youngest in my family. I was protected and didn't see much of what my brother and sisters experienced. They saw the arguments between my parents. They saw the violence. My sisters were treated differently by my mother. They heard my mother accuse my father. They saw my father throw an ashtray at my mom that nearly blinded her and left her bruised and crying for days. They experienced much more of the hardship and the constant upheaval and disruption and change."

"And you don't remember it?"

"I remember bits before the age of ten. I think I blocked a lot of it out. When my parents tell me that I was a recluse, that I refused to talk, that I was sensitive and upset and sullen, hiding in corners and in my room, I don't remember it."

"You were probably processing all the turmoil at the time."

"I see pictures in the photo album of me as a child in Brazil, and I look happy. The family looks happy. There are photos of us playing in Belém and the family being together in restaurants in Copacabana, and we look like we're having a great time. We did have great times. That's how family happens. Happiness one day. Turmoil the next. I do have flashes of memories from when I was six or seven years old. I remember my dad taking me to watch Flamengo play. I held his hand in the stadium. I remember my mom getting a sourball out of my throat that I was choking on. I remember her using red nail polish to glue the head back on a figurine of St. George and the Dragon. I don't remember one plane ride."

"How do you think all the violence and disruption impacted your brother and sisters?"

"That's a question for them to answer. Each of us lives very different lives. We're in distant orbits and we don't share much with each other. Maybe that's one effect of what we experienced. We've created distance for safety."

The red and blue and silver pyrotechnics boomed in the sky and reflected on the bay. We watched the light dance on the water as people cheered around us.

"What I do know," I added, "is that everyone in my family is a good person. We're good people. We're each sensitive and empathetic and caring. Maybe that comes from being a big family. A couple of weeks ago we had the whole family together for dinner at my parents' one-bedroom apartment. Nineteen of us. Three generations. Grandkids playing. My parents were so happy. Everyone was joking and laughing. I don't know if we'll ever have that moment again."

"Why not?"

"Because we will all go away and live our lives somewhere else. We're a good family but we're not a close family. I mean we love each other but we're not involved in each other's day-to-day lives."

"That describes a lot of families, Mark."

"What I can say with certainty is that I am loved. I know that my mother and father love me, despite all the chaos in their lives, or maybe because of it. I feel their love every day like a sword and shield. I feel divinely protected from any evil or harm that comes my way."

"Tell me about the sword part."

"The sword part? Well, I can wield light."

"Like a light saber?"

"Yes, just like Luke Skywalker. That's me." I smiled.

"That must give you a lot of confidence."

"I feel the Force. The Force is with me. It also leads me to hold people responsible."

"Responsible for what?"

"For their choices. For what people do. There are things my father did that drove us apart."

"Like what?"

"Like things I saw. I came home from law school after my first year. I knocked on my parents' door to surprise them. I could hear them arguing. The door was unlocked, and I went inside, and it was as if I wasn't even there. They were in the middle of it. He said things. She said things back. It kept going on with each of them shouting insults. Then my dad threw a milk carton at her. I saw the carton tumbling in the air, until it exploded against the wall, the milk flying onto my mother's clothing and hair. My mother was stunned. I was stunned. My dad was in rage. I yelled at him to stop. He shouted at me to get out. That it wasn't my business. That I didn't understand. I stood there beside my mother. He stared at me, ready to hit me."

"Oh my god, Mark. What happened?"

"He stormed out. Then I helped my mom leave him. I took sides. I helped her pack. I told my brother and sisters about it, and rallied support for my mom. When I returned to Tallahassee, there was a letter waiting for me. From my dad. He typed this blistering letter with typos and words in caps. Saying that I was nothing to him. That I was not his son. That I would regret what I did. That I was tearing the family apart. I read it once and folded it right back in the envelope. To hell with him, I thought. If I wasn't his son, then he wasn't my father. A year of silence went by. He disowned me and I wrote him off."

"How did you feel during that time?"

"Righteous. Indignant. Sorry for him. Sorry for myself. I don't know."

"How did you two start talking again?"

"My mother and I spoke regularly. She said there were things I didn't know. That I should forgive him. That I had only one father. After several months she moved back in with him. She said if she could reconcile with him then I could too. One day I showed up at their apartment and it was as if the months of recrimination between my father and I never happened. I kissed him. He kissed me. They came to my graduation. They were happy for me."

"And that's when you offered to interview him?"

"Yes, to hear his stories. To understand him. To understand myself. I judge him, but I also love him. And I want to document his life and share it with the world. I want his life to add up and be remembered."

On Monday, I had lunch with Steve, Steve, David, and Catherine, associates at Jenner, at Granny Feelgood's beside the courthouse on West Flagler. The restaurant attracted politicians, lawyers, judges, cops, secretaries, and social workers, serving tofu, falafel, smoothies, and mango juice. The place was abuzz with conversation about cases, hiring, firing, sports, politics, money, and who was doing what to whom in Miami. I leaned into everything that everyone at the table said about the firm. About clients. About conflicts. About billable hours. I imagined myself writing motions, engaged in discovery, taking depositions, truly caring about whether a Big Six accounting firm met GAAP standards. I could do it. I could.

Mimi met me for lunch the next day at The Beverly Hills Café on Sunset Drive. We were still spending time together, not dating but dating, or dating but not dating. We set a date-nondate for another round of tennis. I was thinking about taking lessons and new tennis gear I could buy when I started work. Reebok sneakers. A new Wilson ProStaff racket. Once I started at the firm I could even afford to travel to Wimbledon. We could go together. We could sit in the stands near Princess Diana and watch Andre Agassi and Steffi Graff. I would wear sunglasses, and she could wear a silly hat. Mimi shook her head dismissively, making it clear she'd rather go with a future husband than with me.

Two days later, I went to an after-hours cocktail party at Jenner. I rode the elevator to the fifteenth floor of One Biscayne Tower. Beside me stood a young woman in a blue suit. Beside her two young men in pin stripes. In the back an older man with his briefcase. All staring straight ahead in the elevator taking a ride to wonderland. The firm reception area was simple and elegant, promising stellar representation, and money and influence and homes in Coral Gables. Lawyers milled about with crabcake and Bacardi and Coke. I shook hands and said hello to the partners. Be sure to look around, they said, as if I hadn't been there before. I broke away from the crowd. The individual offices were beautiful with sleek blonde Scandinavian furnishing. The latest in design. Each of the lawyers had sliding glass doors that opened to a deck overlooking Bayshore Park and Biscayne Bay. One office was empty, right beside one of the managing partners. I looked at my name on a temporary plate by the door. I entered the office and sat in the black padded chair, imagining my diplomas on the wall. Not quite Harvard or Yale, but Rollins and Florida State would do. I slid open the glass door and stepped onto the wooden deck. My hands grasped the railing as I looked out at the blue and green horizon and traffic below.

I called my dad. We scheduled our next session for the following week. We had years to cover from 1970 to 1992. It was a lot of ground. Years that I remembered. I knew there were a dozen more twists and turns to his life, but there were two or three headlines that mattered most. We would move one more time to Brazil, but that move, one that was very clear in my mind, would end our travels as a family overseas forever.

I spent the night reading in my bedroom. Restless, I turned up *Highway 61 Revisited*. When the last song ended, I left my apartment and wandered outside. I stood at the corner of 8th and Collins, staring at the Tiffany Hotel across from me, thinking about the people inside, wondering what to do next. I walked toward Ocean Drive, past Helium, past the sunglasses shop, past Wet Willies. On Monday nights, the restaurants were quieter. The cars were slower. There were fewer people on the street. For long stretches no one was near me, just the glow of overhead lights that shimmered against the sky. I crossed the road and walked beside the stone barrier wall that ran along Lummus Park. Then past the volleyball nets, past the old wooden fence, past the sawgrass and mangroves, onto the hard and soft sand. Lights from condominiums twinkled in the distance. I kept walking, past the Art Deco lifeguard stands, past seagulls that flew off into the night. I took off my sneakers and socks as I neared the shore, the cool wet sand grainy underneath my feet. The waves from the Atlantic crashed and released. I looked up at the stars against the black night. I wondered what became of the books that Einstein signed for my uncle. What becomes of us? What thousand million things in the universe happen that we know nothing about, that change the course of everything.

CHAPTER SIXTEEN

THE NEXT MORNING the Herald reported that astronomers had detected the most massive black hole ever discovered. It had the mass of a billion suns, making it one hundred times bigger than any other observed black-hole candidate, with matter so dense and the pull of gravity so powerful that no light escaped. Scientists from the University of Hawaii Institute for Astronomy and the University of Michigan showed evidence of an extremely dark and previously unseen mass in the galaxy NGC 3115, thirty million light-years away. I was certain my walk on the beach was tied to the discovery.

My dad and I sat on the balcony of his apartment. It was Tuesday, July 14. The early evening temperature hit 90 degrees. Not an ounce of precipitation. Palm trees sagged as we looked out over the railing. We had come outside after a meal my mom had prepared: steak and onions, potatoes, rice, beans, and oven-toasted buttered bread that melted in my mouth. All the staples. Gravity was bending space-time throughout the universe as my dad had a beer and I drank from a tall glass of orange juice.

"Okay. So, it's 1969. We're in New York," I said.

"Yes, we came from Belém and moved back to New York. We moved into an apartment on 68th Drive in Queens," my dad replied, reporting another momentous fact in our lives, matter-of-factly.

"The James Monroe Building." I had a fleeting memory of the building, of the small, framed picture of President Monroe surrounded by nothing in the lobby, his visage looking out at us from a previous age. I remembered our apartment at the end of the second floor, the last door on the right, the Colony Card Shop on the corner where I bought comic books, Yellowstone Park on Yellowstone Boulevard. I was eight years old. I could recite the presidents. We lived there for almost two years until I was ten. My sisters babysat for families in nearby buildings. My brother delivered Chinese food for Moy's. Once I ran across Queens Boulevard, across six lanes of traffic, darting between buses and cars, and crossed back again to tell the tale.

My dad wiped his forehead in the evening heat and took a sip of his beer. "We got the family back together and I went back to my old hide and skins business without any money."

It's what he did. It's what mattered to him most: keeping the family together against long odds he made longer.

My dad paused, then added, "Devlin had closed his business. He owed money to a financing company and paid them with remnants of alligator skins that we had in inventory in Staten Island from back when we worked together. Devlin's former accountant, a man named Ed Downey, now worked for the financing company. I contacted Downey, and he said the financing company didn't know what to do with the inventory. I told Downey I could sell off the remnants, and that's how I started again."

"Where was your office?" I was still thinking of President Monroe. Then John Quincy Adams. Then Andrew Jackson. Then Martin Van Buren.

"I had no office. I worked from the apartment. I took the subway from Queens into Manhattan, then the ferry to Staten Island, and went into the free zone – the foreign trade zone – of Staten Island, picked up samples, and then went back to Manhattan. I sold to old customers throughout the city. Then back home late at night on the subway to Queens. And Downey, who is in heaven now, became a very good friend of mine. As a matter of fact, he died very young, at forty-two years old."

In heaven now. I loved that. "You were pleased to be back in New York." I said it as a statement.

"Yes, I was pleased to be back in New York, my old New York, the city I was born in spiritually. I started all over again and kept working very hard, and the children went back to school, food was on the table."

Food was on the table. That's what mattered. He provided.

"I remember first grade with Mrs. Hamburger." She was young with short blonde hair. I also remembered second grade with Mrs. Kaplan. Not so young with gray hair. I had report cards my mother kept from P.S. 196. The Grand Central Parkway School. I got high marks in reading and writing. Low marks in spelling. "Mommy wrote in the Parent Comment section, 'We are very happy with Mark's report. I hope he will be good all the time.'"

"That sounds like your mother. This is what she expected of you."

"Then we moved again. To the house on Booth Street in Rego Park." A run-down three-story brick townhouse with a stoop across from P.S. 139. The Rego Park School. Mrs. Ziegler wrote in my report card that I made a nice adjustment to my new school, but I showed lazy habits even though I had perfect attendance. I remembered playing basketball during recess in a fenced-in school playground. I shot just like Earl Monroe.

"You had very good schools. The schools in New York were very good at that time."

I remembered more: "We had a pet spider monkey named Coco on Booth Street. Edison kept it in the basement. I remember Coco swinging from the pipes making a mess. There was a big mimeograph machine in the basement with the smell of ink."

"That monkey was not a good monkey."

"What happened to him?"

"The monkey? I don't know. Ask your brother."

"I will." I wrote down "Coco" on my legal pad. "This is now 1972."

"Yes, we moved again." Again, my dad, reporting the facts.

"That's when we moved to the corner of Burns Street and Thornton Place in Forest Hills. I remember everything about that apartment. You tossed quarters from the balcony when we heard the Good Humor man. I'd get Bomb Pops and Nutty Buddy cones."

I could have gone on. Burns and Thornton. I was ten years old. Our apartment had red carpet and mustard gold furniture covered in plastic that crinkled when we sat on it. My mother played classical music she learned as a teenager in Brazil on an upright piano that two sweaty men carried up the stairs. I shared a bunkbed with my brother Edison, beside a set of World Book Encyclopedia. I listened to the New York Knicks and Marv Albert on the radio. I fell asleep to Three Dog Night. *The ink is black, the page is white.* I spent hours drawing a picture of Eddie Giacomin of the New York Rangers that I taped over my bed. I walked to school, down Thornton, down a rickety metal staircase onto the ballfield, back up to Dieterle Crescent, to P.S. 174. William Sydney Mount School. Fourth grade. I read headlines as a news anchor in class and played tackle football in a neighborhood league. We were the Rams. I wore number 59. I played linebacker in sneakers. Our coach ran laps smoking a cigarette, then collapsed. On one drill I hit a running back with a textbook tackle to his solar plexus. He almost died. Everyone cheered. My friends were Christopher Carr, Robert Narva, and Takashi Tanamora. We got quarts of milk from vending machines and tossed garbage in smelly paper bags down the chute. We played chess, Rock 'Em Sock 'Em Robots, and roller hockey on the streets. I came home with scabs on my knees and went back out again after the sting of Mercurochrome. The medicine cabinet was saltine crackers, Vicks VapoRub, Band-Aids, and ginger ale. I glued Aurora monster models of Frankenstein and Dracula and the Creature from the Black Lagoon. I crossed the 67th Avenue bridge, trains to the city rumbling underneath, and ate burgers at John's luncheonette. Charlie worked the grill. I walked long blocks to Queens Boulevard for hot dogs and knishes. I saw Muhammad Ali at the Forest Hills Tennis Stadium at the end of Burns Street. Arlene, Edison, and Dolores went to Russell Sage and Rachael went to Forest Hills High. They wore hip huggers they bought at Instant Pants and took the green bus to Alexander's department store. My brother and his friends Frank and Mitchell were in Troop 56, meeting at the Jewish Community Center. Edison was patrol leader for the Panther Patrol. They practiced karate with nunchucks and watched Bruce Lee movies at the Midway Theatre. Once I went to the Continental Theater in the fancy part of Forest Hills with all the trees and stone buildings. Teenagers listened to the Beatles and the Stones and NRBQ. We were New Yorkers. Our future was New York.

"Yes, that was your world," my dad said.

"And we had a starburst clock in the kitchen. I remember that too."

My dad looked at the folded paper at his feet with the news of NGC 3115, thirty million light-years away. "Yes, and everything changed again."

"How was your business?"

"I didn't have any problem selling the remnants, but it was not the good stuff. I had to secure new suppliers. The owner of the financing company, Mr. Sasha, a Jewish guy from Iraq, offered me a line of credit so I could establish myself again in the business. The line of credit worked this way: I sold leather that I did not have to a company, I went to Mr. Sasha who gave me the money to buy what I sold, I got the merchandise, classified it and delivered it, Mr. Sasha sent and collected on the invoice, and paid me the difference between the cost and my sales price. I did this for six or seven months. But this was not easy because I was having problems getting suppliers in New York, and Mr. Sasha did not want to open letters of credit to foreign suppliers, so that limited my ability to develop the business. I was struggling to make money every week to take home and keep the apartment. This is why sometimes we had to move."

"Is this when you got into the jewelry business?"

"Yes. But let me tell you something: many things in my life happen that I cannot explain. One day I was in the lobby of the Diplomat Hotel on 43rd Street. The Diplomat is where many Brazilians would get together. I met a man from Spain, I started talking to him in Spanish, and I told him my family was from Morocco and Gibraltar, and I asked what he did, and he said he owned a business in Valencia manufacturing chandeliers. Crystal chandeliers. And he was in New York looking for an agent to sell his chandeliers."

"What was his name?"

"Eduardo Prada. The company was Hermanos Prada in Spain. I offered my services. I had to find something new. I was ready to take on anything."

"Chandeliers? What did you know about chandeliers?"

"Nothing. I took him to Brooklyn. To buyers of chandeliers. I went everywhere around the city to find buyers. And he liked what I did. Then he returned to Spain. After several months, after I had firm accounts, I rented a small office on 46th Street. I got a telephone and sold chandeliers. As a matter of fact, your mother helped me many times, drawing new models of chandeliers. She liked to design. That's why she paints now. And I was doing well. I had established the market. Then Mr. Prada returned from Spain, realized how much I had done, and decided to give the line to someone else from Valencia who had relocated to New York that was recommended by his brother. He said he was very sorry, he was very apologetic, but he had to do it. I got very, very upset with him. I said, 'All you wanted was somebody to open the market for you, and now you come along and take it away.' I told him where he could go. I was very upset."

"Then you got into jewelry."

"Yes. I didn't have anything else to sell. I was out on the street. Then on a very snowy day, a very cold day, I walked into the Americana Hotel in Midtown and stood under the marquis because it was snowing heavily, and I saw a big sign, 'International Jewelry Show.' And I walked into the hotel, the second floor, and I saw what I had never saw in my life, so much jewelry from all the over the world."

"You never really liked jewelry before, did you?"

"No. I still don't. But jewelry was very important historically to the Jewish people because you can take it anywhere and it has value everywhere. I went to the Spanish pavilion and a man asked me in very poor English if he could help me, and I responded in Spanish telling him how amazing and fantastic the jewelry looked. We started talking and talking in Spanish, then a customer came to the counter, and I helped translate. I did not know anything about the jewelry, but I helped make the sale, and he gave a commission on the spot of $100 and said to me. 'Can you come here every day and help me sell?' I said, 'I cannot, but I have a daughter who can.' I was thinking of Rachael. She was sixteen at the time. Rachael was good with languages, and the next day she started working for him after school."

"Do you remember his name?"

"Yes. José Luis Alesandre. Owner of a big jewelry store in Madrid. When the show was over, he came to my office and offered me his line of jewelry to sell in New York. I told him I could not take it because I knew nothing about jewelry. He said, 'You learn on the job. I believe you will be very success-ful.' I said 'Okay, I will help you.'"

"And didn't he leave you all of his remaining jewelry from the show?"

"Yes, he said he was going back to Madrid, and I don't know if he was out of his mind, or I was blessed, but he wanted to leave me with $90,000 worth of diamonds, rubies, emeralds, rings, earrings, and necklaces to sell in New York. I was very surprised. I said, 'You just met me and you're going to trust me with all this jewelry?' He said, 'I can tell by looking at a man whether he is good or bad.'"

"He's in the wrong line of business if he could do that."

"The next day I took all the jewelry to Wachler & Altman on 47th Street. In the Diamond District. Mr. Altman looked at the merchandise and made me an offer for the whole thing. We negotiated back and forth, splitting the difference. I called Mr. Alesandre, and we settled on $65,000. In cash. It took me one hour to count the money. He gave me his account number at City National Bank, and the next day I went to the bank and had to explain where I got the cash and provide proof of sale before I could deposit the money. I got $6500 in commission. All that happened in two days." My dad then added, "Money from the stars."

"This is when you opened Edimar." Edimar was a jewelry and handbag store in Forest Hills my dad named after Edison and me. "I remember when you put peel-and-stick mirrored glass and shelving on the walls. You sold rings and watches and necklaces."

My dad looked quizzingly at me, clearly not remembering the peel-and-stick mirrors that made an impression upon me.

"I would sell wholesale in New York," he said, "and in the afternoon, I would come back to the store. The girls used to help me, your mother helped me, Edison helped me. The store did not do too well because of the location. We were next to a Catholic Church and the Orthodox Jews from the neighborhood would not come to the store because it was near the church. They were superstitious about the location. I was so upset by it."

"You had a partner in the business."

"Yes, Tom Carbone. I met him at the gym. He was very nice, very funny, and he liked me very much. At that time, I was fifty-six. He was thirty-one or thirty-two years old. He was a construction worker. He installed air ducts in skyscrapers and had a lot of money in the bank. This was a side business for him. He liked to be with us all the time. He liked your mother. He liked the kids. He came to our home many times. He encouraged me to start the store, and we started the store together, but it didn't last too long."

"What do you remember about this time?"

"I remember that I was very happy. I was healthy. I was very hopeful, very enthusiastic, I forgot the past, and I was doing well. During this time, I was also making an occasional trip to Brazil to buy precious and semiprecious stones to expand the jewelry business. I was making all my expenses."

"And this is now late 1973?"

"Yes, when everything began to explode."

CHAPTER SEVENTEEN

WE HAD COME back from the balcony inside to my parents' apartment. My mother had cleaned up the table and the kitchen after dinner. She had lowered the lights in the living room before going to her bedroom. On the walls were paintings of ships and the moon over the sea that my mom had painted, and on every table were framed photographs of grandchildren. The furniture was dated but made fresh with throw pillows. Over the couch were the five black and white framed photographs of my sisters, brother, and me.

There was one more move I wanted my dad to discuss that changed the trajectory of our lives. The big one. The one we all remembered.

"What happened in 1973?"

"I got a new line from Brazil. A Brazilian company, a manufacturer of leather handbags, had a very large inventory of handbags in New York. I heard about the inventory, approached the company, and got authorization to sell them. At the end of 1973, there was a leather show in Toronto, Canada, and I went and sold a lot of merchandise. I came back and continued with my jewelry business. I had my office,

I had two or three telephones, and I had a very good inventory of stones. Beautiful inventory. And I had lines of credit with Bankers Trust and Banco do Brasil. When I was in Toronto, I met two guys I really liked, Jim Valentine and Silvio Salgado, who were partners importing Brazilian goods into Canada. I thought we could do business together, so I decided to go back to Toronto. This time I took your mother. It was not a good trip."

"Why not?"

"Things were very, very tense with your mother."

He left it unexplained. He had a choice to say more, and I had a choice to press for an explanation. How much would I risk, and how much more did I want to know? Underneath our entire time together was the undercurrent of arguments between my mother and father, and the possibility that I might hear something that would lead me to once again take sides. I'd spent more time with my father this summer than I ever had. Memories of him in my childhood came to me: images of him shaving and nicking his cheek with a double-edged Gillette removable blade, watching him pack his suitcase and wear his Botany 500 trench coat, hearing the rapid click of his Rolodex and seeing him doodle arrows on the back of business cards. I wanted my time with him to go well. I wanted him to think well of me. It was clear to me that he and my mom had come to an arrangement about what he would share and what he would not. This was a legacy project for them as much as it was for me. And yet I knew much of my dad's explanation for our lives was rooted in the mysteries of their marriage.

"What happened next?"

"The situation at home was very uncomfortable. Very stressed. A couple of months later I made a trip to Brazil, and I went via Belém, and from Belém I went to Sao Luis, because in Belém I was told that Lourdes' mother was very sick, so I went to Sao Luis where your grandmother lived, and she was in very bad shape. She had diabetes and some very bad wounds on her legs that would not heal. I promised her that I would arrange for Lourdes to see her. I called Lourdes and told her that her mother was very ill and got her a ticket to Sao Luis. She flew alone, leaving the children behind in New York. I continued my trip to Rio and Belo Horizonte, then returned to New York, while your mother was with her mother. Then I got a cable, a wire, that Lourdes' mother had died. I told the kids, maybe not you, but I told the kids that I got a cable, and your grandmother had passed away."

"When did she die?"

"April 1974. I called Lourdes at her brother's home in Sao Luis where this happened, and I was told she wasn't there. Her brother wouldn't give me any information about where she was staying. I started calling around long distance, to people I knew in Sao Luis, and found out she was in a hotel there, Hotel Central, but she would not take my calls. I then found out she had left for Rio. I left messages everywhere. One day later she finally called me from Rio. She told me she didn't intend to come back."

"She was leaving you?"

"Yes and also leaving the children in New York."

"What did you say?"

"I don't remember how I reacted, what I said, but I remember thinking one million things. I was upset. I remember telling Arlene and Rachael that we were going back to Brazil. That we had to go."

"We didn't react well, did we?"

"No. Everybody started crying. You didn't want to go. Dolores was crying. Edison kept asking, 'What are we going to do?' I said to all of you, 'Listen, we have to go. Your mother is there, and we have to be together. I am sorry, but we better start packing because we must go.'"

I was eleven. My brother and sisters were teenagers. We were settled into our schools for the first time in what seemed forever. We had friends and routines. My oldest sisters had boyfriends. Our future was Queens. Manhattan. The Village. Chelsea. The Upper East Side. My father didn't give us any time to think about leaving it all behind.

"We had to pack quickly," I said.

"Yes, we did it fast. All of you said goodbye to your friends. I sent Rachael first to talk to Lourdes. To calm Lourdes down. Rachael met your mother in a hotel in Copacabana. A few days later I put everything we owned into a warehouse, all our furniture, and I found a woman who used to run her own jewelry business to run my business, and we flew to Brazil. I was desperate. I couldn't accept leaving Lourdes alone in Brazil or leaving the children without her. I had to swallow my pride."

Within a week, we left. Disappeared. Into the clouds. Varig Airlines. All of us. May 5, 1974. Forever circled on the calendar. Schools gone. Friendships gone. New York gone. Into thin air. We reappeared in Brazil. Materializing as shell-shocked teenagers. "We moved to Copacabana."

"Yes, again we had to live well and above our means in Brazil. I had to get your mother back. We moved to a very nice apartment on Copacabana Street near the beach. And we put the children again into American schools. Hundreds of dollars a month for the children for a private American Catholic school."

The children, again, my father said. As if we were a single tribe of five.

This time I remembered Brazil. Busses passing each other within inches on the winding mountain road of Corcovado while passengers peered up at Christ the Redeemer. Volkswagen Beetles. Motorcycle crashes. Men slicing pineapples with machetes on the beach. *Guarana* soda and *casas de sucos*. Roberto Carlos. Soldiers in green helmets on street corners. Our Lady of Mercy School. Sister Norman wearing a habit. The nuns playing "Lady Madonna" on guitar. Other American and European students. I was given a homework assignment to draw five constellations. I created a book with drawings and a description of all eighty-eight constellations in the sky.

My dad continued, "Lourdes came back home to the children. A lot of emotion and arguments at home. I made three or four trips between Rio and New York to check on the business. I spent thousands and thousands of dollars traveling. On the last trip to New York, I found my office closed and all my merchandise gone. The woman I had asked to watch the business stole my jewelry and disappeared. Your mother accused me and the woman. I didn't have insurance. I went to the banks because I had the jewelry pledged, and they didn't want to hear it. They cut off my lines of credit and began collection proceedings against me with lawyers."

I was still thinking of the constellations I drew. "How were you feeling?"

"Bad. Terrible. We kept on making the same mistakes. Get rich and get poor, get rich and get poor. I told Lourdes what happened. I said, 'I cannot stay in Rio.' I didn't see any opportunity for me."

"And the rest of us?" *Did he notice?*

"Your sisters and brother were older teenagers. They made friends. They went to the beach. They spoke Portuguese. You didn't adjust too well. You were always rebellious about it. You became quiet. You stayed by yourself. Staring at the stars."

I guess he did notice. "That sounds about right."

"I decided after a few months that we would return to the United States, but this time back to Miami. I owed money to the banks in New York, and they were not going to leave me alone. My position in the market, with my customers, was not good. I didn't have merchandise to sell. I didn't have lines of credit. I had to start somewhere new, somewhere less expensive, somewhere where I knew at least a few people and how to get around, so we came back here, to Miami. This was December 1974."

"I started sixth grade halfway through the school year at Miami Shores Elementary School." Mr. Balog was my teacher.

That's when I met Adam. I sat in his chair when he was out of the room, and he made me move to a different chair when he came back in. I also got into fights with classmates, but I didn't mention it.

My dad put his drink down. "At that point I made a promise. I made a commitment, with myself, with God, with the family, with the government of Brazil, to never move the family back again."

CHAPTER EIGHTEEN

WE NEVER MOVED back to Brazil. Our life in Miami began once again. My dad opened an office on N.E. 3rd Street where he sold leather handbags. One year later he opened a store called Boutique Leblon, selling luggage, rings, watches, and necklaces to Brazilian tourists who came to Florida in droves. Two years later the store closed when the Brazilian government restricted who could travel overseas. As time went by my father sold other products: radios, auto parts, computers, electronics, crystals, and semiprecious stones. The names of his businesses changed. Transbras International, Inc. Then KristalKraft, Inc. Every couple of years we moved again. From 82nd Street to 56th Street to 95th Street to 103rd Street. Packing. Unpacking. Furniture bought. Furniture sold. Starting again. Each move a new life. Each move an escape. Each move a prayer into the unknown. Our suitcases were old and battered.

My mom got her first job outside the home, working at K-Mart for minimum wage, where I watched television after school in the Sight and Sound department. She opened her own checking account, her first, at Chase Manhattan Bank, as soon as women could under the law without needing a father or husband to co-sign, carefully handwriting every small transaction into a register. She bought her own clothes and paid bills for the first time with money she earned. She worked several years at Loehmann's department store, wearing her badge that said "Maria," a model employee selling discounted women's fashion in the Back Room. She was meticulous with her responsibilities, never missing work, developing friendships with American women who came to adore her foreign ways and accent. In her apartment building, she would call down to the lobby, directing the porters and staff, raised as she was from a young age to be the lady of the manor.

My father developed emphysema from years of smoking, giving up cigarettes one day after a heart attack scare that wasn't quite a heart attack. I went to see him in intensive care and heard another joke about Joachim Nabuco. Two days later he was back at work. He drove an old car with product samples in the back seat and folders of catalogs and invoices and faxed letters with his doodles in the margin. On birthdays he would give me watches or bracelets and sometimes rings that he said was the latest style that I found strange and didn't wear. I didn't understand his business. Import-export is what I told my teenage friends. I'd come home from school, and hours later my dad would come through the door, his briefcase in his hand, tired from a long day. He'd eat dinner that my mom prepared and watch boxing or the news. *La lucha*, he'd say in Spanish. *The fight*. I'd take my plate to my room.

I went to seventh grade at Horace Mann Junior High, tenth grade at North Miami Beach Senior High School, and eleventh grade at Chaminade High School. My grades were uneven, but teachers saw something in me. I wrote stories, played catch on the streets, bagged groceries, cleaned the ink-stained floors of a print shop, and worked in a camera store. I thought I might be a novelist or a senator one day. My brother and sisters moved out and moved on. I wasn't involved in their lives. Their relationships were a mystery to me. Whatever incidents they had with my parents, whatever they witnessed or experienced, whatever disruption and events they internalized, from moving twenty times in twenty years to becoming themselves in the cauldron of our lives, I never discussed with them. We orbited our parents and each other, bound by family gravity that drew us back no matter how far we broke away.

I went to college and law school. And now here we were. My dad made passing references to those years between 1975 and 1992. Instead, he talked at length about missing his friend Devlin who died of cancer.

The tape came to an end, clicking at the end of the spool. My father looked at the recorder, then at me. "Now all of you are on your own. So that's it. That's the name of the game."

The following Monday, July 20, marked my parents' thirty-seventh anniversary. I stopped by their apartment after a long day in chambers. I arrived with a box of chocolates. My dad said he had something to give me. He asked if I could join him and my mother for dinner on Thursday night. He would give me what he had prepared for me then.

On Thursday, July 23, I met my parents at Olive Garden in Aventura. My dad wore a jacket. My mother wore a flattering dress. The hostess seated us as if we were in Tuscany. I had fettuccine and breadsticks. My father had spaghetti with sausage. My mother had cannelloni with a glass of red wine. She was the only person drinking wine in the restaurant.

"What's this about?" I asked.

"We wanted to know about your decision," my dad responded. "What you plan to do next. We wanted you to talk to us."

"Oh? You mean me answering *your* questions? Okay. Fair enough. I'm going to Jenner. I can pay back my loans. I'll learn a lot. I think I can be a good lawyer."

"That's good, son. It's your job not to be me. But remember, it will be your child's job not to be you."

I smiled. "Is that what your father said to you?"

"That's exactly what he said to me."

"I think I'll write too. I have a story in mind. I've been working on it late at night."

"That's even better," my father said. "That's always been you. It's important that you believe in yourself and that you never give up."

"Are you seeing anyone?" my mother asked.

"I have been," I said. "You'd like her. Her name is Mimi. But we're just friends. And I spend time with Suzanne. Just friends, too."

"Will you tell us if you meet someone?"

"You'll be the first to know." At that moment, after years of not sharing anything with them, hearing them banter, seeing my father smile and the glow on my mother's face, I meant it. I wanted them to know about me. I wanted them in my life. I felt fiercely protective of them and loved them dearly.

Between coffee and dessert, my dad made jokes about my mom, his hand holding hers on the table. My mom shook her head at half his remarks. At the end of the dinner, my father gave me a folder with typed remarks. "This is for you," he said, "to include in the record."

CHAPTER NINETEEN

THAT NIGHT, IN my apartment in South Beach, I opened the folder my father gave me and began to read.

I had a friend in New York, his name was Tom Carbone. We met at the gym, worked out together, and became friends. Tom was a good young man. He was a construction worker who installed air ducts in skyscrapers. He reminded me of those past days in Los Angeles when I was a construction helper. Tom and I became partners in a commercial venture, Edimar, a retail store located in Rego Park, Queens, New York. The store did not last too long. It was not commercially profitable. But Tom and I remained friends.

Tom had an acquaintance in Brooklyn, a mystic man said to have psychic powers which enabled him to tell a person's past. He did this work over a glass of wine. Tom introduced me to this man on a Sunday afternoon. This man told me that my soul was born in Israel 4000 years ago, and I was the Peres mentioned in the scriptures in the genealogy of Jesus (Yeshua), according to the gospel of Matthew. After several incarnations, I showed up in China under Marco Polo's command. Then I was on the caravel of Columbus on his maiden voyage to the new world. Then, as a cartographer, I went to Portugal and joined the armada of Cabral

(Pedro Alvarez) on his trip to Africa, but Cabral missed the route, and ended up discovering Brazil. So, my beginning was in Israel as a Jew and my most recent incarnation was in Brazil, also as a Jew.

I think Tom told this mystical man whatever he knew about me, and his friend concocted this spiritual journey. But he said the journey explains the main traits of my personality. My urge to travel, my love for nature, the instability of my character, all have their roots in my spiritual past. And they are unchangeable because they are the stratification of thousands of years. The mystical man also said that I shall surface again in Israel, and start a new round of incarnations, and about 3000 years from now I shall be on Earth. So be alert!

This enduring spiritual baggage and my 75 years of this present incarnation gave me an inalienable right (a birthright) to request a dialogue with the Lord. After all, he has been with me for at least 75 years. He yielded to my request. I began by telling him that I needed compassionate ears to hear my tale, a kind sounding board. He was very sympathetic, and this conversation followed:

Me: Lord, I want to know myself. I want to get to the root of my personality. I need your help. I have worked very hard and have accomplished very little. I have read a lot and have never written a book. I have bought many houses and own none. My best friends have been called to heaven, and I am still here. What is the problem with me?

The Lord: Son, I gave you a healthy body and a bright mind. I gave you free thinking and free choice. I gifted you with wisdom to distinguish right from wrong, good from bad, light from dark.

I made you a man to spare you the pain of giving birth, but with potential to carry the seeds of life. I created you in my image. What more do you want? You have chosen the wrong, the bad, the dark.

I helped you even further by giving you the Ten Commandments to guide you in your terrestrial passage. To avoid confusion, I divided the Commandments into two categories. The first five for your spiritual rejoicing, the second five for your material and social development. You have chosen only those Commandments that you like. And yet, through your worst hours, I have been with you.

Me: Lord, I feel that you are somewhat angry with me. I realize that I did a lot of distasteful deeds. Although, several times I did wrong to do good. This seems paradoxical and unjustifiable, but too much inflexibility and strict adherence to moral precepts sometimes might make matters worse. A guilty conscience needs no accusation.

As to the Ten Commandments, I confess to you in the hope to clear and calm my mind. Needless to say, you already know these things:

1st Commandment: I never had another God.

2nd Commandment: I never worshiped a graven image.

3rd Commandment: I took your name in vain.

4th Commandment: I have not kept the Sabbath holy.

5th Commandment: I honored my father and mother.

6th Commandment: I never killed a living thing.

7th Commandment: I committed adultery.

8th Commandment: I have stolen, but only in the face of adversity.

9th Commandment: I never accused falsely.

10th Commandment: I have coveted my neighbor's wife.

The Lord: On a scale of 1 to 10, you fared five. Your father Isaac did much better. That's why he accomplished more.

Me: I thank you, Lord, for exalting my father. He really deserves your acknowledgement. However, I know that I am not a bad person. You put a lot of good in me. I can tell by the way I react to my neighbor's suffering, to my friends' needs, to the cry of the afflicted, to the sighs of the poor, to the humble and your beloved. Yet why am I lacking a strong sense of moral balance, of stability and perseverance to get things done correctly? If I am somewhat bright, as you say I am, why am I impatient, restless, aggressive, and act as if I were a peregrine, a wanderer without destination, as a leaf blown by a tempestuous wind? I believe these traits are the source of so many of my failings. Do my past lives have anything to do with my present behavior?

The Lord: Those qualities are not so bad if you use them wisely and to your advantage. I have put on earth men and women with those same traits which have made them great. They would not perform their tasks if they were not impatient, restless, and aggressive, yet these traits are mixed with common sense, perse-

verance, purpose and vision. Just look at the lives and accom-
plishments of the great dreamers and leaders. The elemental
difference between you and them is a quantum factor, an ability
to mix in the right proportions of ingredients to obtain the correct
and proper prescription. You concocted solutions that were too
bitter or sweet. You have done beautiful deeds and ugly deeds.
I sent the Devil to tempt Jesus and Jesus chose me. Why not
you? Both of you are Jews. Both of you are my sons.

Me: Lord, in order to minimize the bitterness and emptiness of my
days, later in my life, I made up my mind to follow your tenets and
'be fruitful and multiply' as commanded in your Book. Through
your grace, I married a beautiful, God-fearing woman and we
begat five children, all precious and blessed. I then realized you
loved me in spite of me. I am very proud of my family. They
sweetened my life. Six diamonds on a crown of thorns.

Let me tell the whole world my emotions about the birth of
each of my children.

When Rachael was born, I saw the miracle of unfolding
life. She was my first child, and the first belongs to you, O Lord.
Your protective wings are with her.

When Arlene was born, her deep dark brown eyes told me
that you gifted her with a penetrating mind capable of under-
standing the mystery of the universe, your creation. She is tender
and sweet, and when she utters that she loves me, I cry for I feel
the honey in her voice.

When Edison was born, I saw in him the continual rebirth
of the Peres name. His name, Edison, had a hidden message,

that light would come into his life. His large, blue eyes reflect a soul filled with hope, kindness, and peace. He is so kind, he accepts me exactly as I am.

When Dolores was born, I saw a beautiful phenomenon for she is her mother, physically and emotionally. She has the mind of leadership and is a dreamer, for all leaders are dreamers. They are the poets of life in action. Above all her qualities are her profound compassion and deep empathy. Her name is properly fitting. Maria Dolores.

When Mark was born, I saw a gift from thee, O Lord, and distinctly overheard your words to him at his birth:

> *"Make your books your companions, let your cases and shelves be your pleasure grounds and gardens. Bask in their paradise, gather their fruit, pluck their roses, take their spices and myrrh. If your soul satiate and weary, change from garden to garden, from furrow to furrow, from prospect to prospect. Then will your desire renew itself and your soul be filled with delight."*

Those words were first expressed through the pen of a Jewish sage of the twelfth century, Samuel Ibn Tibbon. It has been a great joy to see Mark rejoicing with the famous saying of Moses Maimonides, "The advancement of learning is the highest commandment."

A father with children like mine is very, very rich indeed. Thank you, O Lord, for anointing me with so much love. My children have been an endless and powerful source of inspiration, motivation, and strength to face the tribulations and trials of my life. And despite my humble position, I am the victor. I realize that I could be a better father, I could have provided my children with more security and counseling to improve their lot. In a way I am satisfied, for they are well. They are exactly what I felt they would become and have fulfilled the message each of them brought into the world. The prophecies are realities.

Now Lord, what about my grandchildren? Your answer is very important to me.

The Lord: Your grandchildren will be blessed. They are kind and kindness they will give. Your grandchildren are your reward for being faithful to your commitment that you would never abandon your children and that you would exercise your best efforts to keep them together as a family. Do not complain about your lot. It could be much worse had you not been a loyal father. Otherwise, your own conscience would tear you apart.

Me: In my nakedness, I have sinned, I have erred, I have wronged, I have transgressed. But there is a bright side. I have done a lot of good for my fellow man. I am sensitive to my neighbor's needs. I have loved the stranger and the sojourner. I have helped out many without regard for reward. And I have tried my best to be with my children today so to be in their memory tomorrow.

I am a soul in search of peace and happiness. Please be merciful.

I wish to thank you for letting me be born a Jew. To dispel the cloud of darkness that passes over the heads of my people,

I read with great pride the following masterpiece written by Mark Twain in 1899:

"If the statistics are right, the Jews constitute but one percent of the human race. It suggests a nebulous dim puff of stardust lost in the blaze of the Milky Way. Properly the Jew ought hardly to be heard of, but he is heard of, has always been heard of. He is as prominent on the planet as any other people, and his commercial importance is extravagantly out of proportion to the smallness of his bulk. His contributions to the world's list of great names in literature, science, art, music, finance, medicine, and abstruse learning are also way out of proportion to the weakness of his numbers. He has made a marvelous fight in the world, in all the ages; and has done it with his hands tied behind him. He could be vain of himself and be excused for it. The Egyptian, the Babylonian, and the Persian rose, filled the planet with sound and splendor, then faded to dream-stuff and passed away; the Greek and the Roman followed, and made a vast noise, and they are gone; other peoples have sprung up and held their torch high for a time, but it burned out, and they sit in twilight now, or have vanished. The Jew saw them all, beat them all, and is now what he always was, exhibiting no decadence, no infirmities of age, no weakening of his parts, no slowing of his energies, no dulling of his alert and aggressive mind. All things are mortal but the Jew; all other forces pass, but he remains. What is the secret of his immortality?"

My answer is that the Jews are your people, your chosen. You, Lord, have chosen me.

I close with special mention of my wife, Lourdes. My wife was reserved for me by Destiny, as her mother once told me in a letter before her passing. Conscious of her duties, faithful to her principles, she is the 'Unchained Melody' of my life. How much can I say of a person so much more deserving than me? She is a pure source of your love.

And so, Lord, I rest my case. I will be more confident and comfortable appearing before your throne of judgment, and praying, "Lo, I, in thine abundant love, enter thy house, in reverence to thee I bow toward thy holy temple," and I know your judgment will be fair and just.

CHAPTER TWENTY

THREE DAYS LATER, on Sunday, July 26, 1992, my parents hosted an afternoon meal for the entire family at their apartment. My sister Rachael with her two sons, my sister Arlene with her husband and three sons, my brother Edison and his wife and three sons, and my sister Dolores and her husband and two daughters, and me, all filled the small living room. My dad and mom sat on the couch as the grandchildren played and ran between furniture and out to the balcony and into the kitchen and out back again. The table was filled with food that everyone brought, rice and beans, carne asada, salad and lasagna, with my mom's toothpicks beside the olives and salami and strawberries. Everything was loud and busy and bustling as we shared news and asked questions and swapped seats and moved about.

I had spent the morning at Kinkos copying and binding the transcript of the fourteen hours of taped conversation I had with my dad. I typed the last of two hundred twenty-seven single-spaced pages the previous night in chambers, listening to our recorded voices on tape, stopping to type, reversing, going forward, going back, to transcribe every word. I divided the stack of pages into three volumes with subdivided sections for each of the sessions I spent with my father. My mom had given me old black and white photographs that she had hidden away in envelopes in the bottom drawer of her dresser: of my father's father in his office as mayor of Itacoatiara, of my dad's brothers, Leon and José, of my dad in a Brazilian Army uniform outside his barracks, of my mom wearing white gloves descending the stairs of an American Airlines flight in Mexico City, and one more photograph she had set aside of me and my dad on the beach in Rio de Janeiro. I was six years old at the time the photograph was taken. The image showed my father and me from above, both of us looking up at the camera, looking into whatever the future would bring.

Each volume of my transcribed conversations with my father had his name on the cover. *Ambrosio Benchimol Peres*. On the inside page of Volume I, I wrote this Foreword:

> *This is the story of one man's life. It is offered as much to reveal him as it is to reveal us. It is an inventory of impressions on a shelf, of photographs of the mind. Moments are fleeting, elusive to capture, but moments shared are the stuff of lives. Here is a reflection, and a shared memory of a life, and of us.*

At the end of Volume III, I included my father's defense of his life to the Lord that he wanted as part of the record. I made seven copies of the three volumes for my parents and my brother and sisters. I packed the volumes in my bookbag and brought them with me to the family gathering. No one knew

I had them. No one other than my parents knew the extent of the project. After dessert was served and the grandchildren had become overtired and the table had been cleared and photographs were taken and people were ready to go home, I announced that I had something to give to everyone. I took out the volumes from my bookbag and gave a set to my brother and each of my sisters, and a set each to my mother and father. "It's Daddy's life," I said. "So, you can remember," my mother added.

In the minutes that followed, everyone opened the volumes and flipped through the pages. I answered questions: *Did I capture any of Daddy's jokes? Did I interview Mommy? Did I count how many times we moved?* I answered what I could as everyone promised to read it. In the bustle, my dad stayed quiet. He sat at the head of the table with his three volumes unopened in front of him. He just looked down at them. I couldn't tell what he was thinking. I couldn't tell whether he was proud or sad about the life he led and having his stories captured by a son he had momentarily disowned bound in front of him. I did know that he was surrounded by his wife and children and grandchildren, and success meant many things. After everyone left, I was the last to kiss my parents on the way out the door. I told them I would see them again soon as my mind shifted to my own life and things to do.

EPILOGUE I

MY FATHER DIED on September 10, 1999, two months shy of his eighty-third birthday, and four months shy of the twenty-first century, a century of wonder and light he hoped to witness. There was news of a peace accord in the Middle East, the improbability of Jews and Arabs reconciled, at least for a time. The promise of an ever-growing global network of interconnected computers sharing data across devices had Wall Street in a frenzy. Work was underway decoding human DNA. My dad followed the news every night. The fireworks at the end of the year were sure to usher in a new age.

On a late warm and crisp August afternoon in Sunny Isles, my parents were on their way to a doctor's appointment when another vehicle slammed into them, smashing their small compact car. I don't remember whether my father or mother was driving. My father had always been a distracted driver. My mother was more defensive and responsible, believing it was better to lose a minute of your life than your life in a minute. My mother later said that the last sound they heard from each other was the cry of each's others name. *Peres. Lourdes.* In the rush that followed, the details of who was at fault and who was driving became lost to me. In some ways, they were both behind the wheel.

My mother was taken to the emergency room of Jackson Memorial Hospital with crushed ribs and a broken shoulder and torn organs and severe internal bleeding. My father was taken to a smaller hospital across the county with a punctured lung. They would never see each other again. We were certain my mother might die and confident my father would live. Instead, my mother lived, and my father died.

Born near the beginning of the century in the heat of the Amazon jungle, my father died alone at the end of the century surrounded by machines in a cold hospital room in Florida.

My time at Jenner & Block had lasted less than three years. I gave it my best shot, but it was not the right shot. Other attorneys in the office knew and valued the practice of law. What I knew about discovery and depositions and causes of action, after a few months of wanting to care about the corporations we had as clients and business disputes that cost millions of dollars in fees, meant little to me. The politics in the office were contentious. I clashed with certain personalities, and the briefs that I wrote, as good as they may have been on a given day, didn't add up to much in the alternate universe of litigation. I dressed up becoming somebody I was not. After months of tangling with one of the partners, I was let go and given termination papers to sign absolving the firm of any liability. If I was a better lawyer, I would have sued. In the hope of being a better man, I didn't change a word of the settlement.

By then, I had moved to a high-rise apartment on Claughton Island, overlooking Biscayne Bay.

I used my severance package to pay bills and wrote the novel I wanted to write. I wrote late at night and early mornings at the News Café, at the 11th Street Diner on Washington Avenue, and at Books & Books in Coral Gables, where Donna Tartt read from *The Secret History,* her novel of beauty and terror and truth and pretense inspiring a generation of writers. When my severance pay ran out, I moved north to Coconut Creek, a centerless town an hour north of Miami, and joined another firm. Mimi married a businessman, Suzanne married a fellow doctor, and I met the woman who would become my future wife on a blind date on Los Olas Boulevard in Fort Lauderdale. Laura was a paralegal and knew something about lawyers and their dreams. She and I met in 1996, married in 1997, and had a child together in 1998.

I secured a Los Angeles-based agent who shopped my manuscript. Hollywood first, he said, then New York. It had some very good parts, about love and death and sex, and many less-than-good parts, about love and death and sex, and didn't sell, which kept me practicing law.

During those years, my mom had separated from my dad. She found an apartment beside a lake near my sister Dolores that she decorated with flowers and plants and photographs of her children and paintings of seascapes. She would look at the moon and listen to Antonio Carlos Jobim and Rosemary Clooney well into the night. Then she moved to Birmingham, Alabama, to live near my sister Arlene where she stayed for a year, before moving back to Sunny Isles. For several months, while my parents were separated, my dad lived in a small room with a bed, sink, and a shower he rented in a cheap oceanside motel. I visited him once, standing by the doorway, not saying much, as he sat in the lone chair in his room, surrounded by books. I was there to pick up a package. He didn't say much to me. I didn't hear from my dad for the next two years, as he lived in exile, until my wedding day. He surprised Laura and me, dressed in a gray suit and red tie for the ceremony, walking slowly into the fellowship hall just before we took photographs. He was eighty years old. We kissed and started talking again, as if our latest estrangement had never happened.

In their forty-fourth year of marriage, my dad and mom found their way back to each other. My mom had asserted her independence, and my dad had come to his own realizations in solitude. He had been reading the Torah and prayer books in Portuguese. After long conversations over several days, they reconciled. This time for the last time. My mom said they talked about everything. All the years. All the struggles. All the joys. She kept the details to herself, saying only that each of them needed each other, each of them needed to forgive and be forgiven. It was between them, she said. *That the broken heart is the healed heart.* My mom invited my dad to move back in with her, and he arrived with two worn suitcases and a box of books. They positioned chairs side by side in the living room. When I visited, I saw the five framed photographs of my brother, sisters, and me on the wall. I saw them make meals and clean up together. My mom combed his hair. I saw them hold hands.

Laura and I had moved to Rio Vista in Fort Lauderdale, a well-to-do neighborhood of single-family homes near the city, about thirty minutes north of my mom and dad. I gave the law one last go at a boutique firm while Laura worked at a larger regional firm. Our home had wooden floors and vintage furniture and posters from the Edwardian age. We loved our home, the tiny kitchen where Laura cooked warm and nourishing meals, our dogs and cats, the mangoes that fell loudly on our deck in the backyard. My parents came to our house several times, my dad enjoying sitting in an upholstered wingback chair near our fireplace. They brought flowers and pastries. They made jokes about each other. They each held our infant daughter in turn.

In 1999, Laura and I decided to move to North Carolina. After seven on-and-off years, practicing law had run its course for me, and with a new family, I looked for anything else to do. I wanted a new life. Purpose. Meaning. Independence. All those things. I had represented entrepreneurs in legal disputes, and thought I had a few business skills in me. I thought I could lead and communicate and persuade. Professionals were leaving careers and jumping into Internet start-ups, and I jumped in too. I invested the retirement money I had into a website design franchise. I went in with a partner who wanted to live in Charlotte. Laura and I packed up and made the move. I was filled with hope and new beginnings.

The last time I saw my father he was standing side by side with my mother in front of their building in the afternoon sun as we drove away to Charlotte. My mom had her arm around my dad's waist. She waved goodbye. Then my dad did too. I watched them recede in my rearview mirror until I turned away.

Two months later, after moving to Charlotte, I got news of my parents' car accident. I took the call in the office my business partner and I had rented on the sixteenth floor of a high-rise building, our company finances already stretched. I grimaced on hearing the news, asking questions about who and what and when and how, and made plans to return to Florida. After hearing that my mom would recover, and confident my dad would make it through, I decided to wait a few more days. We were on the verge of our first sale at the company. Then late on a Wednesday night, my dad called. We had a wall phone in the hallway of our rented home. He was still in the hospital. His voice was soft and hoarse. He asked if I planned on visiting my mother. I said I was on my way. I asked him how he was. He said not to worry. He had overcome everything in his life, and everything had its time. Then he paused and said he loved me. I felt a wave of emotion come over me, holding the receiver tight. I told him I loved him too. Our call had been brief, maybe five minutes. I hung up the phone, certain I would talk to him again. *Why hadn't I already made the trip?* Two days later, on Friday, the phone rang before dawn. I woke up on the first ring that jolted me out of my sleep. My sister Dolores told me our father had died. I cried out on hearing the news.

We had a simple ceremony for my dad. From the podium I could barely read the words he had shared with me about how he felt when each of his children were born. *My children have been an endless and powerful source of inspiration, motivation, and strength to face the tribulations and trials of my life. And despite my humble position, I am the victor . . . for they are well.* My brother and sisters looked up at me as I spoke. No one else said a word. He left instructions about what to do with his body. He was wrapped in a white shroud and buried in a pine box.

In the last few months of my father's life, he had begun to write. He sat at a small, cluttered glass table in the bedroom he shared with my mom with a yellow pad of paper with books and articles on the floor. Scotch-taped on the glass table were photographs of the family and faces of children with cleft lips from Central America whom he sponsored after watching late-night infomercials. His hair had turned white, and he had stopped shaving. Sometimes he would wear a yarmulke, which he had kept in a drawer along with tallit prayer shawls that his uncle had given him. After several weeks, he finished an essay and sent it to Yeshiva University. He received a letter from the co-founder of the Sephardic Studies program expressing delight and interest in publication.

It was not lost on me that my dad was writing. He had become what he had long wanted to be, but had denied himself being: a scholar, a historian, a philosopher. In his final days he turned back to his youth and to his forefathers. To the ebbs and flows of time.

My dad did not live to see his essay in print. It was published in *Studies on The History of Portuguese Jews*, edited by Drs. Israel J. Katz and M. Mitchell Serels, by Sepher-Hermon

Press for The American Society of Sephardic Studies in 2000.
The book is on my shelf, within reach, the cover of the book
yellow and green, the same colors of the flag of the Brazilian
flag. This is what he wrote:

JUDAISM IN THE AMAZON JUNGLE
By Ambrosio B. Peres

*Over the long and winding course of their history, Jews have settled
in virtually every corner of the world while still managing to abide
by the demanding dogmas and rituals of their faith. No matter
how foreign or strange their new setting, they have demonstrated
a remarkable capacity for adapting to the local culture while continuing to maintain their unique heritage and separateness. With
the knowledge they carried, Jews helped to advance the local arts,
science, commerce, and laws of the region. Yet, in one place their
capacity to adapt was tested beyond measure – a place which, when
they arrived, was totally devoid of electricity, public sanitation,
schools, doctors, roads, newspapers, and telephones – a place where
civilization did not exist at all. Such a place was the immense,
oppressive, primitive, and phantasmagoric Amazon jungle, wherein
this "green hell" a drama unfolded.*

*In the second decade of the eighteenth century, Sephardic
Moroccan Jews set out on an exodus to a remote Brazilian region
called Amazonia. Those who came to the jungle brought not only
their capacity to adapt, but also their embroidered velvet pouches
with tefilim, tallit, prayer books and mezzuzot, taken from doorposts*

of their homes to reaffix on the doors of their homes in Brazil. The majority represented the communities of Tangier, Tetuan, and Rabat, while the others included former residents of Gibraltar, who came via Ceuta.

On the whole, they possessed a substantial level of education. In the international zone of Tangier, the Moroccan Jews had been exposed to a wide variety of languages, including Spanish, Hebrew, Arabic, French, English and Hakatia (an interesting blend of Spanish, Hebrew, and Arabic, and consequently a philological amalgam of Spanish eloquence, ironic Jewish humor, and exacerbated Arabic fatalism, which provided a unique recipe for laughter and sarcasm). The Moroccan Jews acquired a natural ability to learn almost any language. Once in Brazil, Portuguese soon became their daily language.

The Moroccan Jews followed the Sephardic rite, with the singing of prayers, swaying of the body, and covering their heads with the tallit while praying at home or in the synagogue (esnoga).

Historians suggest that the rubber boom in Brazil (El Dorado), then the only rubber-producing country in the world, and the country's political independence in 1882, were the underlying reasons which impelled Jewish emigration from Morocco. However, the ghastly Inquisition still hung like a dark cloud over the heads of Spanish and Portuguese Jewry during the first and second decades of the eighteenth century. Although it had substantially decreased in intensity, restrictions and discrimination still occurred openly. The psychological effects of this inquisitorial holocaust continued to prevail in the minds and souls of the descendants of those who knew the atrocities firsthand. In Spain, the Inquisition was declared extinct by Napolean Bonaparte in 1808, yet the Church reinstated it in 1814 and finally abolished it in 1834, thus completing 352 years of barbarity. In Portugal, the Inquisition is considered by many to be historically benign, for it led to the death and harsh punishment of about 1,500 people, whereas in Spain about 28,000 persons were incinerated or doomed to slow death in the dungeons.

It is important to retrieve historical facts to better understand how the emigration of Spanish Moroccan Jews to Brazil was made possible. In 1808, during the aftermath of Napoleon's invasion of Portugal, the Royal family moved to Brazil, where Rio de Janeiro was chosen as the seat of the kingdom, and remained so until 1821, when the family returned to Portugal. In that same year, King Joao VI abolished the Inquisition throughout the kingdom, including Brazil, and issued a royal decree which opened all the Atlantic ports of Brazil to international navigation and emigration. In 1822, Prince Pedro IV, King Joao's son, declined to return to Portugal and instead, proclaimed, on September 1, 1822, the independence of Brazil. He was crowned the first emperor of Brazil. Pedro was liberal and libertine, more interested in the affairs of love than in the affairs of the State.

Coincidental to these events, the Moroccan Jews, on their own volition and decision, began to arrive in Belém, the capital city of the State of Para, in northern Brazil. In the same city, the first Jewish cemetery – a separate tract within a non-denominational one called Cemiterio da Soledade – was operational in 1823. In 1848, the Israelite cemetery was opened. The first synagogue, called Essel Abraham was established in 1826, and the second, Sha'ar Hashamain, in 1828. Both are still functioning at their original sites, although somewhat renovated to resist the ravages of time. Throughout the nineteenth century, Moroccan Jews continued migrating to Belém, where some settled and became merchants of dry and wet goods, shoes, textiles, home utensils, tools for civilian construction, and extractions of natural resources. Others, however, chose to move into the hinterland (sertao), setting up their homes and shops along the banks of tributaries.

By 1879, they extended their journey farther down into the Amazon itself. Some settled in Manaus, then a small booming city, built principally by the British and soon had amenities such as street cars, electricity, a floating harbor, and running, treated water. Others went further into the jungle, either to small existing villages or to break new ground, erecting new wood-framed or clay structures, which served as their homes and businesses. They were typically tri-level dwellings: the first floor comprising a store front and/or office, with a dock for loading and unloading goods; the second floor, usually a warehouse; and the third, the family's residence. A large sign was placed in front of the structure bearing the name of the homeowner and proprietor, as, for example, Casa Abrao, Casa Isaac, or Casa Jacob. If a business was established in a new location, the name of the local river was made part of its name, like the Casa Isaac do Rio Madeira. If the business was in a town already on the official map, it was registered to include the name of the town, Casa Moyses do Itacoatiara. No other address was needed. It was a unique way to introduce Biblical names throughout the vast jungle. The Jews proudly displayed their identity by advertising their names and surnames. In time their businesses became household names. They became known at Hebraicos, and although its meaning was not quite clear to the natives, the connotation was "different, separate, weird, or smart." Commercial activities in the jungle were more steady than busy.

The Moroccan Jews regularly interacted with the natives, who collected and supplied the local raw materials (rubber, skins, lumber, gums, nuts, fibers, fruits, barks, essentials oils, etc.) and often bought finished products (textiles, shoes, boots, leather sandals, sugar, salt, utensils, tools, fishing and hunting equipment and supplies, medicines, etc.) Most of the transactions were done by barter. The Jews, in turn, sold raw materials to their Moroccan friends or relatives in Belém or Manaus, who worked as overseas exporters.

These exporters were contacted by vessels bearing the British flag as three-to-four-month intervals (SS Hildebrand, SS Liverpool, etc), which carried the raw materials from the Amazon to the industrial centers of Europe and the United States (Marseilles, Lisbon, London, Liverpool, Hamburg, Cologne, New York, etc.) and returned with mail, over-the-counter pharmaceutical products (cod liver oil, balsams, iodine, pain-killers, etc.), books, magazines, The Times of London, wine and olives, olive oil from Portugal, religious calendars and ketuvot from the dayan ("the Chief Rabbi" of Tangier and international spiritual leader of the Moroccan Jews), kosher wines, and matzos from England. These vessels were the only lifeline between the civilized worlds and the world of the jungle. Around 1910, cable telegraphic services (utilizing Morse code) were installed by the British for commercial and official purposes in Brazil.

In the tropics the days are long and boring, and the nights are short and full of eerie sounds and screams. Ferocious animals roam about, seeking food. These wild creatures were attracted to

the chickens, ducks, goats, and lambs that were kept behind the
fences of Jewish homes. Jaguars and ocelots would often leap over
the fences of the Jewish homes to attack their prey. The Jews were
strictly observant of the dietary laws which was their shield against
disease, being solely responsible for their own health since they could
not turn to others for consultation or treatment. They learned the
therapeutic value of roots, leaves, and barks for the home prepara-
tion of teas, potions or balsa. They rejected witchcraft and witch
doctors who abounded throughout the region. They scrupulously kept
to themselves within the boundaries of their own religion and the
dictates of botanical medicines. Their diet consisted of beef, veal,
lamb, poultry, scaled freshwater fishes, freshly picked fruits, and
roasted seeds. Unlike the natives, the Jews did not eat pork of any
kind, or snakes, monkeys, alligator, turtles, shellfish, and such birds
as parrots, toucans, or vultures. Their drinking water came from
the rain or wells, but never from rivers or lakes. By following the
halachic recommendations as close as possible, the Jews protected
themselves against a wide variety of viruses, which, at the time, were
incurable. Their dietary laws also served as a barrier to curtail social
intercourse. Consequently, they usually enjoyed longer and healthier
lives than the natives or other non-Jewish residents.

The family provided the best source for spiritual strength, solidly
based on stern moral principles and reciprocal unconditional love.
A Jewish Moroccan home was God's sanctuary, an idealized nation
of Israel, wherein the word Yerushalayim (Jerusalem) was sacred,
and when uttered, carried profound Biblical significance.

The majestic nature of the Amazon reinforced the Jewish creed
and constantly revitalized their faith. The Jews believed that God

revealed Himself through His creation – and a vast luxuriant portion of it was right there surrounding them; and through the Torah, the infinite wisdom of God immortalized for eternity the inspired sages and scribes of Israel. These Moroccan Jews were assured that God was always there protecting them in the midst of a pandemonium reserved for the best years of their lives.

Life in the Amazon had a selective force. Only the strong survived. It took epic-like courage and determination to survive in the isolation of the jungle. The silence was broken only by the low utterances of family members, short conversations with natives, the paddling of canoes, the singing of the birds, the roaring of beasts, the breathing of cattle and horses, the barking of dogs, or by the occasional whistle of small and slow-moving motorboats (gaiolas) – floating general stores, a recognized Jewish-Moroccan invention – signaling the coming or going of customers or friends.

The intermittent torrential rains permeated the imposing ambiance with spectral monotony. High humidity, scorching sun, and dense evaporation remain constant. But rising against their fate served no purpose. Instead, the Jews convinced themselves of the usefulness of these adverse circumstances. Silence was good for reading, studying, praying, and mind-calming meditation. The rains kept the forest as exuberant as an ever-procreating mother and provided clean, clear uncontaminated water. The sun dried the lumber, skins, furs, seeds – the physical sources of survival. That which was oppressive was also good and sacrosanct. This philosophical attitude proved useful under the circumstances wherein life was always difficult.

The Jews, like the natives, were often fatalistic, but their notion of self-determination and freedom of choice lifted them above the abominable level of the natives. Enduring all difficulties, the Jews somehow attained self-sufficiency and financial security. The Moroccan Jews were quite thrifty, stating that "the chicken fills up her pouch grain by grain." By systematically saving, they amassed resources which, in due time, gave them peace of mind and respectability among their peers. Their word of honor surpassed any personal interest or consideration. Each was successful in their efforts to raise a family. Since there were no schools at any level among the small communities scattered along the banks of the rivers, the children were taught by their parents. When the children reached a certain age, they were sent to a tutor (another Moroccan Jew) in another town, where an elementary school was located. Some children were even sent to southern Brazil or to Europe to receive better, often higher education, while their parents remained in the jungle. What a remarkable demonstration of parental love! Every male child was ritualistically circumcised. A mohel was always to be found. Hebrew was taught at home as a sacred ritual language with mystical connotations. Daily religious services were conducted at home. Tefilin was put on every morning. Evening prayers (arbit) were recited and chanted. Wine and bread (homemade) were blessed at every meal. Candles were lit by the wives each Sabbath. No work or physical activity was performed on this day, but prayers and charity abounded.

The High Holy days were celebrated in towns comprising a few Jewish families. A room in a Jewish home was chosen to serve as a synagogue. Jews came by canoes or small motorboats, carrying their velvet pouches and old prayer books, in some cases those which they brought from Tangier, Tetuan, or Rabat. Wives and children came along as well. Along the Amazon basin, in towns of six or eight families, the Jews gathered to pray, socialize, reminisce, discuss business, and tell old jokes in their spirited and beloved Haketia language. In my hometown (Itacoatiara), which numbered eight hundred inhabitants, and about eight Jewish families, my widowed aunt Esther Ezagui's home was the chosen place of worship among the local Jews, as well as for those located along the Amazon basin. Fasting on Yom Kippur ('the Day of Atonement') was almost beyond human endurance under the severe climatic conditions of high temperatures and humidity. But it was always done with an effusive, self-fulfilling feeling.

Pessah ('Passover') was joyous. The entire household was koshered. Pots and pans, some brand new or kept only for festive days, were cleaned and polished by the women of the household. A roasted lamb was shared by the entire family. The Haggadah was recited in Judeo-Spanish by the patriarch, and the children listened attentively to the historical events which occurred more than three thousand years ago. So forceful was the reading, uttered with eloquence and verisimilitude. After all, they were enjoying full freedom, which is the spiritual message of the Pessah.

My father, Isaac Peres, son of Joseph, came from Tangier around 1870. He married my mother Rachael, daughter of Leon Hilel Benchimol, who came from Gibraltar around 1850. After living several years in Cameta, a small town in the State of Para, they moved to Itacoatiara in the State of Amazonia at the end of the nineteenth century. This town was located on the left bank of the Urubu River, a tributary of the Amazon. Aunt Esther Ezagui, my father's sister, also lived there. She was married to Moyses Ezagui from Tangier. All told, perhaps eight families lived in that small town, all linked by the same orthodoxy. The town was without electricity, phones, pavement, streetlights, sewage, public health care, doctors, and scientific medicines.

I was born at home, the seventh of a family of eight children. However, we were all much better off than the natives and other non-Jewish residents, who were illiterate and lacked ambition, accepting a fate of poverty and intellectual darkness. Among the Jews, those born in Morocco, as well as those born in the Amazon, all enjoyed some education. Some of the Jewish children eventually became professors of the liberal arts and sciences. This included my uncle David Joseph Peres, a scholar in his own right and Professor Emeritus of Latin and Hebrew, who translated the prayer books from Hebrew into Portuguese, whose editions can be found in Portuguese-speaking countries, and J. Jayme Aben-Athar, a scientist of international renown, connected with the Pasteur Institute in Paris, who collaborated in the production of anti-rabies vaccines and in the research of tropical diseases. Many other remarkable men can be cited to augment the constellation of Jewish luminaries of Moroccan ancestry.

My father, a naturalized Brazilian, served as mayor of our town from 1924 to 1930. During his term in office, the town witnessed the first electrical plant to supply light for domestic consumption and power for an incipient lumber mill; the first public school open to every child; the first medical clinic with a physician; the first Catholic Church built in masonry; the first Public Register to issue birth and death certificates; the first silent movie house; the first plant to distill rosewood oil; and the first slaughter house to butcher animals by *cutting the jugular vein (kosher style), although the proprietor was a Christian. Curiously, we had our first automobile, a 1908 Ford.*

Many other Jews became mayors of their respective towns of residence: Eliezar Levy (Macapa), Samuel Benchimol (Baiao), Moses Levy (Igrape-Mirim), and others. Each governed well and introduced major improvements, consigning their names to the pages of local history. The Jews in every village or town, spread over the immense territory, coped with the same unbearable circumstances, yet all were linked together by the invisible presence of the Torah and Talmud.

The Jews eventually built schools not only for themselves, but for the natives. These native children, residing in Jewish households where learning was a commandment, became active and useful members of society. In the Jewish homes, the natives encountered books, pencils, pens, and writing paper for the first time. They were integrated into Jewish family life, although they were not converted to Judaism, because the orthodox Moroccan Jews were against converting persons born of non-Jewish mothers.

The proud descendants of those daring Jews who now live in Amazonia as prominent doctors, lawyers, engineers, writers, teachers, businessmen, public servants, and advisors to their respective local governments, are men and women of remarkable moral caliber, highly respected and admired for their exemplary deeds and accomplishments. The epic and stoic story of the Moroccan Jews in the Amazon calls for the unique talents of a Dante Alighieri, who would better portray the heaven, hell, and purgatory of the immense rain forest, whose days were either majestic, pure agony, or severely unbearable. Yet, as long as they were free to proclaim the words and works of God, the Jews somehow managed to face any challenge, no matter how unique or demanding.

Most intriguing is the underlying reason which propelled the Moroccan Jews to settle throughout the vast Amazon jungle. Why would these Jews of European background choose to live in such an imposing dense and dark region? Why were they determined to isolate themselves in a forest that was almost inaccessible to humans? Why would they prefer to trust such an uncivilized world rather than the splendor of Europe or the promising and rapidly developing country called America? Perhaps they found the uncivilized jungle far more humane than the world they left behind.

The Spanish Moroccan Jews who immigrated to Amazonia realized that stone-age Indians, with their pantheistic beliefs, would allow the Jews to live with dignity. For more than a century, the Jews have honored the kindness, loyalty, and humility of their native neighbors deep within the jungle.

EPILOGUE II

I WAS AT my desk getting ready for the new semester when I received a Facebook message from a person named Pedro Peres. The message came with his photo. He was a young man in his twenties with dark eyes and a rough beard who looked decidedly Brazilian. There were other people with my last name who over the years had sought to befriend me on social media whom I ignored. This message caught my attention. He said he was the great-grandson of my father, and his grandfather was my half-brother.

It took me a minute to process.

Twenty years had passed since my dad died. It was September 4, 2019. I was fifty-six years old. Laura and I had long since made Charlotte our home. After a business start-up here and a recession there, we found our footing in our careers. Laura worked as a paralegal at a law firm, then at a bank, before taking on a project and facilities manager position at a leading nonprofit foundation. I was beginning my thirteenth-year teaching ethics and leadership. I founded and edited an arts and cultural magazine, wrote columns and essays, interviewed artists and executives about their lives and higher purposes, and had begun plans to launch a cultural center celebrating the humanities and civic engagement. My life had become what my dad would have wanted for himself and made possible for me: writing, teaching, mentoring, contributing to the mind and heart of the city.

I was wary about replying, but the message from Pedro reached something in my core. Against all sense of caution, I typed that he was wrong, that he had bad information. He responded immediately. He said we were a DNA match. He included a marriage certificate dated 1939 with my father's name on it, and a birth certificate dated 1940 with my dad listed as the father to a newborn son named Leon. Listed on the documents as my father's wife and mother to his child was a woman named Ioconda Peres. I stared at the message and documents for a long time. Was any of this true? Did my father have another family?

I shuffled the academic papers in front of me. More messages from Pedro began to pop. He said Leon was his grandfather and my half-brother. Leon was seventy-nine years old, living south of Sao Paulo. He said my father had a second son, named Mauricio, now seventy-seven years old. Two images then appeared: an old, colorized photograph of a blonde-haired woman holding two boys who very much had my dad's eyes and ears, and another photo of Leon, now an elderly man, who eerily looked very much like my father.

Pedro said that he lived in New Jersey, that he had recently emigrated from Brazil. His messages were in broken English. He said his father was named Paulo, who was Leon's son. As

Pedro's messages came in, I furiously searched the Internet. Paulo was near my age, an executive at a prominent international financial firm, and if what Pedro was saying was true, Paulo was my nephew. The more I searched, the more evidence mounted that there was a whole other branch of the Peres family who lived in Brazil and the United States that could be my father's descendants. I had cousins, nieces, and nephews I knew nothing about, all of whom might claim – *likely did claim* - my dad in their family tree.

I wrote to Pedro that I would get back to him.

I closed my eyes and thought of my mother. She was now eighty-four years old, living in an assisted living center in Boynton Beach. On the wall across from her bed in her small single room were the five framed black and white photographs of her children. On her dresser were religious candles, photographs of our family, and statues of Mary and Joseph. She received care from an aide twice a day. Her health had taken a turn after a mild stroke that led us to move her out of an apartment she had lived in near the water in Aventura. For fifteen years after my father died she had made a life for herself, quiet, nostalgic, sentimental, listening to music, keeping photo albums, sending cards to grandchildren, talking to us on the phone, making meals when we visited, using her shopping cart to walk, painting seascapes, keeping her apartment clean and beautiful, protective of her memories, until now when she was in a building in the care of people she know little about and who knew little about her.

I texted my brother Edison. *Do you have a minute? It's not about Mommy.* Edison had built a stellar career as a business

executive in technology and sales. He had a large flourish-
ing family. He traveled the world much as my father did and
personified second-generation success. Anything that would
happen next would involve him and his advice and consent.
Within the hour we were on the phone. I told him about the
messages and documents I received from Pedro. My brother
listened carefully, assessing the facts and asking questions in his
probative way. Our conversation was businesslike. Who was
Pedro? What did he want? Why now? I repeated what Pedro
claimed: that I was a DNA match. My brother responded that
he had submitted a saliva sample to Ancestry.com in the last
month. The kit was a birthday gift from his daughter. Pedro
must have gotten an alert. My brother said he might have
received a friend request from Pedro but ignored it. After not
connecting with Edison, Pedro must have messaged me.

We studied the photographs that Pedro had sent. "They
definitely look like family," I said.

"Does that make us bastard children?" my brother asked.

It was odd to hear my brother use that antiquated phrase
to describe our possible family status, but the issue and all
its implications were right in front of us. Brazil was the land
of no divorce. The Brazilian Constitution made marriage an
indissoluble contract. "If Daddy was still married to another
woman when he married Mommy in 1955, his marriage to
Mommy would have been illegal. We would have been illegiti-
mate children. That would have devastated her. Her reputation is everything to her," I said.

"She could have had her marriage annulled," Edison said.

"She would have been an unmarried Brazilian woman with five children in America without financial means living in disgrace." I also knew that Brazilians practiced all sorts of evasions to move on from failed marriages into new relationships. Then I remembered something my dad told me that I never followed up on. "Daddy said he and Mommy remarried in a Catholic church in San Francisco. A second marriage ceremony is unlike something they would do, unless Mommy insisted on it."

"Let's just ask her," Edison said.

Professors and colleagues in the open floor office where I worked were getting ready for a department meeting. I lowered my voice into the phone. "I don't think we should. If she knew that Daddy had another family, she never wanted us to find out. If she doesn't know, it would kill her to hear the news."

The hours and days that followed were a flurry of texts, emails, and phone calls between my brother, sisters, and me. The five of us lived in different cities and led separate lives. We sent each other texts on birthdays, attended weddings of nephews and nieces, but otherwise our communications were limited to managing my mother's care. We had made difficult decisions about moving our mother out of her apartment with the guilt and tension and recrimination and sadness that often brings. Responsibility for my mother kept us talking, and the news about my father brought us together again.

My sister Dolores, who was most like my mother and lived closest to her assisted living center and bore the weight and burdens of her care, had also received a friend request from Pedro and the same documents and photographs. "Good morning, all," she wrote. "I don't know about you but yesterday was a day that brought back Daddy to all my senses. I missed him more than usual and saw him in my dreams and his presence was palpable in my room. I cried and cried uncontrollably last night. I couldn't sleep for a long while. We have a wonderful opportunity now to bring this full circle on his behalf."

My sister Arlene, who lived in Birmingham and who carefully curated photo albums of our family history and who had taken my mother into her home after she fell ill, reacted to the photograph of Leon. "He's beautiful. I'm excited. I want to know everything about him. It fills some missing pieces for me. I'd love to get as much detail as possible. I haven't stopped staring at his picture! The dynamic here might be two sons who were cared for and loved and two sons who feel rejected and abandoned. I hope we embrace them and do not compound the hurt. Maybe we can extend Leon a semblance of accep-tance on our father's behalf."

My sister Rachael, the oldest among us and the most private, who had the deepest memories and most personal experiences of the earliest days of my parents' marriage and our constant dislocation, who carried with her compensations that the rest of us would never know, stayed silent for two days before sending a note. "Of the many questions I have, here are the most obvious: The Peres name and our lineage couldn't possibly have been a difficult thing to research among Brazilians, even if only among Jews in the Amazon, Rio, and Sao Paulo. Why did it take a DNA test to reach out to us now? Does Mommy have a marriage license? Why wouldn't the Brazilian bureaucracy have called it into question? Could the illegitimacy of the marriage be a reason why Daddy flew Mommy immediately to the USA? Is Daddy's first wife still alive? What was her life like with the two boys? I do have to say, though, the photograph of Leon is moving and his resemblance to Daddy is mind blowing."

I wrote a long email recapping everything we knew. I added two options at the end: One, we could contact Leon directly and begin a conversation, understanding that he may feel abandoned and wounded and curious about a father who did not raise him but devoted himself instead to raising another family in America. We could embrace Leon and comfort him in his old age. Or two, we could respect Daddy's wishes. He kept his previous family private for reasons he took to his grave. He established a family with us that became his abiding purpose. Our family was a second chance for him to redeem whatever choices he had made. Our family was the covenant he made with God.

Then the third photograph came in. A photograph we would never have imagined. There it was in front of us. No longer pieces to the puzzle but emotionally convincing proof. The photograph was of a family of four: my dad is in his early twenties wearing a well-tailored suit standing beside an attractive woman with a corsage on her dress. In front of the woman is a young boy about three-years old. In my dad's arms is another boy about one year old dressed as if he had just been christened. The woman and two boys with my dad were the same people in the first photograph that Pedro sent. This time my father and the woman and the boys were all together. My father carried a child just as he carried us. In the photograph my dad looked resolute and proud. Or maybe pensive and burdened.

"Every parent is a mystery," I texted my brother.

"Some more than others," he replied.

On September 10, 2019, exactly twenty years to the day that my father died, I exchanged emails with Leon Peres, living in Curitiba, Brazil.

Dear Leon,

What a strange letter for me to write. I am contacting a brother I never knew existed on the anniversary of our father's death. The news that your grandson Pedro shared with me that Ambrosio Peres was married to your mother before he was married to my mother and that he had two sons who are half-brothers to me and my brother and sisters was a complete shock to me and my siblings. My siblings and I have lived our entire lives not knowing about you.

We are sensitive that you have grown up not knowing your father. We are saddened that this has been the case, but we are hopeful that a connection between you and our side of the family can answer questions for you and provide some resolution. We are curious about what Pedro told us: that Ambrosio left your mother and you and your younger brother. We have many questions about what happened and why it happened and what explanations were given to you. We have questions about what happened in your mother's life and your life. We are curious about these circumstances and what efforts may have been made at contact over the years.

I imagine you have questions too. I can share this: Ambrosio was a complex man who lived a complicated life. He was fiercely independent. He lived life on his own terms. Sometimes this worked out well for him. Other times it led to great struggle. He traveled the world and had many relationships. He knew how to laugh and had many moments of joy, but his life was never easy. His days were filled with great difficulty, often because of decisions he made, or decisions forced upon him. He was a good father to us. The Ambrosio we knew was devoted to his children and had great compassion for other people in distress. He worked very hard and sacrificed to keep his family together. My siblings and I have deep love and affection for him. I do not know what was in his heart about his history with your mother and you and your brother, but I suspect he always carried it within him and it influenced his commitment to me and my siblings.

My siblings have asked me to contact you on their behalf. We are excited to know that we have two new half-brothers. We embrace this moment with curiosity and grace.

All our best,
Mark

Later that evening I received a reply:

Dear Mark,

Thank you for your email. I'm very happy, really happy, that we have this opportunity to contact each other. I won't go into detail now, but we have a lot to talk about.

I have been waiting seventy-six years to know about my father. The last time I saw him I was four years old. I made some attempts to contact my Aunt Semita, your father's sister, and cousins many years ago, but I don't know why they didn't want to give me my father's address. They claimed that he had a new family and five children and that he had a lot of difficulties. It was a shame, but finally the years passed and here we are now.

I'm not surprised by everything you said about 'our' father. My mother always spoke of him that way, but in the end, they are both gone. My mother died in 2017 at the age of ninety-eight, completely lucid. We also had many struggles and difficulties, but we overcame them all. Me and my brother Mauricio, and another half-brother, Gilberto, from my mother's second marriage, are doing well. I will turn eighty in February. It was a long wait. I want to know a lot about my father, and I really want to get to know all of you. I'm a teacher at a technical school. I teach robotics. We're in classes right now, our school year ends in September, when I'll be on vacation, and I'll be able to come to you. My eldest son, Paulo lives in New Jersey, and I'm going to spend ten days with him. I'll be able to meet you then.

Big hugs. Stay with God.
Leon

Four years later, on December 2, 2023, Edison picked me up at Newark Airport, and we drove directly to Paulo Peres's home in New Jersey. Two years of a worldwide pandemic had passed. Waiting inside to greet us was Paulo, his wife, two sons, his sister Monica, and Leon Peres from behind the crowd. Leon was eighty-three years old. He looked very much like my father, shorter in height, with white hair combed back, and a full mustache, dressed in jeans, a blue chambray shirt, and a camel jacket. We hugged and greeted each other with awkward expectation, relying on the Brazilian mannerisms we each knew. Leon spoke broken English, I spoke broken

Portuguese, each of us having an ear for the language we couldn't speak well, understanding more than we could put into words. My brother Edison took the lead. He was fluent in Portuguese and had a way to put people at ease. Paulo served wine and bourbon, and cheese and grapes on a tray just as my mom did the same.

Then dinner around the table. *Feijoada*. The Brazilian national dish of black bean and pork stew topped with *farofa* cassava flour over white rice. The conversation was social, about our careers, about travel, about events in the news, before port and dessert in the living room. We took seats spaced apart from each other in a circle.

Questions turned to my dad. Leon's mother was from a poor Catholic family, daughter of Italian immigrants. My dad met her after leaving the Army sometime in the late 1930's. She became pregnant, which led to the marriage. No one knew how long they lived together. After my father left her and the boys, she reached out to my father's father, Isaac, for support in 1945. Isaac met her during a business trip to Sao Paulo. He seemed genuinely interested in the future of the boys and said he would make sure they wanted for nothing. But then, he died, and there was no further contact between the families. Leon had one clear memory of a surprise visit from my father when Leon was five years old. My dad placed Leon on his lap and gave him a velvet pouch filled with coins. I smiled as Leon told the story. My dad gave me silver dollars in a similar pouch fifty years later before he died. When Leon was ten, Leon's mother remarried, and Leon was raised by an abusive stepfather in the town of Caieiras north of Sao Paulo. Somehow a second marriage on her side occurred, raising more questions about the Brazilian legal system and what my dad was then free to do and what it meant for my dad and mom's own marriage. We sat with the puzzle of it all.

Paulo shared more news: after his bank transferred him from London to New York in 1996, he heard from his uncle Mauricio that Ambrosio was living in Miami. Paulo looked up my father's home number and called him. Paulo asked my father in English if he was Ambrosio Isaac Peres from Brazil. My father answered yes. Paulo then switched to Portuguese and introduced himself as his grandson. Paulo said my father sounded so much like his own father Leon that he had no doubt with whom he was speaking. My father said he must be mistaken. Paulo apologized and thanked my father for his time. When Paulo was about to hang up, my father said, "Wait, don't hang up yet. How are the folks in Caieiras?" Paulo told him about Ioconda and Leon and Mauricio. My father listened intently. The call ended with Paulo leaving his number in case my father wanted to talk or know more, but Paulo never heard from my father again.

The conversation between us in Paulo's home, between Leon and Edison who sat in chairs beside each other as if at a summit, translating English and Portuguese, had an undertone of mystery and diplomacy. Leon was in search of a father he never knew. My brother and I were guardians of receding memories of our dad. All of us in the room were inheritors of the same legacy in profoundly different ways, negotiating emotions and new family obligations. Everyone embraced as the evening came to an end. I felt my dad's presence. I felt him watching and listening, his spirit in the room, incredulous and amazed. This was God's mercy.

We never discussed any of this with our mom. In her remaining months, her words became fewer, and our conversations became briefer. I spoke to her every Saturday by phone. We said the same things to each other. Her world narrowed. The melody of her life became simple notes of love. My brother, sisters, and I had one last gathering with her on her eighty-sixth birthday, with balloons and cake and presents, as she looked at us with wide, tearful eyes. Behind her aged and worn body was the personality of a young woman, vivacious, social, sentimental, ready to give and to take. She wrote these words to my father after he died.

> January 1955. Mardi Gras time in Brazil. Two people met. Ambrosio Peres and Maria de Lourdes. We fell in love and married in July 1955. Two months later we came to live in the United States.
>
> My husband. You had hard times supporting seven people, but you always did. You were proud to be a hard worker and a wonderful salesman. You fell down many times, but you always bounced back. Always making sure to give what your wife and children needed.

44 years passed. 5 children. 14 grandchildren. And now at 83 you are leaving us.

I want you to know that I thank you for everything you did for me and the children. I learned a lot from you, and I am very proud of you. With you goes half of my body, and every time I look at one of our children and grandchildren, I will be seeing you.

This is not goodbye, Peres. *Até logo*, until we meet again.

Our lives are created in the telling. In what we share and withhold. In the stories that mark and bend time. I don't know what my dad felt about events in his life he chose not to disclose. I don't know what secrets weighed on his heart. I don't know what his last thoughts may have been or what final memories came to him alone at night in his hospital room. I do know this: he shared stories that did not spare him. He laid the record before me, speaking more of his failings than his successes. He claimed no victory other than his children. He saw himself humbly, part of a mystical and divine universe from which he sought forgiveness. He felt the sorrows of the world and experienced its delights. He carried on, profoundly, in all too human ways.

There is a moment I come back to when I listen to my dad's voice from so many years ago. A moment when my dad read from his notebook about the wonders of the Amazon, and his brothers Leon and Jośe, and his uncle David, and their achievements. The memories in his notebook were about his native land and the contributions his family and friends made to the world. Along the margins he wrote the names of his wife and children, beside arrows and parallelograms. None of his notes were about him. He didn't see himself as the hero of his story. He revealed what mattered to him, what he treasured, as we all do, in what we honor and recall.

My dad and mom lie side by side now. Buried twenty-two years apart. The cemetery was filled when my mom died, except for one unreserved spot beside my dad. Together they beat self-imposed odds. Their lives add up as all remembered lives do in the scheme of time. Ambrosio Benchimol Peres and Maria de Lourdes Frias Peres are within me, always, as I seek to live a life worthy of them and my own desires.

THE END

AUTHOR'S NOTE

I wrote *The Man Who Lived a Hundred Lives* during a profound period of transition. As my mother's life was coming to an end, I found myself learning about my father's untold past—a discovery that opened an emotional portal. It became clear that telling my parents' story was not just a way to honor them, but a way to make sense of the influences that shaped my own life.

I am now the age my father was when I first began to form clear memories of him, and in some ways, that perspective has given me a deeper understanding of his choices. Having lived long enough to experience more of life's challenges and rewards, I find myself better equipped to grasp the complexity of his journey. Writing this story deepened my love for him—not despite his missteps, but because of them.

When my father and I began our conversations, our relationship was distant and guarded. I kept him at arm's length, unwilling to share much about myself. But something shifted as we talked. His candid reflections—his adventures, failures, and above all, his search for redemption—revealed a man I had not fully known. By the time our conversations ended, I found myself eager for him to know more about me too.

I see the patterns we share now. My father loved history and philosophy, went to law school, and took risks in work and life. He found joy in books, conversation, and storytelling. He had a passion for world affairs and living life on his own terms. He wrote when he was young and returned to doing so later in life. He was far more sentimental than he showed. He likely saw then all that we had in common.

If my father sharpened my mind, my mother shaped my heart, ensuring that whatever wisdom I gained was grounded in loyalty and compassion. My mother taught me how to live. She, like my father, had many dimensions to her character. Everyone in my family has different stories to tell.

We live many lives within our one life. I often wondered where my life would have taken me if I had pursued writing full time after my clerkship ended instead of practicing law. But writing this memoir reminded me of a truth I've long understood: every step along my path has enriched me. I wouldn't have my life any other way.

I wrote this memoir in part to celebrate the immigrant experience—a story that deserves telling now more than ever. We live in a time when the immigrant journey is too often vilified. But America's strength has always come from its newcomers. Immigrants have shaped our communities, strengthened our economy, and infused our nation with resilience, innovation, and cultural richness. My parents' journey is part of that larger story, and I hope readers find echoes of their own family histories within its pages.

The hardest part of writing this memoir was grieving the questions I never asked my father and the moments of deeper connection with my mother that I missed. I suspect that is the bittersweet truth for many of us—we never get all the answers. But perhaps the greatest gift of memoir is that it allows us to piece together the meaning of our lives, to discover grace in our frailties, and to turn the everyday into something sacred.

At its heart, this story is about discovery and the tension between holding on and letting go. My hope is that it resonates with readers who know the struggle of family conflict, the courage of the immigrant's journey, and the possibility of finding grace and connection along the way. Above all, I want readers to feel a deep sense of gratitude for whatever family legacy is their own and to remember that each day is an opportunity to begin anew.

ACKNOWLEDGEMENTS

Writing a memoir is a journey through memory, and I couldn't have taken a single step without the encouragement and guidance of so many.

Thank you to Laura Peres for your constancy and affection, reading pages, reminding me of events, saying what I needed to hear at just the right time, and being patient with my cluttered space in the loft where ideas and ambitions happen. Thank you for being my closest friend and life partner.

Thank you to Shelby Peres, and my nieces and nephews, for the goodness of your hearts, and carrying on the love and legacy of generations.

Thank you to my fellow writers and friends at the Charlotte Center for Literary Arts, especially Paul Reali, who leads with generosity and remarkable commitment to realizing the hopes and dreams of writers. To wise and good-hearted instructors Heather Newton, Megan Rich, and Kim Wright, and to my dear Authors Lab traveling companions, Ellen Powers, Judy Seldin-Cohen, Molly Bollier, Neela McDade, and Amol Kulkarni—you inspire me with your stories, and I am deeply grateful for our time together.

Thank you to Katie Booth for your early editorial guidance, encouraging me to make moves. To Kathy Izard, for every book you have written and every word of counsel that shines a light forward. To Betsy Thorpe for your keen and sensitive developmental and line edits that brought action beats and interiority to life. To Jeff Jackson for pointing to the heart of the story, recommending where the memoir begins, and suggesting the small matter of the title.

To George Stevens for the building of the book. The cover and interior design – from river to dot – is everything I hoped it would be. To Lucy Morton for your detailed and fine-edged proofreading.

Thank you to Rick Thurmond, Eric Davis, Russ Greenfield, Jonathan Fisher, Dael Waxman, Bruce Fritch, and Carlos Salum. You are the best of men.

Thank you to Becky Winkler for sharing the humane and brave stories written by your father, Anthony C. Winkler, and for not reading the first pages I sent you. Your friendship means so much to me.

To Mitchell Schlesinger, thank you for taking me back in time to Rego Park and Forest Hills, for the vividness of your memories, and the kindness in your soul. You brought now and then together.

Thank you to my brother, Edison, and my sisters, Rachael, Arlene, and Dolores—for the ties that bind. Thank you to Leon, Paulo, and Monica for the warmth of your welcome. Thank you to Pedro for sharing what was unknown.

This story is for everyone who ventures.

About the Author

MARK PERES is an award-winning educator and nonprofit leader based in Charlotte, North Carolina. He is a professor in arts and sciences at Johnson & Wales University. He is the founder of The Charlotte Center for the Humanities & Civic Imagination, the Charlotte Ideas Festival, the *On Life and Meaning* podcast, and *Charlotte Viewpoint* magazine. His awards include the Algernon Sydney Sullivan Luminary Award for lifetime achievement. He is a graduate of The Florida State University College of Law and Rollins College. Learn more at markperes.com.

About the Typeface

The text of this book is set in Baskerville, a serif typeface designed in the 1750s by John Baskerville (1706–1775) in Birmingham, England, and cut into metal by punchcutter John Handy. Baskerville is classified as a transitional typeface, intended as a refinement of what are now called old-style typefaces of the period. Baskerville's typeface was part of an ambitious project to create books of the greatest possible quality.